DESIGNING AND MANAGING PROGRAMS

SAGE SOURCEBOOKS FOR THE HUMAN SERVICES SERIES

Series Editors: ARMAND LAUFFER and CHARLES GARVIN

Recent Volumes in This Series

Designing and Managing Programs: An Effectiveness-Based Approach (3rd Edition)
Peter Kettner

Improving Substance Abuse Treatment: An Introduction to the Evidence-Based Practice Movement
Michele (Mickey) Eliason

Effectively Managing Human Service Organizations (3rd Edition)
Ralph Brody

Social Work Supervision: Contexts and Concepts
Ming-sum Tsui

Family Diversity: Continuity and Change in the Contemporary Family
Pauline Erera

Organizational Change in the Human Services
Rebecca Proehl

Stopping Child Maltreatment Before it Starts: Emerging Horizons in Early Home Visitation Services
Neil Guterman

Strategic Alliances Among Health and Human Services Organizations: From Affiliations to Consolidations
Darlyne Bailey

Promoting Successful Adoptions: Practice with Troubled Families
Susan Livingston Smith

Social Work Practice With African American Men: The Invisible Presence
Janice Rasheed

Group Work with Children and Adolescents: Prevention and Intervention in School and Community Systems
Steven Rose

Legal Issues in Social Work, Counseling, and Mental Health: Guidelines for Clinical Practice in Psychotherapy
Robert Madden

Qualitative Methods in Social Work Research: Challenges and Rewards
Deborah Padgett

Understanding Disability: A Lifespan Approach
Peggy Quinn

Self-Help and Support Groups: A Handbook for Practitioners
Linda Kurtz

Social Work in Health Care in the 21st Century
Surjit Dhooper

New Approaches to Family Practice: Confronting Economic Stress
Nancy Vosler

What About America's Homeless Children? Hide and Seek
Paul Shane

Task Groups in the Social Services
Marian Fatout

Third Edition

DESIGNING AND MANAGING PROGRAMS

An Effectiveness-Based Approach

Peter M. Kettner
Professor Emeritus,
Arizona State University

Robert M. Moroney
Arizona State University

Lawrence L. Martin
University of Central Florida

Sage Sourcebooks for

the Human Services

SAGE Publications
Los Angeles • London • New Delhi • Singapore

For information:

Sage Publications, Inc.
2455 Teller Road
Thousand Oaks,
 California 91320
E-mail: order@sagepub.com

Sage Publications India Pvt. Ltd.
B 1/I 1 Mohan Cooperative
 Industrial Area
Mathura Road, New Delhi 110 044
India

Sage Publications Ltd.
1 Oliver's Yard
55 City Road
London EC1Y 1SP
United Kingdom

Sage Publications
 Asia-Pacific Pte. Ltd.
33 Pekin Street #02-01
Far East Square
Singapore 048763

Printed in the United States of America

Library of Congress Cataloging-in-Publication Data

Kettner, Peter M., 1936-
Designing and managing programs: an effectiveness-based approach/by Peter M. Kettner, Robert M. Moroney, and Lawrence L. Martin.—3rd ed.
    p. cm. — (Sage sourcebooks for the human services)
Includes bibliographical references and index.
ISBN 978-1-4129-5194-4 (cloth)
ISBN 978-1-4129-5195-1 (pbk.)

    1. Social service—United States—Planning. 2. Social service—United States—Evaluation. 3. Social service—United States—Finance. I. Moroney, Robert, 1936- II. Martin, Lawrence L. III. Title.

HV95.K428 2008
361.0068'4—dc22   2007020909

This book is printed on acid-free paper.

    08   09   10   11   10   9   8   7   6   5   4   3   2

Acquisitions Editor:	Kassie Graves
Editorial Assistant:	Veronica Novak
Production Editor:	Astrid Virding
Copy Editor:	Jamie Robinson
Typesetter:	C&M Digitals (P) Ltd.
Proofreader:	Ellen Brink
Indexer:	Julie Grayson
Cover Designer:	Edgar Abarca
Marketing Manager:	Carmel Withers

Contents

Contents

Contents

List of Tables and Figures

Preface

The effort to write the third edition of this book began with a contact from Sage to explore our interest in updating the material. After several exchanges, we agreed that it was time for a new edition. What remained was to learn from faculty across the country their thoughts about the second edition, what content still worked well for them, and what needed to be brought into the context of current practice. In preparation for this edition, Kassie Graves, Sage Acquisitions Editor for Human Services, secured agreement to review the second edition from ten faculty members representing a good cross-section of those who were using it at the time. She solicited their feedback and put together a 30-page compilation of reviewer comments which formed the basis of changes made in the third edition.

From reviewer feedback we learned several things. Reviewers made it clear that the primary reason they use this book is to teach students to write program plans or apply for grants in a way that will meet current expectations of funding sources for documentation of efficiency and effectiveness. This was consistent with our thinking in creating the first and second editions of the book. Some faculty liked the practical orientation, while others felt a stronger theoretical framework would help set the stage for the planning process. Some reorganization of content was suggested to strengthen the logical flow. Several reviewers suggested that we put the planning model into a more contemporary context using concepts (such as the logic model and evidenced-based practice) promoted by the United Way and other organizations. Many advised that we bring our discussion of technology up to date by calling attention to the role of the Internet as a resource in problem analysis, and giving recognition to the ways in which software is used in data collection, aggregation, and reporting. We have attempted to respond to all of these suggestions in writing this new edition.

One of the major changes incorporated into this edition was to take a single example and use it throughout the book. We selected a domestic violence situation as the problem to be addressed, and a shelter as our example of the host agency. In response to a suggestion that we emphasize that local agencies often deliver services as a part of county or statewide efforts, we used as an illustration a statewide program (which we called Victims to Victors), and made the local agency (which we called Safe Haven) one of the providers contributing to the achievement of statewide goals for the reduction of domestic violence. This does not mean that we eliminated all references to other populations and problems, but it does mean that in following the logic of the program planning process, students will be able to track from one phase to the next the application to three selected programs offered by the Safe Haven domestic violence shelter. We hope that this will help them to better understand the issues of internal consistency and integrity in program planning—from problem analysis through evaluation—and will enable them to apply the concepts to their own program plans. To further emphasize the importance of a solid foundation and consistency in program planning, we added a new chapter on theory in which we establish the place of theory in the approach to planning as well as in understanding the social problem to be addressed. To reinforce these concepts, we emphasize these themes throughout the book.

While we feel we have made a good faith effort to respond to reviewers' suggestions, we were not able to address every concern. One reviewer proposed that we eliminate the whole concept of process objectives and several suggested streamlining our material on budgeting and leaving out the details of actually creating a cost allocation plan. Our concern in eliminating content is that we might create more problems than we solved. We felt that our description of the process needed to be complete, and that it is easier for faculty to skip over material they choose to exclude than to find a way to include it if it has been dropped. Overall, however, we feel that we have addressed the vast majority of points raised by the reviewers. We hope that they are pleased with the contributions they have made to this edition and that others who continue to use it find that it improves and enhances the learning process for their students. This edition also includes a CD with an instructor's guide providing some suggested assignments and PowerPoint presentations used and continually updated by one of the authors over many years and based on his teaching program planning to over 2,000 students.

We wish to thank our reviewers, Debra Anderson, Rosalyn Chernesky, Kenneth Corvo, Robert Fischer, Beulah Hirschlein, Theresa Roberts, Yvonne Unrau, Karen VanderVen, Beth Warner, and Dale Weaver for their careful and thoughtful feedback on their experiences with the second edition of this book. We are grateful to Armand Lauffer, Professor Emeritus of the University of Michigan School of Social Work and editor of the Sage Human Services Guides and Sourcebooks, for his consistently helpful and practical advice on all three editions of this book. And finally we would like to express our appreciation to Kassie Graves, Sage Acquisitions Editor for Human Services, and to Veronica Novak, Senior Editorial Assistant, who got this third edition off to a very good start with their thorough analysis and organization of reviewer feedback and who have been so helpful and flexible in supporting the completion of this edition.

As with the first two editions, we have attempted to produce a product that will be useful to both practitioners and students. We are aware that many are currently devoting a great deal of time and energy to analyzing social problems, writing goals and objectives, designing programs and data collection systems, preparing budgets, and designing evaluation plans that will be responsive to the new and continuing demands for accountability. One of our most gratifying experiences as authors of this book has been to hear from students who have kept their copies of the book, who still have their old, dog-eared first or second editions on their shelves and constantly refer to them as they encounter various challenges in practice. We sincerely hope that this new edition will support and strengthen future student and practitioner efforts in even more effective ways.

Peter M. Kettner
Robert M. Moroney
Lawrence L. Martin

PART I

Assessing Current Practices

Chapter 1

Contemporary Issues in Social Service Program Planning and Administration

CHAPTER OVERVIEW

The purpose of this chapter is to introduce:

- The major governmental and other initiatives that have prompted the need for program planning
- The relationship between the logic model and program planning
- How agencies and community-wide networks relate to each other in addressing social problems
- The steps that are involved in effectiveness-based program planning
- The elements of a program that are critical to measuring effectiveness

---

The following topics are covered in this chapter:

- The era of accountability
- Designing for monitoring, performance measurement, and evaluation
- The Logic Model
- Community focus
- The issue of effectiveness
- Assessing an existing program
- What is effectiveness-based program planning?
- Using effectiveness principles to understand existing programs
  - Defining programs
  - Problem analysis
  - Needs assessment
  - Selecting a strategy and establishing objectives
  - Program design
  - Data requirements for performance measurement
  - Monitoring, using information technology
  - Budgeting
  - Program evaluation

The Era of Accountability

When it comes to planning, funding, and implementing human service programs at the federal, state, and local levels, times have change dramatically over the last few decades. There was a time when expectations were relatively simple: do your best to meet local needs, manage the budget responsibly, and pass an audit each year. This situation began to change in the 1980s when public, tax-funded support for human service programs began to decline. With decreased funding came more competition between human service providers as well as increased demands for accountability, including the monitoring of service provision, performance measurement, and program evaluation. Fast-forwarding to the present day, human service programs are now embedded in a system of *performance accountability*. The overriding question being asked by both government and private sector funding sources (e.g., United Ways and foundations) is: Do human service programs work? The logical follow up question is: If they don't work, why should they continue to be funded?

The Government Performance and Results Act has become a major driver of performance accountability at the federal level. GPRA, as the law is known, requires federal departments and agencies to annually report their performance to the president and Congress. To facilitate this annual reporting, the "Executive Branch Management Scorecard" ranks federal agencies on several criteria, including how well they have implemented performance accountability and the extent to which performance is linked to the budget process (see www.whitehouse.gov/results).

A second driver of performance accountability at the federal level is the performance contracting requirements of the Federal Acquisition Regulation (FAR). The FAR represents the formal contracting policies and procedures of the federal government. The FAR requires that "all federal service contracts (including human service contracts) be performance based to the maximum extent possible" (www.acqunet.gov/far).

At the state and local government levels, two major drivers of performance accountability are the reporting initiative of the Government Accounting Standards Board (GASB) and the performance measurement requirements imposed by governors and state legislatures. GASB sets financial and reporting standards for state and local governments. GASB has long advocated that state and local governments adopt performance accountability systems that track and report on the outputs, quality, and outcomes of government programs. GASB calls its recommended performance accountability system "service efforts and accomplishments (SEA) reporting" (GASB, 1993). As of 2006, 48 of the 50 states have some form of mandated performance accountability systems (Melkers and Willoughby, 1998); many of these initiatives also tie performance measures to the budget process. Some 50% of municipal and county governments nationwide have some sort of performance accountability system in place (Melkers and Willoughby, 2005). Private sector funding organizations, such as foundations and the United Way (1996, 2006), have also adopted performance accountability systems. Most nonprofit human service agencies that receive government, foundation, or United Way funding through grants and contracts have likewise adopted performance accountability systems in order to satisfy the reporting requirements of their funders (United Way, 2003).

Designing for Monitoring, Performance Measurement, and Evaluation

The primary focus of this book is on designing programs and services in a way that allows collection of the kinds of data that will support responsiveness to funding source mandates for accountability, and at the same time will allow program evaluators to determine whether or not the programs work. This is an important point. If monitoring, performance measurement, and evaluation activities are anticipated at the end of service provision, they will be possible only if certain design elements are incorporated at the beginning of the planning process. The Urban Institute pioneered an effort to establish criteria by which programs could be assessed in terms of whether or not they could be evaluated. They called this effort "Evaluability Assessment." Some of the criteria they specified in order for a program to be considered "evaluable" include: evidence required by management can be reliably produced, evidence required by management is feasible to collect, and management's intended use of the information can realistically be expected to affect performance (Schmidt, Scanlon, and Bell, 1979). The term *evidence* refers to the collection of data around specified variables that define service characteristics and results. Social work has adopted the term *evidence-based practice* to emphasize that clinical decisions must be based on the best available evidence from systematic research wherever possible (Johnson and Austin, 2006; McNeill, 2006). Management's use of evidence simply takes this concept to the next level, defining the parameters within which evidence will be collected, how it will be aggregated, and how it will be used for monitoring, performance measurement, and evaluation. One thing should be made perfectly clear. Designing programs that can be evaluated will mean collecting quantified data on service provision and client response. It will also require that data be captured in a spreadsheet or database to facilitate analysis. Only when data are displayed in some comparative format such as these can the program planner or analyst begin to understand what works and what doesn't.

The Logic Model

The framework for design is a variation of the logic model approach, which is built around basic concepts associated with systems theory. The logic model can be useful in helping the practitioner establish a context for incorporating theory into the planning process (Savaya and Waysman, 2005). The variation of the logic model that we use here uses "program" as the unit of analysis. The purpose of the logic model is to depict the sequence of events that identifies program resources, matches them to needs, activates the service process, completes the service process, and measures results. The sequence is depicted in Figure 1.1 below.

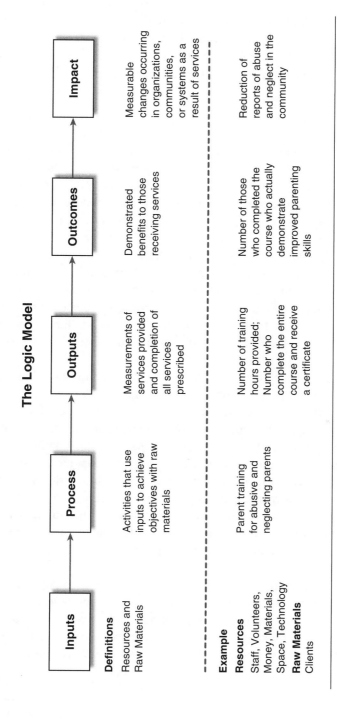

Figure 1.1   The Logic Model

The Logic Model

| Inputs | Process | Outputs | Outcomes | Impact |

Definitions

Inputs: Resources and Raw Materials

Process: Activities that use inputs to achieve objectives with raw materials

Outputs: Measurements of services provided and completion of all services prescribed

Outcomes: Demonstrated benefits to those receiving services

Impact: Measurable changes occurring in organizations, communities, or systems as a result of services

Example

Resources
Staff, Volunteers, Money, Materials, Space, Technology

Raw Materials
Clients

Process: Parent training for abusive and neglecting parents

Outputs: Number of training hours provided; Number who complete the entire course and receive a certificate

Outcomes: Number of those who completed the course who actually demonstrate improved parenting skills

Impact: Reduction of reports of abuse and neglect in the community

This model allows the planner to see the rational flow of addressing a problem and applying a process, while maintaining a focus on the purpose of the entire effort: effecting positive changes in the lives of clients and reducing the size and scope of a problem in a community.

Community Focus

One result of the emphasis on accountability has been to shift the focus from what an agency is providing and accomplishing to what impact a program is having on the community. Most problems addressed by human service programs are community problems, such as children in need of a safe environment, homeless people in need of shelter and rehabilitation, victims of crime and violence in need of protection, family breakdown, the spread of AIDS, and others. These problems are so complex that it is unlikely that services from just one agency can have a significant and measurable impact on an entire community. For this reason, funding sources have learned that they must put resources (primarily money) into a community with the expectation that a number of agencies will collaborate in addressing the problem in the interest of achieving a more comprehensive impact.

The consequences of this approach for program planning are that, early in the planning and proposal writing stages of a program, planners need to know something about the problem and the characteristics of the target population and need to include these data elements in their management information systems. In the following chapters we will examine in great detail the many developmental phases a program must go through and the many elements that need to be included if it is to be considered "effectiveness based." We will also attempt to illustrate how agency management information systems and agency budgets can be structured in a way that allows them to fit into a larger community system and enables the community to measure the impact on the problem while the agency measures the effectiveness of its services.

Basic to all program monitoring, performance measurement, and evaluation is the need for appropriate information technology support in terms of computer hardware, software, and expertise capable of tracking clients and generating program reports. And to achieve the full benefits of effectiveness-based program planning, there must also be a strong commitment from the top and all the way through entry level personnel that evaluation of effectiveness is critical to the success of any client service program, and that evaluation data will be used to initiate changes in the program as it becomes clear that they are needed.

The Issue of Effectiveness

Both efficiency and effectiveness have become major considerations in social service program and agency administration. *Efficiency* can be defined as the ratio of outputs to inputs or, in other words, how much service a program provides in relation to its costs. *Effectiveness* refers to the achievement of client outcomes (quality of life changes) as the result of receiving services. Measuring outputs and outcomes requires that service providers track such factors as the amount of service a client received, whether or not the client completed the program or dropped out, and how much the client improved between entry into and exit from the program.

The term *program* also has some very specific meanings. A program is defined as a prearranged set of activities designed to achieve a stated set of goals and objectives (Netting, Kettner, and McMurtry, 2008). This is an important and sometimes elusive concept for a newcomer to the profession to grasp. If there is an expectation that stated objectives will be met and that monitoring, performance measurement, and/or evaluation will take place at some point, an agency must plan in advance to establish goals and objectives, and to provide clear definitions of services to be provided and results expected. Client requests for help must be categorized in some way, after which clients are directed into services that offer the best possibility of meeting their needs and resolving their problems.

The Commonwealth of Australia has done a particularly good job of applying the concept of effectiveness-based program planning for government-sponsored services. In defining programs, for example, police services are broken down into four areas or programs: (1) community safety and support, (2) crime investigation, (3) road safety and traffic management, and (4) services to the judicial process. Services to the aging are broken down into residential care and community care, with specific indicators identified to track access to service and appropriateness and quality of service. Child Protective Services (CPS), in addition to direct services to children and families, include services from police, courts, education, child care, and health (Steering Committee for the Review of Government Service Provision, or SCRGSP, 2006). The point is that services need to be categorized, defined, matched to client need, and delivered to determine whether or not they have been successful. Data collection systems are closely tied to program definitions.

Programs may be staffed by specialists who work exclusively with a defined population or problem, or staff responsibilities may cut across more than one program. The important issue is that client data must be associated with specific programs and services so that valid and reliable measures are produced.

Assessing an Existing Program

In this opening chapter we will attempt to illustrate, through the use of a series of questions addressed to the reader, that designing effective programs requires a careful, detailed thought process that begins with an understanding of a social problem and ends with analysis of data on effectiveness. Chapters 2 through 13 will focus on the tasks to be accomplished and the elements to be considered and defined in order to create programs capable of demonstrating effectiveness.

The tasks and processes of program development that will be proposed are by their very nature complex, simply because social and personal problems are complex and sometimes well entrenched. The problems and the populations to be served will require thoughtful study and analysis. The purpose of delving into the complexities of social problems and social service programs is to insure there is a good fit of service to need, so that service can be more precisely focused on getting the kinds of results intended. In short, it is a more proactive approach that is more assertive in ensuring service providers produce results rather than merely hoping that things turn out well for the client.

Perhaps in the same way that an understanding of the law is of critical importance to a practicing attorney or an understanding of the body to a physician, so understanding of social problems and programs is central to the practice of social work. This understanding will require that old assumptions be challenged and new approaches to serving clients be implemented as we learn more about effectiveness. In a sense, we will be proposing that programs go through periodic checkups to determine their continuing effectiveness and relevance in a changing environment.

What Is Effectiveness-Based Program Planning?

The idea of conducting periodic checkups is, in essence, what effectiveness-based program planning is all about. Designing effective programs requires that social service professionals develop a thoroughly researched understanding about social problems, people in need, and social services. A commitment to effectiveness requires the collection of new kinds of data—data that will provide information about client conditions at entry into and exit from services, thereby making clear the impact of services on problems. This approach, which we will refer to throughout this book as *effectiveness-based program planning,* will make clear where changes in programs are needed, so that services provided do more of the things that help and fewer of the things that do not. The system is designed to be useful for both direct service and management purposes.

Effectiveness-based program planning involves taking a program through a series of steps designed to produce a clear understanding of the problem to be addressed, to measure client problem type and severity at entry, to provide a relevant intervention, to measure client problem type and severity at exit, and to examine selected indicators in a follow-up study to determine long-range outcomes. The purpose of all these activities is to provide a basis for continual improvement of services to clients and to provide a common database for both clinical and administrative staff for analysis and decision making about program changes. This way, instead of asking clinicians to fill out forms useful only for completing management reports, clinical staff can record data useful for understanding the progress of their clients and, at the same time, provide data and information necessary to good program management.

Using Effectiveness Principles to Understand Existing Programs

In the following chapters we will present a step-by-step process that will enable the reader to begin with a social or personal problem experienced by clients and end with a program designed to get results and be able to document them. Before beginning these chapters, however, we propose that you take a few minutes to take stock of current agency practices in a social service agency with which you are familiar as a means of becoming acquainted with some of the basic concepts of effectiveness-based program planning. This may be helpful in drawing a contrast between the way social service programs are often designed and the way they must be designed for measurement purposes.

The following assessment instrument is divided into sections on each of these topics:

- Defining programs
- Problem analysis
- Needs assessment
- Selecting a strategy and establishing objectives
- Program design
- Data requirements for performance measurement
- Monitoring, using information technology
- Budgeting
- Program evaluation

If you are interested simply in a quick overview of a program's strong and weak areas, you may wish to limit your assessment to checking yes and no answers. If, on the other hand, you wish to conduct a more in-depth assessment, use the instrument as a basis for interviewing key program staff and fill in answers to the follow-up questions. The program planning model discussed is designed for those programs that provide a direct service to clients. It is not applicable for support programs such as fund-raising, lobbying, and advocacy.

Defining Programs

In this section we explore the extent to which agency services are organized into programs. Some social service agencies organize their programs so that each offers a specialized set of services to a defined population (e.g., detox, family counseling, employment services). Others may be designed in a way that all clients come through a common intake point and are systematically assigned to case managers who have room in their caseloads rather than to specialists. This is an important distinction in applying the principles of effectiveness-based program planning, and one of the first elements of design that the practitioner needs to assess. The following two questions are intended to encourage you to think through where your agency stands on its definition and separation of programs.

1. Does your agency provide for clients a number of
clearly defined and distinct programs that provide
specialized services matched to client need
(as opposed to providing undifferentiated casework
services for all clients)?   Yes __ No __

2. If your agency does have separate programs,
can you identify agency staff and resources
that are allocated to each of these programs?   Yes __ No __

3. Do staff have a clear understanding of the distinct
focus and limitations of the services to be provided
to clients within each program (as opposed to
open-ended problem solving)?   Yes __ No __

If the answer to the above questions is no, you may conclude your participation in this survey at this point or select another agency, because the remaining sections focus on questions about programs.

Problem Analysis

In Chapters 2 and 3, we deal with the need for a thorough understanding of the theoretical underpinnings and the etiology (cause-and-effect relationships) of the problem the program is intended to address. Sound practice requires that programs be based on a thorough study and analysis of the problem, but that is not always the case. Programs are sometimes planned and funded for political or ideological reasons without regard for the facts or the realities of the situation. However, as we hope to demonstrate, those programs that have the greatest probability of success will be those that develop a clear understanding of the type, size, and scope of the problem as well as its relevant historical highlights, theory, research findings, and etiology.

For example, if a program is to be designed to treat drug users, it would be important to understand that people use drugs for different reasons, and treatment must be carefully tied to these reasons. Suburban housewives, junior high school kids, and street gang members, for example, each need to be understood in context. Program planners, therefore, must set out to discover how many of each type are in the community, their reasons for using drugs, where they live, and how severe their problems are. This approach provides a solid foundation on which to build an effective and precisely targeted program or intervention.

4.   Thinking of one particular program or service, can you identify the problem(s) this program is intended to address (e.g., teen unemployment; lack of housing for families with temporarily unemployed breadwinners)?   Yes ___ No ___

If yes, state it/them:

5.   Can you define the target population(s) this program is intended to serve (e.g., unskilled, unemployed high school dropouts ages 16 to 21; homeless families in need of temporary shelter for up to 90 days)?   Yes ___ No ___

If yes, define it/them:

6.   Can you identify geographic boundaries for the population served by your program?   Yes ___ No ___

If yes, state them:

7.   If necessary, could you provide a reasonably accurate estimate (based on reliable documentation) of the number of people within these boundaries who fit the description in questions number 4 and 5 for problem and target population?   Yes ___ No ___

If yes, identify the populations and list the estimates:

8.   Can you identify data sources for the above statistics?   Yes ___ No ___

If yes, list them:

9.   Are there commonly agreed-upon understandings among staff who work in your program about the primary or most common causes of this problem and about cause-effect relationships (e.g., limited education, peer pressure, substance abuse, etc.)?   Yes ___ No ___

If yes, list them:

10.   Is there sound theory and research to back up these understandings, and are staff aware of the theory and research?   Yes ___ No ___

If yes, briefly explain:

Needs Assessment

When someone is experiencing a problem, that individual has a need. Sometimes the need is obvious: Someone who is homeless needs a home; someone who is unemployed needs a job. At other times the need is more subtle and more difficult to meet—for example, the need for a permanent and loving relationship with a nurturing parent substitute, the need for a mentor to help build self-confidence, or the need to learn a work ethic in order to succeed in employment.

Accuracy and skill in matching needs to services comes from solid, thorough work on problem analysis. Once you are comfortable that you have an understanding of need, it is time to turn to techniques of needs assessment. There are four different perspectives from which we look at need: *normative need* (as defined by experts in the field), *perceived need* (as seen by those experiencing the need), *expressed need* (from those who seek out services), and *relative need* (needs and resources in one geographic area compared with needs and resources in another) (Bradshaw, 1972).

The following questions will give you an opportunity to explore your understanding of each of these perspectives on need, and to think through the extent to which your programs have taken these perspectives into account.

11. Given the problem you identified in question 4, is there agreement among your clinical staff about the major categories of needs of clients who come to you with these problems (e.g., parent training, shelter, etc.)?   Yes __ No __

   If yes, list the categories of need:

12. Are there any standards that are used to establish normative need (i.e., a point or level defined by experts below which one is defined as being in need in this particular problem area, for example, people below a certain income are said to be in need, children experiencing specified levels of neglect are said to be in need)?   Yes __ No __

   If yes, identify the standards:

13. Can you define what consumers of your services (clients) perceive their needs to be?   Yes __ No __

   If yes, list the major categories of need:

14. Of those people who seek services from this
program, do you know approximately what
percentage is served? Is there a waiting list?   Yes ___   No ___

If yes, state the percentage:

15. Do you know how the volume of services
provided in your community compares with the
volume of these same services provided in other,
comparable communities in terms of percentage
of needy population served? (In other words, do
you serve a larger or a smaller percentage than
other, comparable communities?)   Yes ___   No ___

If yes, cite data that help depict comparative need:

Selecting a Strategy and Establishing Objectives

Once the problem analysis and the needs assessment have been completed, it is time to begin to think about a strategy for reducing or eliminating the problem by meeting the needs of people who have the problem.
This involves a number of steps. By this point in the program planning
process, we are well grounded in history, theory, research, and etiology of
the problem; therefore, we are in a position to propose an appropriate intervention. We then propose one or more program hypotheses—statements
about what outcomes are expected if a person with the problems we have
defined receives appropriate service(s). Program hypotheses, then, provide a framework for the development of precisely stated goals, objectives,
and activities.

The following questions should help in assessing your understanding
of a program's underlying assumptions and expectations.

16. Can you spell out the underlying assumptions
about your client population and the expected
effects of your program in the form of a series
of "if . . . then" statements (e.g., If parents learn
good communication skills and if they use them
with their children, then they are less likely to
resort to physical violence with their children)?   Yes ___   No ___

If yes, state them:

17. Can you identify the following as they relate to
   your program?
   - an independent variable (services provided)   Yes __   No __
   - a dependent variable (expected ultimate or
     long-term results of services)   Yes __   No __
   - an intervening variable (intermediate or
     short-term results of services)   Yes __   No __

   If yes, state them:

18. Looking at the way you assess client need
   in your program:

   Does it permit you to categorize and compare
   clients at intake by type and severity of problem?   Yes __   No __

   If yes, identify the assessment instrument and list
   its categories:

19. Does your program have written objectives that
   specify expected outcomes for clients?   Yes __   No __

20. Is there evidence that your program staff attempt
   to move clients toward these outcomes?   Yes __   No __

   If yes, describe the evidence:

Program Design

It is one thing to understand a need; it is quite another matter to design an intervention that will meet that need. Research in the field has made it clear that certain problems will respond better to certain, more precise interventions. The purpose of the program design phase is to put together that service or combination of services that appears to have the best possible chance of achieving the program's objectives. Program design involves careful consideration of the resources needed to address the needs of clients and attention to the ways in which these resources will be organized. It is a critical point in the planning and management of programs.

If we simply consolidate a great deal of program design under the heading of "casework," we leave decisions about client assessment, service provision, service completion, and outcome assessment to the professional judgment of each caseworker. When this happens, it becomes difficult if not impossible to examine program effectiveness and to modify program design in the interest of improving services to clients. On the other hand, bringing precision to each element of program design allows for constant examination and constructive program change as data and information about effectiveness become available to guide our refinements.

The following questions should help you in assessing the level of precision achieved in specifying the elements of your program design.

21. Does your program have identified problem or need categories that can be checked off at intake and used to help in understanding client needs in the aggregate?　　　　　Yes __　No __

If yes, list the categories:

22. Does your program have some method for quantifying or scaling severity of problems?　　　Yes __　No __

If yes, describe it:

23. Do you collect quantified data on the following?
   - client demographics　　　　　　　　　Yes __　No __
   - client social history data　　　　　　　Yes __　No __
   - client problem type and severity　　　　Yes __　No __

24. Do you itemize service tasks for each service you provide and record the amount of time or volume of each task provided for each client?　　Yes __　No __

If yes, list the service tasks:

25. Do you specify acceptable service methods for each type of service (e.g., one-to-one counseling, group treatment, classroom instruction)?　　Yes __　No __

If yes, list them:

26. Do you have some way of identifying those who complete your program and those who drop out so that you can do some analysis of these as separate populations?　　　　　　　　　Yes __　No __

If yes, describe how they are tracked:

27. Do you quantify and measure results with clients using some sort of a pre-post measure?　　Yes __　No __

If yes, describe it:

28. Do you follow up with clients and collect data that indicate long-term effects of treatment?　　Yes __　No __

If yes, list the follow-up variables:

29. Do you have a formally defined unit of service
that you use to measure the amount or volume
of service provided by your program?   Yes __ No __

   If yes, describe it:

30. Do you have written standards to which you adhere
that protect the quality of service provided to clients?   Yes __ No __

   If yes, cite them:

Data Requirements for Performance Measurement

Data collection is the *sine qua non* of effectiveness-based program planning. All the effort put into the development of a program hypothesis, goals and objectives, and design will mean little if the correct data are not collected, aggregated, and reported. Data collection systems must be designed to answer questions about meeting community need, program implementation, productivity, costs, and achievement of outputs and outcomes. Principles associated with performance measurement should be understood before attempting to design a management information system. The following questions may be useful in understanding the data requirements effectiveness-based program planning:

31. Do program planners have a common
understanding of the community need that
is intended to be met by the program?   Yes __ No __

   If yes, state the need:

32. Is there agreement about how data on service
delivery requirements, such as service definition,
service tasks, and standards, will be collected?   Yes __ No __

   If yes, describe data collection plans:

33. Is there agreement about how data on
products/services, quality, and service
completions will be collected?   Yes __ No __

   If yes, describe data collection plans:

34. Is there agreement about how data will
be collected to measure program success?   Yes __ No __

   If yes, describe data collection plans:

35.   Is there agreement about how unit costs
for services provided, service completions,
and client outcomes will be calculated?   Yes ___ No ___

Monitoring, Using Information Technology

Once program data elements have been designed and implemented in accordance with the guidelines established for effectiveness-based program planning, they can be collected, processed, and aggregated in a manner that informs both clinical staff and administrators. Programs can be said to meet objectives and to bring about positive changes in clients' lives only if the data generated from the program provision process can support such statements.

In contemporary social service agency management, computerized data management is absolutely essential. Narrative case recording is useful for individual case analysis, planning, supervision, and documentation, but virtually useless for purposes of program management and administration. In effectiveness-based program planning, we propose a client data system that is capable of producing data and information about the progress of clients throughout each episode of service and the effects of these services at termination and follow-up. This information, we believe, should be used by all levels of staff, each from its own perspective.

The following questions may be useful in assessing the strengths and weaknesses of an existing monitoring system.

36.   Do you have a computerized data collection
and data processing system that is used
for client data?   Yes ___ No ___

37.   Do you collect, enter, aggregate, and cross-tabulate
selected variables (such as those listed below) to
help you achieve a better understanding of your
clients and their problems?   Yes ___ No ___
- client demographics   Yes ___ No ___
- client social history data   Yes ___ No ___
- client problem type   Yes ___ No ___
- client problem severity   Yes ___ No ___
- staff characteristics   Yes ___ No ___
- material resources provided to clients   Yes ___ No ___
- service type   Yes ___ No ___
- service tasks   Yes ___ No ___

- unit of service   Yes __   No __
- method of intervention   Yes __   No __
- service completion   Yes __   No __
- intermediate outcome   Yes __   No __
- long-term outcome   Yes __   No __
- financial data   Yes __   No __

38.   Do you produce tables of aggregated data
        about clients and client services on a regular basis?   Yes __   No __

39.   Do appropriate groups such as the following
        use these tables to better understand the effects
        of services provided?   Yes __   No __
        - clinical/direct service staff   Yes __   No __
        - supervisors   Yes __   No __
        - program managers   Yes __   No __
        - administrators   Yes __   No __
        - board of directors or political body to whom the
          program is accountable   Yes __   No __

40.   Do you periodically discuss what changes
        should be made to improve your program based
        on data produced by your monitoring system?   Yes __   No __

Budgeting

All programs and services depend on funding for their continuation, and for many funding sources there are no guarantees that the same level of support will continue year after year. It is, therefore, in the interests of clients and staff to ensure that the best possible results are being achieved for the lowest possible cost. A well-designed budgeting system is capable of generating important and valuable information for use in making program changes in the interest of providing better quality services for clients at a lower cost. Unfortunately, many budgets in human service agencies reflect only categories for which dollars are to be spent. These are called line-item budgets. In effectiveness-based program planning we propose, instead of or in addition to this simplistic type of budgeting, methods for calculating costs for items such as provision of a unit of service (e.g., an hour of counseling), completion of the full complement of prescribed services by one client (e.g., 10 parent training sessions), achievement of a measurable outcome by one client (e.g., improved parenting skills), and achievement of a program objective (e.g., at least a 50% reduction in child abuse reports on those who complete the class).

For example, by costing out services we may learn that it costs just $1,500 per trainee to complete a training program. However, if we also find that there is a 50% dropout rate, the cost then doubles to $3,000 per "graduate." These kinds of calculations help staff keep focused on using resources in a way that steers clients in the direction that offers them the best possible chance of success at the lowest cost. These types of calculations should ultimately lead to more cost-effective and cost-efficient operation of social service programs.

The following questions should help you in assessing the strengths and weaknesses of your current budgeting system.

41.   Can you calculate the following from the budget
         data you collect?
         • line items by program   Yes __   No __
         • direct costs by program   Yes __   No __
         • indirect costs by program   Yes __   No __
         • total program costs   Yes __   No __
         • cost per intermediate output (unit of service)   Yes __   No __
         • cost per service completion   Yes __   No __
         • cost per client outcome   Yes __   No __

Program Evaluation

One of the most exciting features of effectiveness-based program planning is that it produces information that informs staff about how successful the program was in relation to expectations as expressed in objectives. How many abusing and neglecting parents completed parent training? How many can demonstrate improved parenting skills? How many have stopped abusing and neglecting and are progressing toward more effective relationships with their children? This information can bring together direct service staff, supervisors, managers, administrators, and board members around a common set of concerns and interests. It is always more satisfying to be able to say, at the end of a program year, "We helped 75% of our clients to master at least 10 techniques of effective parenting" than simply to be able to say, "We provided services to 100 abusing and neglecting families." Furthermore, the database produced can provide the raw material for an ongoing research and development function within the agency, a function usually reserved for only the wealthiest organizations.

In this section we will explore methods of evaluating social service programs from several different perspectives.

42. Do you regularly use any of the following
    approaches to program evaluation?
    - evaluation of the amount of staff time and
      resources used in direct client services and
      ways to reduce costs   Yes __ No __
    - evaluation of the service provision process
      and the extent to which it fits the program
      design as originally intended   Yes __ No __
    - evaluation of the cost of outputs (units of
      service) and ways to reduce costs without
      adversely affecting service quality   Yes __ No __
    - evaluation of outcomes achieved with clients
      and ways to improve them   Yes __ No __
    - evaluation of the costs of outcomes and ways
      to reduce costs without adversely affecting clients   Yes __ No __
    - evaluation of the contribution made by your
      program to the total community in terms
      of its impact on the social problem experienced
      by the community   Yes __ No __

The foregoing questions are intended to provide a very general overview of a particular program in terms of its fit with the principles of effectiveness-based program planning. The purpose is to familiarize you with some of the more important concepts, but applying the questions to a program can also provide some clues to where the major work needs to be done to allow for monitoring, performance measurement, and evaluation.

The following chapters are intended to explain each of the phases of effectiveness-based program planning. As you proceed through these chapters we encourage you to think through and apply the concepts to a specific program, perhaps the program you have assessed using the foregoing questionnaire. While the most ideal application of these principles is in designing new programs, you may also find that existing programs can be converted with careful attention to the details of each phase of the planning process.

References

Bradshaw, J. (1972). The concept of social need. *New Society, 30,* 640–643.

Government Accounting Standards Board (GASB). (1993). *Proposed statement of the Governmental Accounting Standards Board on concepts related to service efforts and accomplishments reporting.* Norwalk, CT: Author.

Johnson, M., & Austin, M. (2006). Evidence-based practice in the social services: Implications for organizational change. *Administration in Social Work, 30*(3), 75–104.

McNeill, T. (2006). Evidence-based practice in an age of relativism: Toward a model for practice. *Social Work, 51*(2), 147–156.

Melkers J., & Willoughby, K. (1998). "The state of the states: Performance budgeting requirements in 47 out of 50." *Public Administration Review, 58*(1), 66–73.

Melkers, J., & Willoughby, K. (2005). "Models of performance-measurement use in local governments: Understanding budgeting, communication, and lasting effects." *Public Administration Review, 65*(2), 180–190.

Netting, F., Kettner, P., & McMurtry, S. (2008). *Social work macro practice* (4th ed.). Boston: Allyn & Bacon.

Savaya, R., & Waysman, M. (2005). The logic model: A tool for incorporating theory in development and evaluation of programs. *Administration in Social Work, 29*(2), 85–103.

Schmidt, R. E., Scanlon, J. W., & Bell, J. B. (1979). *Evaluability assessment: Making public programs work better.* Washington, DC: U.S. Department of Health, Education and Welfare.

Steering Committee for the Review of Government Service Provision (SCRGSP). (2006). *Report on government services 2006.* Canberra, Australia: Productivity Commission.

United Way of America. (1996). *Measuring program outcomes: A practical approach.* Arlington, VA: Author.

United Way of America. (2003). *Program outcome measurement: Outcome measurement in national health and human services and accrediting organizations.* Arlington, VA: United Way of America.

United Way of America. (2006). *Outcomes measurement resource network.* http://national.unitedway.org/outcomes/resources (7/03/06).

PART II

Problem Analysis/Needs Assessment

Chapter 2

The Contribution of Theory to Program Planning

CHAPTER OVERVIEW

The purpose of this chapter is to explain:

- Why the use of theory is important in understanding social problems
- Why and how theory is used in program planning
- How to differentiate between theory of practice and theory in practice
- How to differentiate between theory of program planning and theory in program planning
- The differences between strategic, management and program planning

The following topics are covered in this chapter:

- The use of theory in program planning
- Theory of practice
- Theory in practice
- Theory of program planning
- Types of planning
- Theory in program planning

The Use of Theory in Program Planning

A reviewer in 1991 had this to say about this book:

> A well organized discussion of an effectiveness-oriented approach to social service program design, management and evaluation. . . . Essentially it is a cookbook approach in which Step A must be completed before Step B, and each of the remaining activities follows from completion to the previous one. This is a very good cookbook. (Community Alternatives, 1991)

While we appreciated this review of our first edition, we wondered over the years whether we should make a more explicit case that our book is more than an ordinary cookbook that identifies the ingredients that the cook needs to assemble as well as the order of their introduction and how much of each ingredient to use. We always assumed that our "cookbook" provided another dimension. It was more than just a methodology or a set of activities that, if followed, should result in the development of more effective programs. A professional wants to know *why* these activities in specified amounts and in a specified order produce the desired products.

We hoped that the reader would see that our approach was based on the assumption that program planning is *theory* driven, and that the methodology produces effective programs because it incorporates theory on at least two levels.

To paraphrase Karl Popper (1959), a preeminent social scientist of the 20th century, researchers who collect data without a road map are merely on a fishing expedition. They hope that if they collect enough data and examine them long enough, not only will there emerge answers, but even questions. These researchers are often referred to as "rank empiricists," many of whom subject data to statistical techniques such as correlational analysis and seek to find answers by finding statistically significant correlations. Popper argued that social science research needs to begin not only with the development of hypotheses that will guide the collection and analysis of data, but with hypotheses that can be verified and falsified, tested and refuted. To develop hypotheses a researcher draws on existing theories. Testing hypotheses may also lead to a modification of those theories.

We agree with Popper and maintain that a *program*, which we define as a set of activities to produce some desired outcomes, is basically a hypothesis and that a hypothesis, which we define as a set of statements about the relationships between specified variables, is derived from an understanding of relevant literature and theory.

Faludi (1973), a well-recognized planning theorist, distinguished between "theory of" and "theory in" a problem-solving process. The first, "theory of" (in this case, theory of planning) is concerned with the process the planner uses, the *how* of problem solving. In program planning we need to introduce and implement a series of steps or activities that guide the planner. The second, "theory in" (as used in this book, theory in planning) attempts to provide the planner with an understanding of the problem he or she is attempting to resolve, the *what and why* of the problem.

Theory of Practice

Before we discuss theory and planning in more detail, we will begin examining theory at a more basic level—the clinical level. When working with a client/patient, a case manager carries out a set of activities or a process:

- Collection of data and information
- Assessment of the problem based on the assessment data
- Development of a treatment plan
- Implementation of that plan
- Monitoring of progress
- Evaluation

Initially there is gathering of data and information and an assessment of the situation to better understand what the problem is and what might be done to resolve it. Intake data are collected to understand who the client is. These often include:

- *Demographic or descriptive information*, such as age, gender, ethnicity, marital status, education, income, etc.
- *Social history data*, including information relevant to the presenting problem such as previous substance abuse, mental illness, etc.
- *Etiology of the presenting problem information*, which is collected when the therapist attempts to identify those factors that either cause the problem or place the client at risk for developing it.

These assessment data help the therapist make a diagnosis, develop a treatment plan, and so forth. The six activities in this process—collection of data and information, assessment of the problem based on the assessment data, development of a treatment plan, implementation of that plan, monitoring of progress, and evaluation—make up the *problem-solving methodology*, the "theory of" dimension.

Theory in Practice

"Theory in" the problem-solving process relates to that part of the assessment process that attempts to identify the etiology of the problem and the factors associated with the presence of the problem.

In the first two editions we used a number of different illustrative examples drawn from the human service field. In this edition we will use a single issue—domestic violence. In this way, we hope that the reader will more clearly see how each activity builds on a previous activity, how a problem statement is translated into a hypothesis, and how a hypothesis is translated into a hierarchy of goals and objectives, and so forth.

While there are many points of intervention in the case of domestic violence, such as (1) prevention, (2) early intervention when the abuse has begun, and (3) support for a woman who is seeking help to escape from her abuser, the following is an example of the last event. Each of these three will draw on different literature bases at times and offer different theoretical positions. Here we are looking at the literature that identifies the intrapersonal and external issues that often create barriers to her seeking help.

When a woman seeks help after being abused by her partner, she brings a number of issues that need to be addressed if she is to achieve a level of independence and self-sufficiency, as measured, for example, by her not returning to her abuser, holding a meaningful job, and obtaining a permanent place to live (Campbell and Lewandowski, 1997).

Women in abusive relationships often experience depression, generalized anxiety disorder, posttraumatic stress disorders (Tolman and Rosen, 2001), and lower self-esteem (Kirkwood, 1993). They may have been socially isolated, living in an environment controlled by their abusers to the point where they might feel stripped of a sense of self-worth and dignity (Johnson and Ferraro, 1998). Often the consequences of being abused are substance abuse and chemical dependency (Fishback and Herbert, 1997). Finally, many have little or no income, little education, few marketable skills, and a sketchy employment history (McCauley, Kern, Koladron, and Dill, 1995).

Each individual client will not be experiencing all of these risk factors, and it is the task of the case manager to determine which of these are present. Once this is accomplished, a treatment plan can be developed to target these specific factors, appropriate services (chosen from a list of services) can be provided, and progress can be monitored and eventually evaluated. While it is not often expressed in these terms, the case manager is testing a hypothesis.

Theory of Program Planning

Program planning as a methodology has its roots in a number of planning theory streams, some of which go back to the beginning years of the 20th century. This does not mean that planning did not occur before this time. The megaliths found at Newgrange (built around 3200 BCE), the Pyramids at Giza (2500 BCE), and Stonehenge (1800 BCE) were built by skillful workers following a plan. Even the canals built 2,000 years ago by the Hohokam Indians of the Southwest were carefully planned. But it was only recently that planners began to write about planning. Most planning efforts prior to the 20th century were developed in response to the then current tensions. Laissez-faire economics dominated decision making, allowing a few very powerful men to do as they pleased, with little outside interference by government. Uncontrolled development was the norm and cities such as New York, Boston, and Chicago experienced the rise of slums.

For example, by 1910, 3 million people in New York lived in tenement houses. Of these, 1 million had no bathing facilities in their homes, 250,000 used outside privies, and 1 family in 2 shared a bathroom. Surveys conducted by social reformers highlighted crime, overcrowding, inadequate water supplies and waste disposal systems, filth, and disease. Moreover, existing green space in these cities was taken over by developers to build more and more tenements.

Progressives in these cities formed coalitions and were able to convince city leaders that development needed to be regulated and controlled. Housing codes were introduced to require builders to meet certain standards of safety and public health. Comprehensive land use plans balanced residential and commercial interests and set aside land for parks. Government passed child labor laws, and factories were made safer for the worker.

The initial planning was rudimentary, however, in that the reformers began their social investigations with the solutions as a given. They knew what to do and used data to persuade others to support their recommendations For the first time, citizens argued that government needed to become involved when the public's interest was threatened. Eventually this concern became the basis for planning, and the professions of city and regional planning as well as public administration emerged.

A second stream is referred to as the era of scientific management. In 1911, Fredrick Taylor published his work, *The Principles of Scientific Management*, which introduced, among other things, the idea that planning should be based on the notion that there always will be a single best way to achieve desired goals. Since he worked in a steel mill, he was primarily interested in meeting production goals with the least cost, finding the best fit between ends and means. He emphasized the importance of *efficiency* through "rational" planning.

These streams of thought merged in the middle of the 20th century, when academicians and practitioners began to offer different theoretical formulations about the "theory" of planning. Based on Taylor's research, Banfield and Meyerson (1955) concluded that effective planning must be comprehensive in its scope. Analysis needs to identify the cause or etiology of the problem. When this is completed, the planner needs to identify *all* possible means to solve the problem and evaluate each alternative in terms of its efficiency and effectiveness (later this was translated into benefit-cost analysis). Once the alternative has been chosen (Taylor's single best way), the planner needs to develop goals and objectives, which in turn lead to the design of a program and so forth.

Other theorists, such as Herbert Simon (1957) and Charles Lindblom (1959), basically agreed with this process but recognized the impracticality of identifying and analyzing all the alternatives. They suggested that comprehensive planning, although ideal, was neither feasible nor useful. Simon argued that "suboptimizing," the selection of an alternative that achieves some of the desired goals, was a more reasonable criterion than "optimizing," the selection of the single best solution after examining every possible alternative. He further argued that decision makers look for a course of action that is good enough to meet a minimal set of requirements. Lindblom introduced the concept of "incrementalism" and suggested that, in practice, the decision maker be concerned with improving the shortcomings of the existing system. Our basic approach to program planning can be characterized as suboptimizing or incremental rather than as the more demanding comprehensive approach with its requirement to identify and analyze all possible alternatives.

Types of Planning

Three major types of planning are used in the human services: (1) strategic planning, (2) management planning, and (3) program planning. While the three are used for different purposes, they all build on the above discussion of "theory of" planning.

All three assume a "rational" approach to decision making or problem solving. They are concerned with the relationship between ends and means, goals and intervention strategies. Furthermore, to act rationally, the planner needs to identify a course of action that lays out the most efficient means—the best solution.

The first type of planning is referred to as *strategic planning*. To be effective organizations periodically need to step back, examine what they are doing, and determine whether changes should be considered if they are to be effective especially in ever-changing environments. Strategic planning involves a process of deciding on the future of an organization, setting goals and objectives, and identifying resources needed to achieve these goals and objectives and what policies are needed to govern the acquisition and disposition of these resources. This process often produces, among other products,

- A vision statement
- A mission statement
- A statement of strategic direction
- Strategic analysis
- Strategic goals

Strategic planning takes a long-range view and may establish a vision for as much as 10 years ahead, with detailed plans for about a 3- to 5-year period.

The second type of planning is referred to as *management planning.* Here, the focus is on the process by which managers assure that the resources, once obtained, are used efficiently and effectively in the accomplishment of the goals identified in the strategic plan. The focus is on the entire organization, with the manager being able to expand, modify, or terminate programs as needed.

The third type of planning is *program planning.* Here the focus shifts from the organization as a whole to the development of a discrete set of activities that focus on one aspect of the overall mission of the organization.

Program planning to address a specific problem or need is the focus of this book. We recognize that many newer theoretical aspects of management planning, reflective practice, marketing theory, networking, and even critical theory are important in exploring the full range of management and planning theories. However, our primary concern is to create a model of program planning that can enable students and practitioners to understand and incorporate effectiveness-based principles into client-serving programs. We recognize that broader concerns, such as agencywide administration, management planning, and developing community partnerships, are critical in human services, but we consider them to be important in their own right and beyond the scope of this book.

While the terms are different, the following theory of planning is basically the same as that described above in the clinical example:

- Problem analysis and needs assessment

The first planning task is to assess the state of the system. Moreover, all conceptual approaches of problem analysis emphasize the need to identify the causes of the problem.

Needs assessment follows the problem analysis step. The planning task is to estimate the target population, the numbers at risk. A final phase of this activity is to develop a hypothesis, a series of "if-then" statements that provides a road map of what you hope to achieve and how this will be accomplished.

- Establishing goals and objectives

The second planning task is to translate the hypothesis into goals and objectives. Note that the extent to which these objectives are measurable will determine the extent to which the program can be evaluated. Moreover, just as the hypothesis is a series of statements in hierarchical form, so also are the goals and objectives, demonstrating that the accomplishment of higher level objectives are dependent on the achievement of lower level objectives.

- Designing the program

The third task is to develop the intervention—the program. Just as the goals and objectives section is a translation of the hypothesis in another format, the description of the actual program is a reformulation of the goals and objectives. However, rather than using a descriptive narrative, the framework used in planning is a systems framework developed initially in the business sector.

- Developing a data collection system

Once the program design section of the plan has been completed, program elements listed in the design section need to be translated into a data collection system that allows managers to monitor what is happening in the program on an ongoing basis.

- Developing an evaluation plan

The data collection system also provides the data needed to evaluate the effectiveness of the program. This section also needs to address the evaluation design that will be used.

Theory in Program Planning

In an earlier section we discussed theory from a clinical perspective and suggested that a clinician needs to understand the problem that a client brings to the encounter. In the example of domestic violence, the clinician will explore those factors that are standing in the way of the client's achieving self-sufficiency and then will provide services that target these factors. The process that helps a clinician understand the problems an individual experiences is essentially the same process the program planner uses. The specific services provided to the client are drawn from a larger list of services, since not all program participants will have the exact same needs. Those barriers identified in the earlier section can now be translated into a set of services a community might develop.

- Shelter
- Case management
- Crisis counseling
- Medical care
- Legal services
- Child care
- Financial planning
- Training and employment services
- Short- and long-term counseling

This chapter introduced the notion that theory not only is an important aspect of program planning, it is an essential component. We use the concept in two ways, *theory of* and *theory in* planning.

The former provides the planner with an approach to problem solving, a series of activities that begins with problem analysis and ends with a strategy for evaluating the program once it is implemented.

The latter is concerned with identifying those factors that cause or are related to the presence of the problem. This provides the planner with an understanding of what the intervention should be—what services should be provided.

The next chapter will begin laying out those set of activities related to problem analysis.

References

Banfield, E., & Meyerson, M. (1955). *Politics, planning and the public interest: The case of public housing in Chicago.* Glencoe, NY: Free Press.

Campbell, J., & Lewandowski, L. (1997). Mental and physical health effects of intimate partner violence on women and children. *Psychiatric Clinics of North America, 20,* 353–374.

Faludi, A. (1973). *Planning theory.* Oxford: Pergamon Press.

Fishback, R., & Herbert, B. (1997). Domestic violence and mental health. *Social Science Medicine, 45,* 1161–1176.

Johnson, M., & Ferraro, K. (1998). Research on domestic violence in the 1990's. *Journal of Marriage and the Family, 62,* 948–960.

Kirkwood, C. (1993). *Leaving abusive partners: From the scare of survival to the wisdom of change.* Thousand Oaks, CA: Sage.

Lindblom, C. (1959). The science of muddling through. *Public Administration Review, 19,* 79–88.

McCauley, J., Kern, J., Koladron, D., & Dill, L. (1995). The battering syndrome: Prevalence and clinical characteristics of domestic violence in primary care. *Annals of Internal Medicine, 123,* 737–745.

Popper, K. (1959). *The logic of scientific discovery.* New York: Basic Books.

Simon, H. (1957). *Administrative behavior.* New York: Macmillan.

Taylor, F. (1911). *The principles of scientific management.* New York: Harper & Row.

Tolman, R., & Rosen, D. (2001). Domestic violence in the lives of women receiving welfare. *Violence Against Women, 7,* 141–158.

Chapter 3

Understanding Social Problems

The purpose of this chapter is to explain:

- The importance of carefully thinking through the social problem(s) to be addressed
- Common mistakes that have been made in the past in defining social problems
- A more productive way of defining social problems
- How standards are used in defining problems
- How a social problem can be better understood and more clearly defined by answering a series of questions about the problem and the population affected

The following topics are covered in this chapter:

- Addressing social problems
- Stating problems as solutions
    - The limitations of this approach
- The need for a new approach
- Identifying a social condition
- Defining problems
    - Social problems and standards
- Frameworks for problem analysis

Addressing Social Problems

Most social programs are justified on the basis of one intention: to address identified social problems, which become translated into the needs of a target or client population. Once implemented, programs often drift from their initial focus and are adjusted to meet the demands of agency and staff. Nevertheless, in their original design it is important that programs develop a clear focus on client need and that the extent to which it is met becomes the barometer for measurement of program integrity and effectiveness. This is the "bottom line" for social service programs because we cannot use profit or loss as the measure of the success or failure of a program. Though considerations of profit and loss are important in business, in the social services we need to go beyond these and give primary consideration to meeting client need in a way that is cost-efficient and cost-effective. In the following pages, we explain how one develops an understanding of a social problem in a way that makes explicit the relationship of problem, client need, and program.

Problem analysis and needs assessment can be viewed as the first of a number of related activities that, in sum, constitute the planning process. Such a process, according to this perspective, would also include the formulation of a policy framework expressed in goals and objectives; the selection and implementation of a particular intervention or program; the calculation of resources needed to implement the program; and the management of monitoring, evaluation, and feedback procedures.

These activities often require the participation of many, including professionals familiar with the problem, administrators familiar with service capabilities, consumers or potential clients who have experienced the problem firsthand, and others knowledgeable and influential in this area of concern. We will frequently refer to this group as *program planners*. Most human service professionals, at one time or another during their careers, serve in the role of program planner. Perhaps in some large, well-funded agencies there are professionals specifically designated as planners. For the most part, however, planners in human service agencies are those involved in the direct provision of services, supervisors, or administrators who have a special assignment to develop a program plan and who draw on a variety of people for their special talents and perspectives.

An orderly, systematic approach to program planning suggests that planners begin by asking: What is the problem? What are its facets, and what are its causes? What are the characteristics of those who can be defined as having the problem? How many people are affected? Can they be located geographically? Effectiveness-based planning presumes that needs can be responded to if, and only if, such questions can be answered.

Pursuing answers to these questions appears at first glance to be both logical and necessary. In a typical agency, however, both the phases of the process and the questions asked are often likely to be ignored or treated in a perfunctory fashion. Why might this be so?

Stating Problems as Solutions

The answer might be found in the following scenario. Whether it resembles your experience or not, it describes an all-too-common occurrence in many communities.

A planning agency concerned with the problems and unmet needs of women who have been abused (e.g., an interagency coalition on domestic violence) brings together representatives of all agencies offering services to these women. The convener hopes that the process will not only identify these problems and needs but also provide the basis for establishing priorities and a blueprint for long-range planning. After introductions are made and the purpose of the meeting is stated, each participant is asked to share with the group his or her perceptions of problems, needs, and priorities.

The first person, a program manager for a shelter, describes that agency's programs and the number of women and children it serves and concludes that, on the basis of these data, there is a pressing need for many more beds. The next person at the table, a social worker from a local counseling agency, speaks of the large numbers of women who are in need of individual and group counseling. She concludes with a plea that priority be given to recruiting and training social workers to more effectively work with this target population. A third person, a nursing supervisor in the county hospital, points out that many of these women are brought to the emergency room by police officers who really know very little about how their initial contact can have a positive or, in many cases, a negative effect. She suggests that the plan give some priority to a series of training sessions. The next person, a representative from child protective services, speaks of the tragedy the children experience even if they only observe the violence, and their need for specialized therapists. As the meeting progresses, a case for additional legal services is articulated by the representative of the county's legal aid services, and for job training by the local employment agency center. At the end of the process, the facilitator thanks the members and promises to draft a report based on their "planning."

Many planning efforts are initiated with the implicit assumption that the problems are fully understood and their solutions known. In fact, the problems are frequently stated in terms of solutions, and often qualified by the word *more,* as in "more physicians" (or nurses, social workers, counselors, day care facilities, hospital beds, or training slots). The common denominator to this approach, regardless of the problem in the community or the target population, is a strong belief that the major problem is basically a lack of resources. We know what to do and would be able to solve most, if not all, problems if we had sufficient resources.

The Limitations of This Approach

Additional resources are not necessarily always the solution. Times change, conditions change, people change, and problems change. The assumption that "business as usual" with additional resources is what is needed may well prove to be faulty. A fresh analysis of condition and problem may well lead to a number of different interventions or programs.

Commitment to business as usual is certainly understandable. As human service professionals, we have come to believe in the efficacy of our profession and therefore advocate for an increase in numbers. But these services tend to take on lives of their own, thereby reducing the potential for flexible approaches to problem solving and inhibiting efforts to initiate change through experimentation.

The emphasis on planning is too often on organizational survival or program maintenance and expansion. Administrators who are responsible for the management of programs often structure their agencies in such a way that the purpose of the organization becomes defined as the sum total of the services provided. Staff tend to view potential clients in terms of those services the staff are in a position to offer. The elderly, for example, are often grouped into those "needing" homemaker services, meals on wheels, institutional care, and other services. Likewise, persons who are mentally disabled may be seen as those who "require" institutional care, special education, training, and other services. Such views may continue long after these approaches have outlived their relevance for these groups.

Whatever the system, this labeling has the potential to begin at intake and to continue throughout the client's contact with the agency. All too often, services that were initially introduced as "possible" mechanisms to assist people in need quickly become the "only" way to do things. Services initially developed and seen as potentially beneficial for certain people with particular needs take on a life of their own and are rarely questioned. There is a universal tendency when we approach planning with a focus on the existing service delivery system to emphasize management aspects—the efficiency of our system. We rarely step back and examine the purposes of these services or question their effectiveness.

Looking only at existing programs and services serves to maintain the status quo, and the process generally discourages experimentation. Change, when it does occur, offers minor modifications to the existing system. The problem with the approach, however, is that although the system has grown exponentially over the past 30 to 35 years, and although expenditures have mushroomed, many of the social problems that these expenditures were to alleviate remain unchanged. The persistence of serious problems despite monumental financial efforts has brought renewed pressure for experimentation with new processes and changes in the existing system. The expectation that resources will continually expand to meet need as defined in the existing system is not realistic.

The critical considerations in developing an understanding of a social problem, then, are these:

- Problem analysis should be seen as the first of a series of related activities in the planning process.
- Problem analysis initially should focus on understanding the problem—not on generating the solutions.
- Problem analysis should involve a fresh look at issues, free of assumptions about services.

The Need for a New Approach

These pressures, in part, have stimulated a growing recognition that there must be a better way to understand and address problems. The need for data to justify predetermined service planning decisions is being replaced by a need for data that will lead to a clearer understanding of social problems and will help in identifying the most effective directions for planning decisions. This, in part, has been the impetus for developing a model for effectiveness-based program planning.

Current decision making is not, and probably will never be, a purely technical process removed from the political environment. This does not mean, however, that decisions should not be influenced by sound technical analysis. Attempts need to be introduced that establish more rational decision-making processes that take into account both the political and the technical.

The appropriate first activity, then, is problem analysis and the assessment of need. It is one that seeks to stimulate independence from the status quo by focusing on the problems and needs of people rather than on the existing network of human service programs. Figure 3.1 illustrates the differences between the "business as usual" approach and planning based on current problems and needs. This activity begins with the recognition of a social condition.

Identifying a Social Condition

The temptation in problem analysis is to move directly to a definition of a problem. Premature definitions, however, can lead to premature conclusions about the nature of the problem. Instead, program planners should begin with an understanding of a condition: the facts, or a statistical representation of the phenomenon under study. The facts may tell us, for example, how many people are experiencing the condition, who they are, where they live, and for how many the condition is mild, moderate, or severe. This begins to present a profile or portrait of a condition. From there we can move to an understanding of a problem.

The concept "social problem" needs to be understood as relative, in that an individual brings a frame of reference, shaped by a value system, to a condition and labels a condition as a problem. *Webster's* defines a problem as a "source of distress." A condition, on the other hand, can be defined as a social fact: that is, a datum that stands independently and is without value interpretation. An example may clarify this distinction. To report that a particular family's income is $18,000 for the year 2006 is to describe that family's income condition only. An income of $18,000 is a social fact and only a social fact. To label a family's income of $18,000 as a social problem requires bringing some frame of reference to that social fact.

Defining Problems

A problem that is inadequately defined is not likely to be solved. Conversely, a problem that is well defined may be dealt with successfully, assuming that adequate resources are made available and appropriate services are provided. Still, it must be understood that problem analysis is by nature more an art than a science. If it were a science, there would be only one approach to it, and no matter how many program planners were

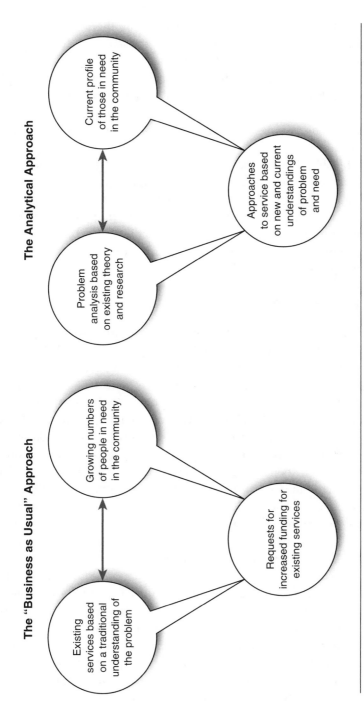

The "Business as Usual" Approach

The Analytical Approach

Figure 3.1   A Comparison of Two Approaches to Problem Analysis

43

involved in this phase, collectively or individually, the analysis, grounded in objective methods, would always result in the same conclusion.

Although it involves a good deal of creative activity, problem analysis still has its foundation in an orderly approach based on proven principles. What we find, however, is that different program planners can assess the same situation and produce quite different analyses insofar as each shapes the problem in terms of his or her background, training, experience, and values.

Scientific objectivity in the analysis of a community's problems would be, in fact, an unrealistic and possibly undesirable goal. It would be unrealistic in the same way that social science has recognized that objectivity in science is not possible. It would be undesirable, moreover, in that existing attempts to translate this "scientific objectivity" tend to result in the application of dominant values under the guise of neutrality when labeling a situation as a "problem."

Social Problems and Standards

One way to move from fact to problem is to bring some standard to assessing the individual situation. If the family with the $18,000 income in 2006 was made up of four or more members, they would be defined as living below the federally defined poverty level with that income in that year. A family of four was judged to be poor if their income fell below $20,000. If, on the other hand, the family was made up of a parent and a child, or two parents and no children, their income of $18,000 in 2006 would place them above the poverty level. A family of two was considered to be poor if their income was less than $13,000 (Federal Register, 2006). The fact of the income has not changed, only the size of the family, and thus the label that applies to that level of income. The standard by which we determine whether a particular family is poor, or living in poverty, is a judgment that there is a level of income under which a family of a particular size cannot meet basic needs.

A second way of looking at this labeling of an income level (a social fact) as constituting poverty (a social problem) is to go beyond the absolute definition using an income figure and demonstrate how poverty is related to a number of other conditions that have been labeled as problems, such as ill health, poor school performance, substandard housing, dependence on welfare, and teen pregnancy. Conditions become problems when they are judged by someone or some group to be negative, harmful, or pathological. Furthermore, whereas one individual or group may label a condition to be a social problem, another individual or group may argue the oppo-site. One group may describe the existing housing stock in a neighborhood as "substandard" because the social facts or conditions fall below the pub-lished standards (the federal definition of substandard relates to various aspects of plumbing, heating, electricity, and space as it relates to over-crowding). Another group may look on that same housing and draw a dif-ferent conclusion; in fact, that housing may be viewed by the homeless as superior to their existing situation. A third group may feel that if the own-ers (assuming they are absentee owners) were required to upgrade the housing, they might raise the rents to the point that some low-income families might find themselves forced to vacate.

Given varying perspectives on social conditions, therefore, it is critical that all views be taken into account during the planning process. To do otherwise opens up the possibility of an incomplete analysis and the prob-ability of future political backlash during the implementation phase.

In summary, in problem analysis it is important to remember the following:

- The first point of focus is on conditions or social facts.
- Conditions become problems when they are judged to be negative, harmful, or pathological.
- It is important to know who is judging the condition as a problem and why.

Frameworks for Problem Analysis

The framework used in this book offers a number of questions as guides in this phase of the planning process. In general, they deal with the nature of the situation, the social values being threatened, the extent to which the situation is recognized, the scale of the problem, and the etiology of the problem. These concerns can be reduced to the questions listed below, each of which is discussed in turn.

1. What is the nature of the situation or condition?

In pursuing an answer to this first question, program planners need to collect facts and impressions from as many different individuals and groups as possible—including service providers, community leaders, and those affected by the problem—to ensure that all perspectives are consid-ered and that the problem is not labeled prematurely. If, for example, we are concerned with the increase in the incidence of domestic violence, we will want to collect information not just from human service professionals but also from others who are affected—for example, the abused women and their children, community leaders, police, and clergy.

2. How are the terms being defined?

One of the reasons that many planning efforts either terminate prematurely or result in ineffectual programs is that the problem is not clearly understood in the same way by all who participate in the planning. For example, the planning effort might be concerned with the problem of unemployment in the community. The term *unemployment*, however, may refer only to those actively looking for work or may include "discouraged jobseekers" and the "underemployed," that is, those working part-time or fewer than 50 weeks each year. Common understandings must be achieved on all terms so that there is a shared definition of the problem and the target population.

3. What are the characteristics of those experiencing the condition?

This question closely follows the previous question. In answering it, we are able to describe those experiencing the problem in sociodemographic terms. Who are they, and what do they look like? If the planners are concerned with the domestic violence problem, for example, and have achieved agreement on their definitions, their next task will be to describe who these women are. In most communities, we are likely to find that many different subpopulations make up this group. They cannot be thought of as a single homogeneous group. A percentage is likely to be families with young children, another group will probably have psychological problems, and still another will be individuals with substance abuse problems. Without these data, the planning effort is likely to produce programs and services that may be appropriate to only one or a few of the subgroups experiencing the problem of domestic violence.

4. What is the scale and distribution of the condition?

This question addresses the need to estimate the numbers affected and the spatial distribution of the condition under study. These data provide two figures: (a) an estimate of the numbers, which is important for deriving some notion of the level of effort needed to deal with the condition; and (b) the distribution of the condition, whether it is concentrated in specific geographic areas or spread out. This might give program planners some beginning direction in terms of intervention strategies.

5. What social values are being threatened by the existence of the condition?

There is a need to explore, to the extent possible, how people in the community would respond to the presence of the condition if they knew that it existed. For example, how would the general community react if the situation involved the number of abused women and their children? Would people be concerned with the safety of these families? Would they support the position that anyone who is being abused needs protection and assistance to achieve a stable life for themselves and their children? Perspectives of community people, community leaders, the media, and various special interest groups are important for later use in determining whether this particular condition will be seen as a problem that should be addressed.

6. How widely is the condition recognized?

It is valuable to have some idea of potential community support for later action. Furthermore, if the situation is not widely recognized, there may be a need for community education before an intervention can be implemented. If the condition is known only to some professionals or agencies and those who have experienced it, it is unreasonable to expect the larger community to respond favorably to a request for support. The problems of homelessness and AIDS demonstrate this point. In the early 1980s, few people were concerned with these problems; many saw them as both small in scale and involving narrowly defined populations. Community action occurred only when the general public and community leaders became more aware of and knowledgeable about these conditions. Such is the case for domestic violence as more and more people recognize it as a growing problem.

7. Who defines the condition as a problem?

A corollary of this is the question: Who would support and who would oppose resolution of the condition? It should be apparent that problem analysis in a planning context is different from problem analysis in a traditional research framework. It includes an analysis not only of who, what, and where but also of the political environment. This assessment of the readiness to deal with the problem and to commit resources to its resolution is an important part of problem analysis.

In any situation, there is likely to be one group of people who define the condition as a problem, another who have no opinion, and still another who oppose any resolution or change in the situation. When facing demands to improve substandard housing, for example, those opposing change may include landlords and others who are benefiting from the status quo. Whenever money is involved, which includes almost all areas of social services, there is likely to be competition for scarce resources and therefore opposition. Whatever the situation, it is critical to identify these possible opposing forces. To do otherwise could result in failure during later stages of the planning and implementation processes. Force field analysis offers one strategy to carry out this task (for discussions of this strategy, see Netting, Kettner, and McMurtry, in press).

8. What is the etiology of the problem?

This question raises concerns that are the most critical part of these frameworks—the need to identify the cause(s) of the problem. Interventions that target the causes of the problem will result in positive outcomes; others may not.

Typically, etiology emerges from a review of the theoretical and research literature on the topic and from an understanding of the history and development of the problem. The epidemiological model can be helpful in determining etiology. An epidemiological approach hypothesizes the existence of causal chains and assumes that if a link in that chain can be altered or broken, the problem can be dealt with, at least with partial success.

Two classic examples are found in the literature on communicable diseases: response to a cholera outbreak in the 19th century and the yellow fever campaign of the early 20th century. In the first case, John Snow, a physician noticed that those who contracted cholera in London were likely to have used water from a single source—the Broad Street pump. The epidemic abated after the source was sealed and closed (Summers, 1989). In the second example, Walter Reed and his associates found that yellow fever existed only when three essentials were present—a human to contract the disease, a mosquito to carry the disease, and a swamp to breed the mosquitoes. Assuming a causal chain, efforts were initiated to eradicate the breeding grounds, and the incidence of yellow fever was dramatically reduced (see www.wramc.amedd.army.mil/welcome/history). More recently, epidemiological thinking has been helped us better understand current communicable and infectious diseases such as sexually transmitted diseases and AIDS.

Although the model has been less successful in dealing with multi-causal problems and problems that do not involve infection, it has great value as a framework for thinking about problems. Cloward, Ohlin, and Piven (1959) incorporated this approach in their proposal dealing with juvenile delinquency. They hypothesized that delinquent behavior resulted from "blocked opportunity" and that "blocks" included a nonresponsive educational system, an inaccessible health care system, discrimination, poverty, and substandard housing. Their intervention, then, focused on removing these blocks.

Some risks may have to be taken in speculating about etiology in multicausal social problems. The amount of knowledge and information program planners have about the problem will have a major influence on the accuracy and validity of their common understandings of cause and effect. Reaching agreement is extremely important in that it is around these common understandings of cause and effect that interventions are designed.

9. Are there ethnic and gender considerations?

Although not a part of the early analytical frameworks, this question has taken on a new significance in the past few years. As the bodies of literature on culture and gender grow, it is important that program planners be aware of the ways in which the problem and the proposed intervention will affect and be affected by ethnic and gender considerations.

Though the general intervention may be the same for many different groups, the way the intervention is packaged is shaped by these considerations. Several authors have developed feminist and ethnic-sensitive interventions (see, e.g., Anderson and Carter, 2003; Appleby and Colon, 2007; Cross, Bazron, Dennis, and Isaacs, 1989; Lecca, Quervalu, Nunes, and Gonzales, 1998; Locke, 1992; and Weil, Gamble, and Williams, 1998). Where programs will affect and be affected by these populations, this literature should be explored.

In summary, it should be apparent that problem analysis in a planning context is different from problem analysis in a traditional research framework. It includes not only an analysis of the who, what, and where issues but also an analysis of the political environment, an assessment of a community's readiness to deal with the problem, and a measure of the resources the community is willing to commit to its solution. Finally, it is critical that program planners understand history, theory, and research related to the problem so that cause-and-effect relationships can be hypothesized and areas of need for gender and ethnic sensitivity can be identified.

References

Anderson, J., & Carter, R. (2003). *Diversity perspectives for social work practice.* Boston: Allyn & Bacon.

Appleby, G., & Colon, E. (2007). *Diversity, oppression, and social functioning: Person-in-environment assessment and intervention* (2nd ed.). Boston: Allyn & Bacon.

Cloward, R., Ohlin, L., & Piven, F. (1959). *Delinquence and opportunity.* New York: Free Press.

Cross, T. L., Bazron, B. J., Dennis, K. W., & Isaacs, M. R. (1989). *Towards a culturally competent system of care.* Washington, DC: Georgetown University Child Development Center.

Federal Register, Vol. 71, No. 15, January 24, 2006, pp. 3848–3849.

Lecca, P. J., Quervalu, I., Nunes, J. V., & Gonzales, H. F. (1998). *Cultural competency in health, social and human services: Directions for the twenty-first century.* New York: Garland.

Locke, D. C. (1992). A model of multicultural understanding. In D. C. Locke (Ed.), *Increasing multicultural understanding: A comprehensive model.* Newbury Park, CA: Sage.

Netting, F., Kettner, P., & McMurtry, S. (in press). *Social work macro practice* (4th ed.). Boston: Allyn & Bacon.

Summers, J. (1989). *Soho: A history of London's most colourful neighborhoods.* London: Bloomsbury.

Weil, M., Gamble, D. N., & Williams, E. S. (1998). Women, communities, and development. In J. Figueira-McDonough, F. E. Netting, & A. Nichols-Casebolt (Eds.), *The role of gender in practice knowledge* (pp. 241–286). New York: Garland.

Chapter 4

Needs Assessment

Theoretical Considerations

CHAPTER OVERVIEW

The purpose of this chapter is to explain:

- What is meant by the term *need* and why it is important to be precise when using the term
- How the term *need* has been defined historically
- The importance of incorporating both qualitative and quantitative dimensions into the definition of need
- How the definition of need can change depending on factors used in defining it
- How different perspectives can change the definition of need
- Why it is important to be cautious in identifying at risk groups
- Why it is important to seek out supporting data but also to verify the reliability of data sources

The following topics are covered in this chapter:

- The concept of need
- Theoretical understandings of need

- Needs assessment and the planning process
- Factors influencing the definition of need
- Different perspectives on need
    Normative
    Perceived
    Expressed
    Relative
    An application
- Need categories and the planning process
- Determining who is in need
- Two major problems: Reliability and availability of data

The Concept of Need

To illustrate the concept of need and its application to human services, we present a brief, and not uncommon, scenario. A task force is appointed to explore and to make recommendations about alarming increases in reported drug use in a community. A study is undertaken, and key community leaders share their perspectives with the task force. The police chief believes that the community needs stronger law enforcement capability. A major corporation executive believes that there is a need for widespread drug testing in places of employment. A social service agency executive sees a need for more treatment and rehabilitation of drug users. A legislator believes there is need for harsher sentencing and more jail cells. Without some framework for understanding need, the task force will probably end up recommending a little of each of these suggestions, or it may simply choose to define need as it is perceived by the most powerful individuals and groups. Neither solution really pursues a serious understanding of the concept of need.

In determining that individuals or groups have a need, it is important to evaluate existing conditions against some societally established standards. If the community is at or above those standards, there is no need; if it is below those standards, there is need. The difficulty comes in defining the standards. They are often vague, elusive, and changing. We discuss a number of perspectives on standards in subsequent sections of this chapter, but first we examine two theoretical perspectives on need.

Theoretical Understandings of Need

Two theorists—Ponsioen and Maslow—have offered a number of useful insights on need. Ponsioen (1962) suggested that a society's (or community's) first responsibility is to meet the basic survival needs of its members, including biological, social, emotional, and spiritual needs. Although these needs may be defined differently over time, each society or community will identify a level below which no one should fall. Within this framework, social need exists when some groups do not have access to these "necessary" goods and/or services whereas others do. Need, in this sense, is relative, and the planning issue becomes one of distribution and redistribution.

Maslow (1954) took a slightly different approach: He argued the value of discussing need in hierarchical terms. Accordingly, people become aware of their needs in a prescribed manner—from the bottom up—and only when the more basic, or lower, needs have been satisfied can higher ones be attended to. More specifically, until physiological survival needs are met (e.g., food and shelter), a person cannot be overly concerned with safety and security. Achievement of this second level of need then allows attention to higher levels—the need for love and self-actualization.

Although this discussion of concepts may seem far removed from the practical problems of planning, it is in fact incorporated into much community and societal planning. For example, the British have developed their National Health Service with a keen understanding of Ponsioen's argument. Rather than spending their resources on developing the more sophisticated medical technologies and then making them available to patients, the official policy is to give priority to making primary medical care and health services available to the general population. It is only when this level of basic service is available to all that other forms of medical technology will be supported.

An example of how Maslow's hierarchical framework has been applied can be found in programs dealing with family violence. The first level of service provision is the shelter—a place a woman can turn to when she has been abused. Initially, basic survival needs are addressed—food, housing, and, if necessary, medical care for the woman and her children. Only when these have been addressed can the staff turn to the next level—*security* (the shelter provides safe housing, but legal services, a cell phone, emergency contact numbers, and other resources are often needed for longer term security). When these survival and security needs have been met, the staff can then turn to higher level needs—helping the woman achieve a *sense of belonging* (the shelter actually creates a "community" of families and staff who are supportive of each other) and a sense of *self-esteem* (through participation in support groups), and finally, *self-actualization* (self-reliance, autonomy, and self-governing) through finding meaningful employment, child care arrangements, child support, and permanent housing. Figure 4.1 illustrates Ponsioen's and Maslow's approaches to defining need.

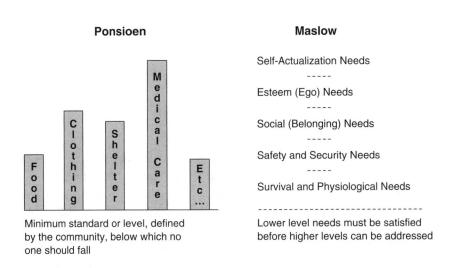

Figure 4.1   Two Definitions of Need

Despite the above applications, need as a concept remains somewhat vague, often buried in phrases so global that it has little value for placing boundaries on the planning task. Alternatively, it is at times employed so narrowly that specific services are mandated and analysis is unnecessary. Moreover, although the word *need* is used frequently by program planners and managers, it is rarely operationalized. All too often, the professional assumes that it is understood and therefore requires little elaboration, only to discover later that the program has targeted neither the "real" needs nor the "right" group. In the following sections, we explore the importance of the concept of need and argue from a number of perspectives that needs-based planning is not only possible but necessary for the design and implementation of effective human services.

Needs Assessment and the Planning Process

Once problems have been identified and defined, they have to be translated into needs (eventually the needs will be translated into services or other interventions) that are to be addressed through the planning process. As a concept, need is not only difficult to define but, once defined, difficult to measure. One of the first "official" definitions in the human services arena was introduced in 1974, when the federal government consolidated a number of social service programs through the creation of the social service block grant. The legislation, commonly referred to as Title XX or the Title XX Amendments to the Social Security Act (Pub. L. No. 93–647), required each state, as a condition of the receipt of federal funds, to initiate a planning process that included the assessment of need as the beginning point. The legislation defined a need as

> any identifiable condition which limits a person or individual, or a family member in meeting his or her full potential. Needs are usually expressed in social, economic or health related terms and are frequently qualitative statements. Need assessment refers to the aggregation of similar individual needs in quantified terms. (20 U.S.C. § 228.31)

Although need is defined globally and rather ambiguously in the regulations, Title XX did advance our thinking and practice by asserting that need has both *qualitative* and *quantitative* dimensions. The qualitative statement implicitly requires the labeling of the situation as a problem to be corrected or ameliorated. This, of course, was the major thrust of the previous chapter.

Quantification or tabulation of that problem represents the second dimension of need. Planning assumes that it is possible to identify similarities among people or groups of people who are experiencing problems and that these problems can be translated into needs that can be categorized and aggregated. In turn, once these aggregations have been tabulated, they can be further transposed into service budgets and appropriate service delivery structures. However, the ability to group or aggregate is a sine qua non for effective planning for the human services.

In summary, thus far we have tried to illustrate the following:

- Problems must be translated into needs.
- Need is a normative concept shaped by social, political, and economic environments.

- Theorists differ on the interpretation of the concept.
- Ponsioen defined need in terms of a level below which no one should fall.
- Maslow defined need in terms of a hierarchy in which higher level considerations become needs only after lower level needs are satisfied.
- Need has both quantitative and qualitative dimensions.

Understanding need requires that we address a number of key issues. The first is understanding what we mean by the term *need*, with specific emphasis on the complexity of need as a planning concept. The second is examining factors influencing need. The third involves exploring categories of need, and the fourth deals with general problems of reliability and validity of data used to determine need.

Factors Influencing the Definition of Need

At the beginning of this chapter, we introduced the idea that need involves statements of values and preferences and that these are influenced by existing social, political, and economic institutions. We expanded this argument by suggesting that Ponsioen and Maslow accepted this reality when they attempted to describe levels of need and the development of priorities. This position is built on a number of important assumptions.

The first assumption is that need itself is elastic and relative rather than static and absolute. If need were absolute, the planning task would be relatively straightforward. Once we had defined the need and quantified its scope, the primary task would be to develop a plan for services and programs to meet the defined need and then to acquire sufficient resources to implement the plan. Experience shows otherwise. At best, needs assessment assists the planner in estimating what the need is at that moment and what it may be at some time in the future if attitudes, expectations, conditions, and values do not change dramatically.

As attention is focused on a problem and services are provided, expectations are raised and demand increases. The homeless, for example, do not necessarily create a demand for housing in a community. Homelessness exists side by side with thousands of vacant houses. It is only when affordable housing becomes available and the means are found to enable the homeless to afford that housing that a demand is created for this limited type of home.

In short, expanding services tend to raise expectations in the target population. We now realize that many people who might need services seek them only when they believe there is a real possibility of actually receiving them. Planners, then, must begin with the assumption that need is elastic—that it is likely to change over time—and that this elasticity extends also to demand: that is, demand is likely to increase with increased service provision. This influence, furthermore, can have unintended consequences. For example, if we allocate a greater share of social welfare resources to institutional services at the expense of funding community services, people who are experiencing mental illness may need to be institutionalized even if they are good candidates for community-based care.

A number of factors emerging from existing social, political, and economic considerations influence the phenomenon of elasticity. Three of these—the standard of living, the sociopolitical environment, and the availability of resources and technology—are discussed in turn below.

The first and most obvious factor is the *standard of living*. Housing without indoor plumbing or toilets, considered to be adequate in the past, would be classified as substandard today. The housing itself has not changed, but expectations have. An example of a similar shift is the official definition of poverty used in the United States. In the early 1960s, the Social Security Administration developed a series of poverty profiles. These were based on particular standards that made allowances for different circumstances that families were experiencing. In all, 124 different poverty thresholds (e.g., large versus small, rural versus urban, young versus elderly) were identified. The poverty line was tied to the amount of money a family was thought to require to obtain basic necessities (this approximates Ponsioen's level below which no one would be allowed to fall and Maslow's first and possibly second levels). Allowing for inflation, the poverty line has been raised a number of times over the past 35 years. Whereas the poverty line for an urban family of four was $3,100 in 1963, in the late 1980s the line for that same family was over $11,000, and by 2005 that family needed more than $19,350.

A second factor influencing the definition of need is the *sociopolitical environment*. Public attitudes and expectations are constantly shifting. A generation ago, for example, the notion of universal day care would have been rejected out of hand. It was expected that mothers would remain in the home to raise their children, entering the labor market only when this function was completed. Mothers who did work during this earlier period did so out of necessity, and many professionals, including those at the Children's Bureau of the U.S. Department of Health, Education and Welfare, argued that this had a negative effect on the family and on child development outcomes. By the 1970s, attitudes had changed considerably, and as of today, little, if any, stigma is attached to placing a child in day care. In fact, some research actually suggests that for some children these arrangements can have a positive impact. As these sociopolitical attitudes have changed, the definition of need has changed.

A third factor influencing the definition of need is the *availability of resources and technology.* If people do not believe that the available resources are adequate to meet the particular social needs under consideration, it is unlikely that they will follow through on their concerns and take any significant action. For instance, before there were heart transplants and artificial hearts, there was no expectation of extended life for a person with a diseased heart. New technology in this arena created a demand. An example of how this affects social services can be seen in programs for the elderly. From 1935 to 1960, income maintenance programs represented the major national effort on behalf of this group. Since then, however, the move has been to develop and support programs that emphasize not the just the economic but also the social needs of the elderly. Examples of such programs include adult day care centers, foster grandparent programs, and special employment opportunities, as well as programs focusing on the physical needs of the elderly (e.g., meals on wheels, home care and homemaker services, and comprehensive health maintenance programs). Our knowledge about the aging process has changed, along with the resources and technology available to improve the quality of life for the aged. As resources and technology have changed, the definition of need has changed.

Need, therefore, is a concept deserving of careful analysis by those responsible for the planning of human services. As has been indicated, vague or implicit use of the term can lead to ill-conceived programs or inaccurate predictions. It is important to keep in mind that need is shaped by values and that it possesses an elasticity affected by changing standards of living, changing sociopolitical environments, and changing resources and technology. Bearing this in mind, we can now move on to a consideration of the categories of need: that is, the *what* of need mentioned earlier.

Different Perspectives on Need

Conceptually, four distinct approaches to measurement of need can be identified: Need may be conceived of as normative, perceived, expressed, or relative (Bradshaw, 1972). (The issue of how to measure need is the focus of Chapter 5.) The categories are useful in that they offer different perspectives on need and different but complementary approaches to understanding the concept.

Normative Need

By definition, the term *normative* implies the existence of standards or norms. When we add the concept of need, we posit the existence of some standard or *criterion* established by custom, authority, or general consensus against which the quantity or quality of a situation or condition is measured. Program planners working within this framework do not collect new information but rely on existing data. Surveys from comparable communities or opinions from knowledgeable professionals can produce suggested targets, usually expressed as ratios against which existing levels of services are compared. If the actual ratio falls short of a particular standard, a need is said to exist. Examples of these ratios are the number of beds in hospitals or nursing homes that a particular community might need (often expressed as numbers per 1,000 population), the number of home-delivered meals per 100 elderly population, and the number of case managers for each 100 chronically mentally ill persons. The strength of this approach is that it allows program planners to generate objective targets. Its limitations are those discussed above: Need levels are likely to change as knowledge, technology, and values change.

Perceived Need

Need can also be defined in terms of what people *think* their needs are or *feel* their needs to be. Although the idea of felt need is important, it can be unstable. Depending on the current situation, people's expectations may fluctuate in that they are susceptible to change. Moreover, people who have a higher standard of living (by objective standards) may feel they need more than do those who are living in poverty. Program planners must be sensitive to what consumers state and, of equal importance, must be able to interpret this in the context of other perspectives on need.

Need as perceived by the potential consumer of the service provides program planners with information that will be useful in designing a more responsive service delivery system. A fine balance must be maintained, however, between the professional's judgment of client needs and potential consumers' perceptions of what those needs are. Consumers may express what in reality are symptoms of problems and not causes, and professionals may provide what they consider to be the client's "real" needs.

The major drawback of using perceived need in planning is that whereas with normative need a single standard exists, with perceived need the standard changes with each respondent. In addition, experience has demonstrated that in actively soliciting consumers' perceptions of their needs, program planners are likely to raise expectations in that they leave the impression that those needs will be met. This can raise levels of frustration and even alienate potential consumers if the services are not provided.

Expressed Need

Need can also be discussed in terms of whether it is met or unmet. Economists are most comfortable with this approach in that the critical variable is whether the individual actually *attempts to obtain a service* rather than whether or not some "expert" judges that the individual needs that service. Either way there is a drawback. On the one hand, there is evidence that a major deterrent to seeking a service is the absence of the service. On the other hand, individuals may not perceive or feel that they need a service and may not use it even if it is made available, despite what the experts say.

Relying on "demand statistics," program planners attempt to determine how many people actually have sought help. Of this group, a percentage have been successful (met need or demand), and a percentage have failed (unmet need or demand). The strength of this approach is that it focuses only on situations where people actually translate a feeling into action—and the unmet need or demand then becomes the basis of planning targets. The limitation of this approach is its lack of concern for overall community need, especially if program planners assume that all persons with needs seek appropriate help. In this instance, the standard (the level of met need or demand) is influenced by people asking for help, and not all people with well-documented needs actually seek services. In fact, community survey after community survey has provided sufficient data to demonstrate that "expressed need" or demand statistics represent only the tip of the need iceberg.

Relative Need

The definition of relative need does not begin with the assumption that there are existing standards or desirable levels of services that should be met. Relative need is measured as the gap between the level of services existing in one community and those existing in similar communities or geographic areas. The analysis must, of course, take into account differences in population as well as social pathology. Unlike a measure of normative need, which provides an absolute standard to work toward, programs based on relative need are concerned with equity. Given scarce resources, how are criteria best developed that give priority to population groups or geographic areas in "greater need" than other groups or areas? In some instances, this means that a poor community that already is receiving many resources may be favored over a more affluent community with fewer resources if it can be demonstrated that the relative unmet need is greater and that they are at higher risk. Table 4.1 provides a comparison of the four types of need.

To illustrate the different possible conceptions of need further, we present below an example showing how all four might be applied in a particular community.

An Application

The director of the Franklin County Department of Human Services has been informed that the number of new cases of family violence, especially spouse abuse, has been increasing in the county over the past few months. After meeting with a number of community leaders, she establishes a task force to analyze the situation and recommend a course of action that would proactively address the community's "need." She has assigned one of the agency's professional staff members to assist the task force. After initial discussions, the task force decides to explore this need using the framework described above.

Normative Need

The staff member contacts the director of the National Coalition Against Domestic Violence as well as a number of people with the National Institute

Table 4.1   Four Types of Need

Type of Need	Definition	Example
Normative Need	Need defined as falling below a standard or criterion established by custom, authority, or general consensus	The number of people in a community who live in substandard housing as defined by federal housing standards
Perceived Need	Need defined in terms of what people think their needs are or feel their needs to be	The number of people in a community who define themselves in a survey as being in poor health
Expressed Need	Need defined in terms of the number of people who actually have sought help	The number of people in a community who are on waiting lists to receive family counseling
Relative Need	Need measured by the gap between the level of services existing in one community and those existing in similar communities or geographic areas	The percentage of homeless people placed in shelters in community X compared to the percentage in community Y

of Mental Health (both in Washington, D.C.) and finds that another state—New Jersey—has completed a similar planning exercise. The New Jersey plan includes guidelines for a comprehensive community service delivery system for women who have been abused. The staff member contacts the New Jersey Department of Human Services and requests any material that might be available on this issue; within a week she receives a copy of the New Jersey plan, *Physically Abused Women and Their Families: The Need for Community Services* (Department of Human Services, 1978).

At the next meeting of the task force, the staff member discusses her analysis of the New Jersey plan and its possible implications for Franklin County. First, the New Jersey planners, using a number of studies, estimate that 6.1% of all couples engage in serious violence in any given year. If this rate were applied to Franklin County, we would estimate that 6,100 women are being abused each year by their spouses (i.e., 6.1% of 100,000 couples). The New Jersey report also discusses various theories of causation found in the literature and the problems of and services needed by abused women and their children. Finally, the report outlines the components of a comprehensive system as developed in New Jersey system:

- Crisis intervention
- 24-hour hotline
- 24-hour crisis intervention unit
- Shelter
- Crisis counseling
- Crisis financial assistance
- Crisis transportation
- Crisis day care
- Crisis medical care
- Immediate police assistance
- Crisis legal assistance
- Ongoing services
- Information, referral, and advocacy
- Self-help groups
- Short- and long-term counseling
- Transitional housing
- Financial planning
- Training and employment
- Medical services
- Long-term child care
- Parent education
- Children's services
- Medical services
- Education
- Counseling
- Recreation
- Program development support
- Public/community education
- Training
- Coordination
- Preventive services
- Education in schools
- Law revision

If the task force concluded its efforts at this stage and recommended that Franklin County implement the above system for an anticipated 6,000 women each year for the near future (assuming that preventive efforts would reduce the numbers in the long term), the needs assessment would incorporate only the normative need approach.

Perceived Need

One of the task force members, a woman who has been abused and now serves as the president of Franklin County's major advocacy group, raises a number of questions at this point and suggests that, although the New Jersey program is an excellent beginning point, it may need to be modified to fit the particular needs of the area. She points out that because many women who are abused delay seeking help or do not seek help at all, the task force should attempt to identify specific reasons the abuse is occurring in the community and whether these barriers are related to cultural expectations and values, feelings of shame, embarrassment, powerlessness, fear, or even previous negative experiences with human service agencies. This approach incorporates perceived need. In talking with women who have been abused, the task force will be able to design the program(s) so that clients' perceptions of what their needs are will be incorporated.

Expressed Need

At the next meeting, one of the members, an administrator from the Franklin County Mental Health Department, states that although he is in agreement with the strategy the task force has decided to use—that is, using the New Jersey plan and its estimates of the prevalence of spouse abuse (normative need) and undertaking a survey of women who have been abused (perceived need)—he suggests that the task force go beyond these two sources of information and collect data from the existing programs in the community. In this way, the task force will be able to assess the capacity of the existing system as well as to establish short- and long-term priorities. It is agreed that the programs will be asked to provide data on the numbers and characteristics of the women and children they served over the previous 12 months and the numbers and characteristics of those on their waiting lists. A survey of the major community programs in the county shows that 2,000 women (and their children) were provided services during the past year. Specific services (e.g., shelters, counseling, child care, employment) and utilization rates were documented. This suggests that approximately 4,000 women were not receiving services and were "in need." This approach incorporates expressed need in that it looks at demand for services.

Relative Need

At a later meeting, after the staff member has presented the results from the above data collection efforts, another member of the task force points out that she is concerned that whereas 94% of the women who received services or who were on waiting lists were White, 18% of the county population is Hispanic and 9% is African American. Moreover, in the task force's survey of women who have been abused, it was found that a significant number of the respondents were from these two minority groups. On the basis of these and similar findings, the task force recommends that immediate priority be given to the development of two new shelters that will be accessible to neighborhoods where there are large numbers of Hispanics and African Americans, that these shelters be staffed with workers sensitive to the needs of minority women, and that bilingual workers be placed where needed. This approach incorporates relative need by diverting resources to those with lower availability of resources.

Need Categories and the Planning Process

It should be apparent that need cannot be measured adequately by selecting only one of these approaches. Because each is limited and provides insight into only one facet of the phenomenon, a serious exploration should account for all four dimensions.

Given that needs assessment is conceptually ambiguous, that need is elastic and subject to shifts in scale over time, and that most social service agencies are experiencing demand levels greater than the resources available at any one time, why should agencies and program planners spend scarce resources and energy on this activity? Despite these "realities," there are clear and compelling reasons for utilizing the needs assessment process. In practice, managers must constantly review the money and resources available to them and employ techniques that make the best use of this information. If they do not, they are likely to end up not knowing what the needs of their communities really are. The needs assessment process can feed a well-organized and pertinent flow of information into the overall management decision process. It can show what the actual demand on human service agencies is and what potential demand might be. It can provide useful information as long-term goals and capital budget programs are reviewed. Further, it can provide a useful early warning system regarding potential changes in demand. And once key data sources are identified and data collection systems are organized, all four perspectives on need can be incorporated in a low-cost and efficient manner. Without this information, managers are likely to find scarce resources being squandered on programs that may well serve to further the bureaucratic status quo rather than to address the concerns of the community.

Needs analysis, then, in both its qualitative and quantitative aspects, is an activity that begins with problem analysis as outlined in Chapter 3 and provides the agency with an idea of what is to be done and the size of the target group. Needs are then translated into measurable objectives, resources, and the criteria necessary for program evaluation.

Determining Who Is in Need

The concept of "at-risk" populations is fundamental to any discussion of needs assessment. It has been inherent in the development of such programs as those dealing with poverty, as well as programs for the homeless, families at risk of abusing their children, and persons with AIDS. These activities are based on the principle of channeling resources to "high-risk areas" in which there are concentrations of "high-risk families and individuals." Needs assessment, then, consists of establishing standards of need and devising some methodology of counting the number of people in a given community who fall below the standard and therefore are in need. The methodology is discussed in Chapter 5.

It should be emphasized that to identify a group of people as vulnerable is not to argue that all members of that group have problems or that all members have similar problems. Rather, to identify such a group is only to document a high statistical correlation between that group's characteristics and specific types of problems. For example, to show a high correlation between advanced age and poverty, chronic illness, mental illness, and social isolation in a community does not mean that every person over 65 in that community is poor, ill, and unable to function socially. What it does mean is that an aged person is more likely to have one or more of these problems than is a younger person. Dangerous stereotyping can occur if we are not sensitive to these concerns. Many individuals have suffered discrimination in obtaining home mortgages, automobile insurance, or bank loans because they happen to live in neighborhoods that have been described as "high-crime areas," for example; assumptions about an area tend to attach to everyone from that area.

Two Major Problems: Reliability and Availability of Data

There are two major problems in conducting a needs assessment. First, current methods are useful only for deriving estimates, and decision makers often prefer greater precision. They need to be informed that such expectations are perhaps both unnecessary and unrealistic and that estimates are of considerable value in providing targets. For example, a program planner may estimate that 10% of a state's elderly population of 100,000—that is, 10,000 people—may need homemaker services. The actual number may fall somewhere within the range of 9,000 to 11,000. With the introduction of various eligibility standards and criteria, the number of eligible elderly may be reduced to 7,000. Although exact numbers cannot be generated at a reasonable cost, targets can be established, and they can be modified later as additional data become available.

A second problem planners face in conducting needs assessment is that of data availability. For example, the analysis undertaken to estimate the number of elderly persons needing homemaker services requires considerable data—data that some would argue are not available in most situations. It may be pointed out that information does not exist or that even if it does, it is not easily accessible or usable in its present format. The existing database may be criticized also in that it is not specific to the particular planning issue—it does not contain the right kind of data. The response is often to delay needs assessment until "more appropriate" data are available. It is, however, unlikely that a perfect or ideal data set will ever become available. Program planners must accept these limitations and use existing data sources creatively. Although the data are imperfect, they can still be used to generate targets.

Following this line of argument, that existing data are better than no data, program planners often must identify surrogate measures of needs. The percentages of working mothers with children under 6 years old, single-parent families, and families with incomes below the poverty line have been used as indicators of day care need. Although it is reasonable to assume that these variables are highly correlated, they do not directly measure these needs. The problem is twofold: to identify appropriate surrogates (the theoretical requirement) and to develop the best possible argument that those surrogates are valid (the political argument).

The next chapter identifies a number of methodologies that have proven useful in identifying indicators of need and collecting data. In summary, this chapter has attempted to make the following points:

- There are four different conceptions of need: normative, perceived, expressed, and relative.
- All four should be considered in any assessment of need.
- Identifying at-risk populations is fundamental to any needs assessment.
- Reliability and availability of data are important considerations in needs assessment.

References

Bradshaw, J. (1972). The concept of need. *New Society, 30,* 640–643.

Department of Human Services. (1978). *Physically abused women and their families: The need for community services.* Trenton, NJ: State of New Jersey.

Maslow, A. (1954). *Motivation and personality.* New York: Harper & Row.

Ponsioen, J. (1962). *Social welfare policy: Contributions to theory.* The Hague, the Netherlands: Mouton.

Chapter 5

Needs Assessment

Approaches to Measurement

CHAPTER OVERVIEW

The purpose of this chapter is to explain:

- Various approaches to measuring need
- How to use available data and information in assessing need
- How data from local agencies can be used as a resource in determining need
- The pros and cons of conducting an original survey
- The pros and cons of holding public meetings to determine need
- Ways to be sure that the needs of groups to be served are incorporated into the assessment

The following topics are covered in this chapter:

- Methodologies used in measuring need
- Extrapolating from existing studies: normative need
    Strengths and limitations of surveys
- Using resource inventories: normative need
    Strengths and limitations of resource inventories
- Using service statistics: expressed need
    Strengths and limitations of service statistics
- Conducting a social survey: perceived need
    Strengths and limitations of social or community surveys

- Holding a public forum: perceived need
   Strengths and limitations of public hearings
- Selecting the best method
- Approaches useful for locating concentrations of high-risk groups
   An overview of the issues
   An example of the need for spatial analysis
   Spatial analysis defined
   Factor analysis: An example
   Human service applications
- Concluding comments on needs assessment

Methodologies Used in Measuring Need

The discussion of such concepts as at-risk populations, estimations of need, and data availability in the previous chapter underscores the fact that needs assessment is more than just the application of technique in a predetermined cookbook fashion. Furthermore, just as we discussed four different but complementary perspectives on need in Chapter 4 (normative, perceived, expressed, and relative), we find that there are different methodologies available as we attempt to measure need. Each of these, however, has its own strong and weak aspects, and program planners need to be aware of these as they consider what resources are available for the needs assessment, how soon the assessment has to be completed, and how accurate or precise the assessment has to be. Five methodologies are explored: (1) extrapolating from existing studies, (2) using resource inventories, (3) using service statistics, (4) conducting a social survey, and (5) holding a public forum.

Extrapolating From Existing Studies (Normative Need)

All too often, program planners assume that any attempt to assess need must be based on primary data sources (i.e., data they themselves collect). In doing so, they ignore the value of using secondary sources (data collected by others in other geographical areas or for other purposes). In ignoring secondary sources, planners often confuse specificity with accuracy—thinking, for example, that because the studies were not carried out in their county they cannot accurately describe their situation. Not only can these studies be useful, they often provide the most efficient and effective strategy for assessing need when time and resources are a factor.

Furthermore, the number and subject matter of these studies cover most of the issues of concern to local communities. For example, the National Center for Health Statistics (NCHS) (www.cdc.gov/nchs) is one of four general-purpose statistical agencies of the federal government charged with collecting, compiling, analyzing, and publishing data for general use. The other three are the Bureau of Labor Statistics (www.bls.gov), the Bureau of the Census (www.census.gov), and the Department of Agriculture's Reporting Service (www.nass.usda.gov). Within the NCHS, the Health Interview Survey (HIS) is one of three major survey programs, the other two being the Health Examination Survey (HES) and the Health Records Survey (HRS). These surveys provide estimates of the prevalence of specific diseases and disability in the United States.

For example, national surveys have been carried out in this country and others that estimate a prevalence rate for the severely mentally disabled of 3 per 1,000 population, with more age-specific prevalence rates of 3.6 per 1,000 persons under 15 years of age and 2.2 per 1,000 persons aged 15 and over. Application is then fairly straightforward. Table 5.1 presents an example of a county's age distribution.

The number of those in Franklin County's population under the age of 15 is 111,251. When we apply the prevalence rate of 3.6 per 1,000, we can conclude that the number of severely mentally disabled children is approximately 400 (111,241 x .0036). Similarly, the number of people in the county aged 15 and over is 388,540. When we apply the prevalence rate of 2.2 per 1,000, we can conclude that the number of severely mentally disabled people aged 15 and over is approximately 855 (388,540 x .0022). The total number across all ages would be approximately 1,255.

There are also special topic surveys covering such areas as child abuse (e.g., the National Center for Child Abuse and Neglect, www.childwelfare .gov), children (e.g., Hobbs, 1975), the elderly (e.g., www.aoa.gov/statistics), and mental illness (e.g., www.nimh.nih.gov/topics/statistics.shtml). The prevalence rates in these surveys can be useful for estimating need and for serving as benchmarks against which proposed targets can be measured.

Table 5.1   Age Distribution, Frankin County

Age	Male	Female	Total
0–4	17,896	17,072	34,968
5–9	18,891	18,025	36,916
10–14	20,273	19,364	39,637
15–19	20,103	19,338	39,441
20–24	17,411	17,124	34,535
25–29	15,641	15,811	31,452
30–34	16,951	17,304	34,255
35–39	19,061	19,835	38,896
40–44	19,448	20,343	39,791
45–49	17,630	18,463	36,093
50–54	15,544	16,429	31,973
55–59	11,834	12,824	24,658
60–64	8,876	10,120	18,996
65–69	7,639	9,553	17,192
70–74	6,402	8,935	15,337
Over 74	8,851	16,918	25,769
Total	242,451	257,248	499,699

Strengths and Limitations of Surveys

Two important qualifications need to be introduced at this point. First, it must be noted that the data from these surveys will not be specific to the geographic area of concern. Before the rates can be applied, differences in population characteristics must be weighted. For example, most prevalence rates are age and sex specific: that is, different rates are given for different groupings. Functional status and ability are highly correlated with age: The elderly, for instance, are much more likely to be physically disabled. Yet an overall rate for the population over 65 years of age can be misleading. Program planners need to apply differential rates—that is, rates for the "frail elderly" (those over 75 years of age) as well as rates for those 65 to 74 years of age, or the "young elderly" (see Table 5.2). This refinement will generate more sensitive and precise estimates.

The next task is to apply these rates to our own data (Table 5.1). Table 5.3 provides estimates only for the total number of the disabled as an example of how the rates might be applied to a local community.

Table 5.2   Impairment and Disability, by Age (rates per 1,000)

Age	Very Severely Handicapped	Severely Handicapped	Appreciably Handicapped	Total
16–29	0.46	0.41	1.02	1.89
30–49	0.86	2.28	4.18	7.32
50–64	2.65	9.59	16.47	28.71
65–74	8.28	23.99	50.67	82.94
>74	33.91	52.95	74.90	161.76
Total	3.47	7.68	13.37	24.52

SOURCE: Adapted from Harris (1971); see Moroney (1986) for a discussion of the methodology and definitions of terms.

Table 5.3   Estimates of Total Disabled, Franklin County

Age	No.	Rate per 1,000	No. Handicapped
16–29	105,428	1.89	190
30–49	149,043	7.32	1,088
50–64	75,627	28.71	2,170
65–74	32,529	82.94	2,167
> 74	25,769	161.73	4,167
Total			9,782

A second caveat is related to the definitions behind the estimated rates. How is the condition operationally defined? For example, a number of epidemiological studies over the years have suggested wide-ranging estimates of the number of people who have suffered mental illness.

- 1930s - A study by the United States Public Health Service estimated that 3.5% of the population experienced mental illness (National Resources Committee, 1938).
- 1960 - Leo Srole estimated that 40% of the residents of New York City were experiencing mental health problems (Srole, 1962).
- 1978 - The President's Commission on Mental Health estimated that 10% of the population experienced mental health problems.
- 1998 - Applying the *Diagnostic Statistical Manual* definitions, it was estimated that 18.5% of the population experienced mental health problems (Tonja, Overpeck, Ruan, Simons-Morton, and Scheidt, 2001).
- 1999 - The Surgeon General of the United States Public Health Service reported a mental illness prevalence rate of 20% (U.S. Department of Health and Human Services, 1999).

Although all five studies used the term *mental illness*, they used different definitions. In the earliest study (done in the 1930s) assessment tools were primitive and only the more seriously and obviously ill would have been counted. Srole, a sociologist, built his assessment largely on Durkheim's notion of anomie and related that to signs of depression. The President's Commission estimates were based on an analysis of existing studies that used more stringent criteria than the earlier studies, and the final two were similar in their estimates.

On a theoretical level, none of these studies is more *correct* than the others. The program planner must choose that study that incorporates definitions that are the most meaningful for program development in his of her community. To only use prevalence rates and not evaluate the appropriateness of definitions can be dangerous. The definitions used must correspond to the specifics of the planned intervention.

A complementary approach to the above also addresses the category of normative need and is based on professional or expert judgment. In the previous chapter, for example, we introduced the *New Jersey Plan for Physically Abused Women and their Families* (Department of Human Services, 1978). Rather than relying on the published document, we could have invited someone from the program to translate the New Jersey system to our community. His or her expertise would not be the processes of planning or administration, but would be in a specific substantive area such as family violence. Such specialists are likely to be most familiar with existing surveys and relevant research in their area of expertise and are usually in a position to propose specific strategies and suggest reasonable levels of service provision.

The strengths of expert judgment are numerous. Costs are likely to be reasonably low (consultant fees can be as low as $800 to $1,000 per day), and the time required is likely to be short. The planning effort will benefit in that parameters of need are established by recognized experts and the credibility of subsequent budgetary requests will be fairly high.

Although the limitations of using experts are considerable, they tend to be subtle. Professionals, even experts, are often biased and at times view problems through a form of tunnel vision. In fact, the very successes that have gained them recognition can limit their problem-solving abilities should they take on the attitude that experience has provided them the "solutions" before any new analyses are undertaken.

For example, we estimated that of the 25,769 elderly persons in Franklin County 75 years of age and over, 13,710 were disabled. Expert A might recommend a home care program with a public health nursing emphasis, Expert B might suggest a new program with a strong case management focus, and Expert C might propose a program based in the local senior center that would provide both nutritional and social interaction services. Each of these experts brings recommendations with him or her, and this is to be expected.

To counter this possibility, such consultations should be initiated only after a basic programmatic strategy has been outlined by the planning staff: community support services, residential care, respite care, nutritional programs, and so on. Consultants, then, are relied on to offer suggestions based on their substantive expertise: estimating numbers at risk, establishing feasible targets, and designing relevant programs or interventions.

Using Resource Inventories (Normative Need)

A resource inventory is basically a mapping strategy in that it attempts to amass a considerable amount of information so that the total system can be identified and its boundaries established. The inventory usually begins with an identifiable at-risk population group, such as the aged, single-parent families, the mentally disabled, or substance abusers. Program planners attempt to identify all agencies, public and private, that offer service to these subpopulations. To carry out an inventory (for planning purposes) requires going beyond a simple listing. Optimally, this activity involves the development of discrete and meaningful categories so that services can be grouped by function and purpose, by the eligibility criteria they use (in a standardized format), and by their perception of their overall capacity to meet greater demand.

Table 5.4 presents an example of the type of form that might be used as the first step in conducting a resource inventory attempting to identify and assess the capacity of a community system for women who have been abused. In this example, all agencies that possibly offer services to these women in Franklin County are contacted (more often than not by phone)

Table 5.4   Resource Inventory, Franklin County Services for Women Who Have Been Abused, Franklin County Community Action Agency

Service	Available and Adequate	Available but Inadequate	Not Available
Transportation			X
Case management		X	
Individual counseling		X	
Legal services		X	
Group counseling			X
Employment referral	X		
Housing assistance	X		
Job training			X
Information/referral	X		
Crisis financial assistance			X
Self-help groups			X
Parent education			X
Crisis counseling			X
Socialization/recreation			X

and asked whether they offer any of the pre-identified services listed on the form. The interviewer (a) checks those services provided by the agency and (b) asks the respondent whether the agency is in a position to meet the needs of all who request that service, as well as meet the agency's eligibility criteria, or whether it has waiting lists or refers clients to other resources. The information in Table 5.4 shows that the Franklin County Community Action Agency offers six of the listed services. Moreover, it has sufficient resources to provide information/referral, employment referral, and housing assistance to all who have requested assistance in those areas, and although it does offer legal services and case management services, it is not able to provide these services to all who request them. Following this analysis, the information is aggregated by service: The planners are in a position to document how many agencies in Franklin County are providing transportation services, counseling, information/referral, and so forth. This is the planner's equivalent of the geologist's surface survey. After program planners have completed this phase, they are in a position to collect more detailed information from each agency providing services to the population.

Strengths and Limitations of Resource Inventories

The critical problems in developing resource inventories are in the areas of standardization and of applying mechanisms to reduce definitional disagreements. What is "case management"? What is "counseling"? Do all service providers define the activity the same way? We have found that it is not uncommon for agencies to use the same terminology but carry out quite different activities under those headings. Many communities have resolved this problem by designing a taxonomy of common terms covering problems, needs, and services. This was partly a response to purchase-of-service contract requirements and partly a realization that without such a system, effectiveness-based program planning on a community-wide basis would be impossible.

Through the resource inventory, the program planner is in a position to evaluate whether the existing system is functioning to capacity, whether specific agencies in the system are capable of serving more people, and whether there is an overlap of services. This assessment may result in the conclusion that there is a need for growth and expansion or, just as likely, that better coordination can meet increased demand. For example, rather than each agency providing case management services or information and referral, agreements for sharing this function might be negotiated, thus reducing the need to develop more of these services.

It is useful to include a survey of service providers under the heading "Resource Inventories." Asking service providers to identify the problems or needs of at-risk groups is quite different from both asking people themselves what their needs are and analyzing utilization data. A survey of providers generates statements of normative need—what the providers consider the problems to be—based on their day-to-day practice.

In that many new initiatives are likely to build on the existing system (i.e., modification and/or expansion), program planners seek more than the opinions of the existing human service leadership. Indirectly, these providers are invited to become members of the planning team, a strategy that could potentially generate a sense of cooperation and reduce the likelihood of domain or turf protection when the implementation stage is reached. A resource inventory may provide formal information on the system, but the provider survey may give insight into the real capacity of the system to change.

Finally, it is important to recognize that service providers are likely to make recommendations based on their knowledge of consumers and not necessarily based on the nonuser population. This perspective emphasizes demand and not need. Despite this limitation, the information received can be extremely useful for needs assessment as long as those analyzing the findings understand the context in which the data were collected.

Using Service Statistics (Expressed Need)

Using service statistics involves analysis of utilization data, which builds on the previous activity, the inventory of resources. Whereas the task in the above section was to identify whether an agency was providing services and, if so, whether that provision was adequate (the agency was expected to respond yes or no in Table 5.4), the program planner now uses that information as the basis for collecting service reports from direct-service agencies. The reports provide a rough measure of agency effort expended and are valuable for the maintenance of support activities and for establishing monitoring procedures. These data, often referred to as *utilization data*, reflect activity under each category or service of the inventory (Table 5.5), such as transportation, counseling, and legal services and are descriptive of (a) who was receiving, (b) what, (c) from whom, and (d) at what cost.

Table 5.5   Service Utilization Survey, Franklin County Community Action Agency

Service	No. of Clients Served/Month	No. of Units Delivered/Month	Cost per Unit
Transportation			
Group counseling			
Job training			
Legal	25	25	$37.50
Crisis financial assistance			
Self-help groups			
Parent education			
Crisis counseling			
Information/referral	75	100	$18.75
Case management	50	225	$18.75
Individual counseling	20	30	$40.00
Employment referral	5	5	$25.00
Housing assistance	15	15	$20.00
Socialization/recreation			

NOTE: One unit is defined as follows: Legal services = 30 minutes; information/referral = 15 minutes; case management = 15 minutes; counseling = 1 hour; employment and referral = 30 minutes; housing assistance = 30 minutes.

Following the initial resource inventory, the Franklin County Community Action Agency was asked to generate more detailed information on the six services they offer to women who have been abused. These data identify the number of clients served in an average month, the number of units of specific services provided, and the cost per unit of service. As with the initial data (Table 5.4), these data can be aggregated across agencies, giving the planner a fairly comprehensive picture of capacity of the current "human service system."

The "who" data describe the characteristics of the utilizers. Although in theory all agencies in this example would provide services for our target population, services may be restricted to a subset of women who have been abused, whether it is defined by age, presence or absence of teenage members, family status, or income. Or within an agency some services are more likely to be targeted to one subgroup, whereas others are targeted to another: For example, basic training for employment may be given to those with no prior employment experience, while more advanced training would be given to those women with work experience, and support groups may be available to all.

The "what" data describe not only the services provided but also the volume of those services. How many units of services are provided to what types of clients with what type of problems over some agreed-on standard period (e.g., monthly, quarterly, semiannually, or annually)? For example, we might find that one agency provided 45 hours of parent training to 30 families over a 15-week period, while another provided 30 hours over this same period. The "from whom" data document staffing ratios or caseloads. The average caseload for a caseworker providing counseling services might be 15, whereas that for a case manager might be 25.

The "at what cost" data are gross financial data that can be used to demonstrate the level of commitment for a specific service across agencies and to extrapolate the level of resources that might be necessary if services were to expand. For example, we found that one agency in an average month provided 30 counseling sessions to 20 abused women. The agency spent $27,000 annually for this service (this includes both direct and indirect costs), or $2,250 per month. Using this as a base, we can derive a unit cost of $75 per session ($2,250/30). These concepts are discussed in greater detail in Chapter 11.

In using this approach to a resource inventory, program planners are now in a position to aggregate the above data across agencies and produce a comprehensive picture of services currently being provided by the human service delivery system at the community level.

Strengths and Limitations of Service Statistics

The obvious advantage of this approach is the availability and accessibility of the data, assuming that the issue of confidentiality can be resolved. It is clearly more economical in terms of resources and time to rely on existing data than on newly collected special survey data. Needs assessment using available data can be described as a "low-profile" activity that minimizes the potential problem, already discussed, of increasing expectations among recipients or potential recipients. Furthermore, agencies will have data that cover extended periods of time, thus allowing the planner to analyze trends in service delivery and demand.

The major limitation of service statistics is that they do not provide adequate data about *prevalence* or *unmet need*—data that are essential for effectiveness-based program planning. From a planning perspective, the practice of using data that are descriptive of service utilizers and those on the waiting lists to "plan" for the total population is fraught with danger. In fact, it is possible that the characteristics of the groups are markedly different, and often these differences are what determine utilization.

Waiting lists are affected by actual service provision. For example, in one community, waiting lists for residential care placements had remained fairly constant over a 10-year period. Although there had been significant increases in resources over that period, these facilities were always operating at full capacity. As more places became available, they were filled from the existing waiting lists; as people moved from the waiting lists, their places were filled by others. Although the factors associated with this situation are complex, one reason was that increases in service provision raised expectations, and this, in turn, was translated into demand. If it is known that there are limited resources and that the waiting lists are lengthy, many people will see no value in even applying for help. If, on the other hand, people find that additional services are available, they are more likely to apply. This is precisely what happened in England in the early 1970s. One local authority was approached by a few women who sought help in leaving an abusive situation. The agency, not knowing the extent to which this was a problem, agreed to set up a small shelter to provide these women with a safe place to stay. Once the shelter opened its doors, more and more women sought help.

Service statistics do, however, have value. Utilization data can be used to identify the characteristics of the subpopulations in contact with the human services agencies: who they are, where they live, the types of services they receive, and the extent to which they are helped. These data can be used to assess the capacity of agencies to deliver services and, if the program planners anticipate increased demand, the capacity to expand.

Such information can produce census lists, admission and discharge statistics, and other types of population reports useful for planning and policy formulation. It is then possible to extract information indicating trends in caseloads, client characteristics, and program needs for forecasting and research activities. Such information can also provide the basis for examining the treatment process. As information on individuals and families is accumulated, it becomes possible to identify service needs for total populations and potential caseloads. It also becomes possible to determine cost patterns incurred in providing services to recipient groups with common problems or needs and, as a result, to offer a more rational basis for adjusting priorities and program plans.

Conducting a Social Survey (Perceived Need)

Of all the approaches, the social or community survey is, in many ways, the most powerful method available for assessing need. In that it is concerned with collecting information from people residing in the community, it provides original data tailored to the specific needs of the geographic area in question. Furthermore, it is the one strategy that can produce information on the attitudes of consumers and potential consumers.

The social survey usually has two foci: (1) the identification of the respondent's perception of need and (2) the determination of knowledge about existing services. Both are important for planning. The first provides information useful in the delineation of targets; the second may identify barriers to utilization, whether financial, physical, or attitudinal. Information about these barriers might indicate a need not only for a particular service but also for various supportive services (e.g., outreach, transportation, advocacy, education) that could be instrumental in achieving program success.

The purpose of a survey is to provide a valid description of a situation. It begins by defining the problem in conceptual and operational terms. Program planners can then construct appropriate data collection instruments, draw a sample, conduct interviews, analyze the data, and produce planning recommendations. (It is beyond the purview of this book to discuss the technical aspects of survey research, but interested readers are referred to such texts as Babbie, 2004, which are listed in the references section at the end of the chapter.)

A survey also offers other benefits. If a survey identifies shortages or barriers to utilization, it can serve to legitimate change. In this sense, it becomes a tool for action and a stimulus for marshaling support. As a process tool, it can heighten the awareness of a community and thus serve an educational purpose. To achieve this, the community survey must involve agency representatives, community leaders, and actual and potential consumers in the planning and implementation of the survey itself. Involvement of this kind can produce support for the recommendations that will follow. Finally, although most surveys offer only a static description of a community at one point in time, they establish baseline data and reference points for evaluation at a later time.

Strengths and Limitations of Social or Community Surveys

Time and expense are major considerations in conducting social or community surveys. The amount of time and effort involved in the initial phases of the survey are usually underestimated. To many, a survey is equated with the actual fieldwork, the interviewing of respondents, and a program planner may spend little time on the design of the survey itself. Data items and questions are often included with minimal thought given as to their usefulness for the planning task.

The analysis strategy, however, is not something to put off until after the data are collected. It should begin in the design phase of a survey. Before any data item is included, the program planner should know why the information is being sought (the rationale) and how it will be incorporated in the analysis. This requires careful design preparation and much discussion. Otherwise, it is likely that the analysis will become a fishing expedition, and those responsible for the analysis may become lost in a morass of information.

A number of technical concerns need to be addressed in the creation of survey instruments. Pretests need to be conducted to determine whether the questions are understandable, whether they elicit the types of responses desired, and whether they motivate the respondents to participate. These matters touch on the issues of validity and reliability. A critical concern is the sampling procedure used. All too often, surveys are based on methodologically and statistically inadequate samples. Rather than discussing such a technically complex issue here, we will merely suggest that a sampling expert be brought in to develop an appropriate strategy. Without some confidence in the final sample, it is impossible to generalize to the total target population, a requirement essential for the planning of social services.

Although the social survey is probably the most powerful method of determining need in a community, it does have severe limitations that should be weighed. The more information (variables) you add, the more respondents you will need in the survey. Sample size is a function of the number of variables to be used in the analysis, and in a survey of social service need, the required number of respondents can be relatively large. Sample size is directly related to costs. A final concern is the time involved in designing and implementing a survey. A conservative estimate would be 6 to 9 months from design through analysis.

Given these limitations, program planners should exhaust available data sources before finally deciding on the survey. Is it really necessary? Planners should consider the time and financial costs as well as the potential danger of raising expectations that might not be met. If these are not outweighed by the benefits to be derived, then an original survey should not be conducted.

Holding a Public Forum (Perceived Need)

The public hearing approach to needs assessment usually takes the form of an open meeting to which the general public is invited and at which they are welcomed to offer testimony. Quite apart from political or community relations aspects, such meetings may be required by law. Since the 1960s, such hearings have been conducted through neighborhood meetings first encouraged by Office of Economic Opportunity (OEO)-organized community action agencies. Later public forum activities were stimulated by programs such as Model Cities and revenue sharing (especially community development programs). Since the mid-1970s, the Title XX amendments to the Social Security Act have required public forums as a part of some planning processes.

Ideally, those attending the meetings are able to articulate their own needs, to represent the concerns of their neighbors, and, in some instances, to speak for organized constituencies. Needs and priorities are then determined by a consensus of those involved in the process or through tabulation of articulated concerns to be prioritized at a later time.

Strengths and Limitations of Public Hearings

Public meetings have the advantage of compatibility with democratic decision making. They are less costly than surveys in terms of both money and time, and they tend to encourage clarification of issues and cross-fertilization of ideas through open discussion. The major problem in this approach is the issue of representation. Do the elderly who attend a meeting represent their individual needs or those of the broader group? Do all interested (or potentially affected) groups attend the meetings, or are some (such as the homeless or welfare recipients) self-excluded because of perceived stigma attached to their needs? Is it possible that those with the greatest need feel uncomfortable or embarrassed in attempting to articulate their concerns in the presence of more educated professionals? Experience to date suggests that attendees usually are not representative, that some groups are more aggressive than others and more familiar with lobbying strategies, and that different communication patterns are often a barrier.

Program planners need to anticipate these possible problems before deciding to hold these meetings. First, planners should recognize that an announcement of a meeting in the press or on radio and television will not produce a cross-section of the community. Use of the media in traditional ways will not prove successful if our concern is to attract consumers or potential consumers of human services. Resources should therefore be allocated to help reach important target groups, resources that include outreach and community organization activities in places such as neighborhood shopping centers, churches, social service agencies, and the schools, to name only a few. Second, planners must assume that attendance per se will not necessarily result in equal and effective participation by all present. Process techniques that attempt to structure participation should be introduced. Delbecq, Van De Ven, and Gustafson (1975) described in considerable detail a number of group techniques for needs assessment and problem analysis. Two of these approaches are the nominal group technique (NGT) and the Delphi technique; these are useful for involving various participants early in the analysis phase and helping them to identify problems, clarify issues, and express values and preferences.

Selecting the Best Method

None of these methods should be seen as "better" than the others. The methods are not mutually exclusive, and by choosing one, program planners do not automatically reject others. Each contributes distinct information. What is important is that in each planning effort, those responsible for planning determine available resources and constraints and then decide what is feasible.

Approaches Useful For Locating Concentrations of High-Risk Groups

The preceding section was concerned with approaches for estimating the needs of high-risk target populations. The primary focus was on the determination of the characteristics and numbers of specific population groups, such as the elderly, the disabled, or abused spouses. For human service planning, the emphasis was on the aggregation of people with similar needs. Another task for the program planner is to locate concentrations of these high-risk groups by carrying out a spatial or geographic analysis.

An Overview of the Issues

Program planners are expected to formulate plans, develop policies for plan implementation, formulate criteria for priority setting and resource allocation, and establish a monitoring system. Needs assessment, though related to all of these activities, has a major input to priority setting and resource allocation considerations. In general, this assumes that when resources are scarce, the decision maker is interested in identifying concentrations of subpopulations in need; furthermore, it assumes a commitment to channeling resources in such a way that areas with greater need will receive larger amounts of resources. This concern falls into the category of relative need, discussed earlier.

An Example of the Need for Spatial Analysis

County-based indicators, to take one example, though useful for state planning, have proven to be inadequate for local planning. A county might be ranked relatively low (in terms of risk) compared with other counties but still have geographic pockets of high need. County indicators are usually made up of averages, and statistical averages often mask subcounty conditions. For example, in a study of five southern counties, various health and social indicators suggested that their status was similar to the overall state average (Moroney, 1973). After subareas (or neighborhoods) were delineated, however, it was found that, in some subareas, mortality rates were almost twice as high as those found in others, the crude death rates were almost three times as high, the out-of-wedlock pregnancy rates were 10 times higher, residential fire rates were three times higher, and arrest rates were six times higher. Social problems and social needs are not uniformly distributed in geographic space, and part of the planning task is to find these variations.

Spatial Analysis Defined

Spatial analysis is the use of social indicators to classify geographical areas into typologies. The construction of these social indicators of need involves combining more than one variable to form an indicator. The process can be viewed as a device helping planners to assess the status of a community, to establish general priorities, to measure program impact, and to document change over time.

The underlying assumption of indicator construction is that no one variable by itself is capable of tapping into complex social phenomena. Rather, what is needed is a construct that can summarize large amounts of data that are a part of these phenomena. In this sense, a health status indicator might include a combination of such factors as mortality rates, morbidity rates, and accessibility of medical care. An indicator of social equality might include measures of access to educational resources, employment, housing availability, and participation in community decision making.

Program planners are faced with multiple databases and literally hundreds of variables that may or may not be important in determining need levels and in developing programs to meet these needs. It is inefficient, if not impossible, for the planner to obtain a coherent and easily understandable picture of the character of a geographic area by dealing separately with these variables and their permutations. Quite apart from the issue of efficiency is the concern for clarity and comprehension. Decision makers not involved in planning and faced with a deluge of information have considerable difficulty in perceiving its relevance. It would be naive for those who participated in the planning to expect them to wade through the data morass that these planning efforts tend to produce. Carefully selected information and succinct display are more likely to have an impact on decision making.

Factor analysis is a statistical technique that can be used to take a large number of variables and reduce them to a smaller number of constructs or indicators. Underlying factor analysis is the notion that if a large number of variables are intercorrelated, these interrelationships may be due to the presence of one or more underlying factors. Those variables that are most highly correlated with the underlying factor should be highly related to each other. However, it must be emphasized that if the factors cannot be interpreted—if the related variables do not make conceptual sense—factor analysis is of little value to program planners.

Factor Analysis: An Example

The data shown in Table 5.6 are taken from Bell's (1955) classic study of census tracts in San Francisco. Bell chose these seven variables as important measures of different urban characteristics. The results of the correlation analysis show that all of the variables are interrelated, some more strongly than others.

To determine whether these seven could be reduced to a smaller number of factors, Bell subjected the data to a factor analysis and found three distinct clusters (see Table 5.7). Bell then argued that Variables 1 through 3 were components of "socio-economic status," Variables 4 through 6 measured "family status," and Variable 7 measured "ethnic status."

Since that time, and building on Bell's work, a sizable body of literature has emerged, initially in developing approaches to classifying cities and gaining knowledge of political behavior (Berry, 1972) and later as a

Table 5.6   Correlation Matrix

	(1)	(2)	(3)	(4)	(5)	(6)	(7)
(1)	1.0	.780	175	.678	.482	.190	.135
(2)		1.0	196	.490	.126	.255	.488
(3)			1.0	.555	.260	.051	.360
(4)				1.0	.759	.476	.205
(5)					1.0	.753	.066
(6)						1.0	.248
(7)							1.0

NOTE: Key to variables (+, positive correlation; –, negative correlation): (1) Occupation (+), (2) Education (+), (3) Income (–), (4) Fertility Rate (+), (5) Women in the Labor Force (–), (6) Single-Family Dwelling Units (+), (7) % in Ethnic Groups (+).

SOURCE: Adapted from Bell, W. (1955).

Table 5.7   Factor Analysis

	Factors		
Variable	*1*	*II*	*III*
(1) Occpation	.635	.070	.178
(2) Education	.467	−.105	.209
(3) Income	.602	−.071	−.028
(4) Fertility Rate	.097	.630	.215
(5) Women in the Labor Force	.031	.711	−.029
(6) Single-Family Dwelling Units	−.031	.573	−.183
(7) % in Ethnic Groups	−.098	.106	.496

SOURCE: Adapted from Bell, W. (1955).

support methodology for the planning of human services (Moroney, 1976; Redich and Goldsmith, 1971; U.S. Bureau of the Census, 1971; Wallace, Gold, and Dooley, 1967). The basic units of analyses are the census tracts, which tend to be relatively small geographic areas (averaging populations of 4,000 to 5,000) and are left unchanged from census to census. In some cases, the analysis is complemented by the examination of smaller spatial units such as blocks or block groupings.

Human Service Applications

It was only in the 1960s that the factor-analytic approach was used for human service planning. Wallace, Gold, and Dooley (1967) reported on a study in San Francisco that used a combination of factor analysis of census data, expert judgment, and existing health and social data to identify the city's high-risk areas. Five human service professionals independently reviewed the indicators to achieve "consensus indicators." The data were then subjected to a factor analysis. One factor (a general measure of socioeconomic status) accounted for 43% of the total variance and was found to be highly correlated with 29 health and social indicators.

In 1967, a dress rehearsal of the 1970 census was carried out in New Haven, Connecticut (U.S. Bureau of the Census, 1971). Census data were combined with other information to develop a health information system, which, in turn, was to be used to construct social indicators describing health and social conditions at the census tract and block group levels. Using factor analysis, the researchers were able to identify one strong factor, "socioeconomic status," or SES, that was highly correlated with the prevalence of a large number of human service problems. Five variables made up the indicator (income, occupation, education, family organization, and overcrowding). The census tracts were ranked on each of the five variables separately, and then the ranks were added and averaged to generate a composite score (see Table 5.8).

After the ranking, the tracts were divided into quartiles designated as SES 1, SES 2, SES 3, and SES 4. Data from human service agencies were then transposed against these quartiles; the results are illustrated in Table 5.9.

More recently, with the readily accessibility of census data and the Census Bureau's TIGER (Topologically Integrated Geographic Encoding and Referencing system), planners have demonstrated the value of mapping through the application of Geographic Information Systems (GIS).

Table 5.8   Rank Ordering of Census Tracts, by Level of Risk

Census Tract	Income	Occupation	Education	Family	Overcrowding	Sum/5
001						
002						
003						
. . .						
. . .						
095						

NOTE: Key to variables: Income, median family income; Occupation, % semiskilled and unskilled workers; Education, % adults with high school completion; Family, & % two-parent families; Overcrowding, more than 1.01 persons per room.

Table 5.9 Indicators, by Socioeconomic Statues (SES) Areas

Variable	SES 1	SES 2	SES 3	SES 4
Infant mortality per 1,000 population	35	25	19	14
Crude death rate per 1,000 population	11	7	5	4
Out-of-wedlock pregnancies (%)	34	16	9	3
Residential fires per month	18	7	5	4
Arrests/1,000 population per month	12	7	4	2

GIS software allows an agency to produce meaningful, attention grabbing maps that visually show important administrative, policy and practice issues . . . to uncover new insights (for example) gaps in service delivery, areas of low service take-up rates, transportation problems, and location of areas of new demand. (Queralt and Witte, 1998, p. 466)

The strengths of the above approaches are as follows: They are efficient in terms of time and money; they will produce rankings of relative social need and risk; they can be used to predict need clustering as well as to provide insight into issues of service design; and they provide baseline data for evaluation. A particular disadvantage of using census data is the data's relatively infrequent updating, although the decennial census is now being updated through special studies between the scheduled periods of data collection. Moreover, the Census Bureau is in the process of arranging for the data to be eventually available through the Internet.

It should be emphasized that the techniques described in this section can be of real significance when properly integrated into local decision-making and political processes. Correct and timely identification of high-risk populations by geographic areas, when coupled with the proper use of other techniques described in this chapter, promotes more effective administrative control of limited resources.

Concluding Comments on Needs Assessment

The position outlined in this chapter is, in essence, that needs assessment has both qualitative and quantitative dimensions. It involves more than measurement of need, and attention has to be given to what is to be counted. Needs assessment, in this context, begins with problem analysis; only after this is completed can the quantitative aspect be addressed.

In this chapter, a number of methodologies were explored that are useful for determining levels of need. These methods are interdependent insofar as none by itself provides a total assessment and each can be classified under one of the four definitions of need. Strengths and limitations for each approach were identified, and it was argued that the critical factors in determining which of these will be used are time and resource constraints.

We argued that even though needs assessment techniques can produce estimates of need rather than exact numbers, these estimates can be used both to educate the general public and to marshal support from decision makers and elected officials. Furthermore, targets can be translated into resources and budget estimates. The formulation of goals and objectives is directly influenced by the needs assessment task. Insofar as objectives have to be stated in measurable, time-bound terms, the needs assessment provides target data. Finally, estimates of need become the basis for the evaluation of program adequacy.

The next chapter builds on the preceding chapters and takes us, step by step, through the process of developing a program hypothesis—the linchpin of effectiveness-based program planning.

References

Babbie, B. (2004). *The practice of social research* (10th ed.). Belmont, CA: Wadsworth.

Bell, W. (1955). Economic, family and ethnic status: An empirical test. *American Sociological Review, 20,* 45–52.

Berry, B. (1972). *City classification handbook: Methods and classifications.* New York: John Wiley & Sons.

Delbecq, A., Van de Ven, A., & Gustafson, D. (1975). *Group techniques for program planning: A guide to nominal group and Delphi processes.* Glenview, IL: Scott-Foresman.

Department of Human Services. (1978). *Physically abused women and their families: The need for community services.* Trenton, NJ: State of New Jersey.

Harris, A. (1971). *Handicapped and impaired in Great Britain.* London: HMSO.

Hobbs, N. (1975). *The futures of children.* San Francisco: Jossey-Bass.

Moroney, R. (1973). Use of small area analysis for evaluation. In R. Yaffe & A. Zalkind, (Eds.), *Evaluation in health service delivery.* Washington, DC: Engineering Foundation.

Moroney, R. (1976). The uses of small area analysis in community health planning. *Inquiry, 13,* 145–151.

Moroney, R. (1986). *Shared responsibility.* New York: Aldine.

National Resources Committee. (1938). *Problems of a changing population: A report of the Committee on Population Problems to the National Resources Committee.* Washington, DC: Government Printing Office.

President's Commission on Mental Health. (1978). Report of the President's Commission on Mental Health: A summary of recommendations. *Hospital Community Psychiatry, 29,* 468–474.

Queralt, M., & Witte, A. (1998). A map for you: Geographic Information in the human services. *Social Work, 43,* 455 –469**.**

Redich, R., & Goldsmith, H. (1971). *Census data used to indicate areas with different potentials for mental health and related problems.* Washington, DC: Government Printing Office.

Srole, L. (1962). *Mental health in metropolis: The mid-town Manhattan study.* New York: Harper & Row.

Tonja, R., Overpeck, M., Ruan, J., Simons-Morton, B., & Scheidt, P. (2001). Bullying behavior among US youths: Prevalence and association with psychological adjustment. *Journal of the American Medical Association, 285,* 2094–2100.

U.S. Bureau of the Census. (1971). *Health information systems, Part 2.* Washington, DC: Government Printing Office.

U.S. Department of Health and Human Services (USDHHS). (1999). *Mental health: A report of the surgeon general.* Rockville, MD: Author.

Wallace, H., Gold, E., & Dooley, S. (1967). Availability and usefulness of selected health and socioeconomic data for community planning. *American Journal of Public Health, 57,* 762–771.

PART III

Planning, Designing, and Tracking the Intervention

Chapter 6

Selecting the Appropriate Intervention Strategy

CHAPTER OVERVIEW

The purpose of this chapter is to explain:

- Why programs should be conceptualized and designed around their underlying hypotheses
- How to move from an understanding of a social problem to the construction of a hypothesis
- Why it is important to think through and understand the appropriate level of intervention
- The logical process and the steps involved in developing a program hypothesis
- The relationship between causal factors and effects to be tested through program design and implementation
- How to ensure that services provided focus on the barriers that were identified in the program hypothesis

The following topics are covered in this chapter:

- The program hypothesis
    A maternal and child health example
- Types of program hypotheses
    Where to intervene
    Example 1: Political economy as a factor contributing to unemployment
    Example 2: The presence of a disabled child as a factor contributing o child abuse
    Example 3: Sexuality and teenage pregnancy
- The process of developing a program hypothesis
    Statement of a condition
    Statement of a social problem
    Needs assessment
    Mothers working in marginal jobs
- Program hypotheses and the idea of consequences
- From program hypothesis to service
    Incorporating problem analysis into program design

O ver the last three chapters, we have defined and made distinctions among conditions, social problems, and social need. Furthermore, we have demonstrated the importance of not deciding on a solution prematurely, but instead beginning with a condition, transforming that condition into a social problem, and then translating a problem into a social need that will be targeted for action. Finally, we have discussed ways to generate estimates of the numbers with particular social needs, to describe the characteristics of those with these needs, and to locate geographic areas with high numbers of those with needs.

The next task is to take all of the above and devise an intervention strategy. In this chapter, we introduce the *program hypothesis* and its central function in shaping the goals, objectives, and design of the program and, eventually, the monitoring and evaluation of the program.

The Program Hypothesis

Most human service professionals would probably argue that because they are action oriented and not researchers, their primary concern is to solve problems and not to test hypotheses. The fact of the matter is, however, that when they design programs they are also proposing hypotheses. Granted, most administrators and program planners do not explicitly offer and document tentative assumptions that are then translated into testable logical or empirical consequences. Still, most design their programs with hypotheses in mind, albeit simplistic ones at times. The most rudimentary form of a hypothesis would be the administrator's "hunch," based on practical experience, that a particular problem or situation will respond to a particular form of intervention—for example, that parenting classes will prevent child abuse.

We can think of hypotheses as nothing more than a series of "if-then" statements. Effective program design should be viewed as a hypothesis-generating activity (e.g., "If we provide parenting classes, then we will prevent child abuse"). The "if-then" statement then provides the mechanism for program evaluation, which is a hypothesis-testing activity (e.g., was child abuse prevented after parenting classes were provided?). In generating a hypothesis, the program planner is able both to identify meaningful objectives and to structure these objectives in a hierarchical series of statements—objectives that are, in fact, a series of means-ends (or if-then) statements.

We find the basis for these "informed hunches" in the research literature—the literature that identifies the etiology of the problem. It is at this point that theory is joined to practice. (See Chapter 2 for a more detailed discussion of this point.)

A Maternal and Child Health Example

The following example of a program hypothesis might be helpful. In the mid-1960s, the U.S. Department of Health, Education and Welfare (now the U.S. Department of Health and Human Services), concerned with the problems of infant mortality and mental retardation, provided funds for the development of a number of maternal and infant care projects. Although this new program seemed, on the surface, to resemble a number of previous programs, at least in terms of services, the underlying or implicit assumptions and hypotheses were quite different. In summary form, the assumptions were as follows:

- Infant mortality and mental retardation are related to the incidence of low birth weight (prematurity).
- Low birth weight is related to untreated illness, trauma, and nutritional deficiency experienced by the mother during the pregnancy.

- These conditions are more likely to be found among certain population groups, such as teenagers, women over 35 years of age, women with histories of multiple births, women who have had previous premature births, and women with low family incomes.

On the basis of these interrelated assumptions, the following program hypothesis was formulated:

- *If* we are able to locate high-risk mothers, and • *if* we are able to recruit them to our program, and • *if* we are able to offer services that will effectively deal with those factors associated with prematurity, • *then* we should see a reduction in the incidence of prematurity, and • *then* we should see a reduction in the incidence of infant mortality and mental retardation.

One can easily take the above and translate the terms into a more traditional research framework (this is basically what one does when concerned with program evaluation—the hypothesis-testing function).

We introduce the issue of program evaluation at this point in the process rather than at the end of the process (where it usually is discussed) because it is here that the foundation is laid for the monitoring and evaluation of the program. All too often, planning, design, and evaluation are viewed as loosely connected but separate processes. This failure to connect different parts of the program planning process can produce disastrous evaluations by producing findings that simply do not reflect what a program has produced. Findings from an evaluation that has not been through a disciplined planning process tend to be unrealistically positive, inaccurately negative, or inconclusive. The situation becomes disastrous when these flawed findings are treated as accurate reflections of program performance and are used to extend or discontinue funding, and therefore the life of the program. We do, of course, devote a number of chapters to the issues of monitoring and evaluation later in this volume, but at this point we want to argue the importance of laying the necessary foundation for those functions.

Evaluation begins with our stating a proposed relationship between a program or service (the independent variable) and some desired outcome (the dependent variable). In the example cited above, comprehensive prenatal care (including aggressive case finding and outreach) was the independent variable, and infant mortality and mental retardation were the dependent variables.

Variables may also be intervening variables (in a later chapter, we refer to these as *intermediate outcomes*) insofar as some variables appear in a causal chain between the independent variable and a dependent variable and influence the causal pattern. The concept of intervening variables recognizes the existence of multicausal models in understanding the complex problems that human service professionals encounter. Often, there is a long and complicated chain of events between treatment and outcomes. To test the program hypothesis, this chain must be explicated.

In the maternal and infant care example, the relationship between the services and the lower incidence of infant mortality is complex. The program affects these outcomes by improving the nutritional and health status of high-risk mothers. These, then, are the intervening variables: a series of steps or events, each of which is the result of a preceding event and a precondition of the next event. These relationships are illustrated in Figure 6.1.

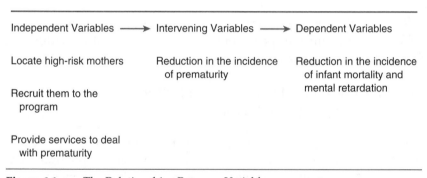

Figure 6.1   The Relationships Between Variables

Types of Program Hypotheses

Where to Intervene

Throughout these chapters, the notion of causation has been discussed. We are using the term *cause* in the sense of factors associated with the existence of a condition and not in the more classic sense of "cause and effect." Smoking, for example, is a factor associated with cancer, heart disease, and emphysema, but it is not a "cause" in that nonsmokers also experience these problems and some smokers do not. Furthermore, linear cause-and-effect relationships are rare when one is dealing with social problems. Multiple causation or multiple factors associated with social problems tend to be the rule.

If one hopes to deal successfully with a problem, one should modify or remove those *factors associated with the condition*. One of the purposes of the analysis, then, is to identify those factors or preconditions—the etiology of the problem. There are, however, special considerations about certain of these factors. Some do not lend themselves to intervention at the community level. For example,

- Certain preconditions can be dealt with only at the regional or national level (see Example 1 that follows).
- Some preconditions do not lend themselves to intervention because we lack the knowledge and/or technology to change them (see Example 2 that follows).
- Other preconditions may not be addressed because they cannot be controlled, in that controls would be either socially or culturally unacceptable (see Example 3 below).

These distinctions are critical; the following examples are offered only to illustrate the different paths and perspectives generated by different formulations of the problem.

Example 1: Political Economy as a Factor Contributing to Unemployment

It has been argued that many of the problems facing a particular society are "caused" by the specific form of that society's political economy (e.g., capitalism). If one were to begin at this level, proposed solutions would be likely to involve a radical transformation of the existing system or at least its modification. Although the analysis can be theoretically and technically correct, it is unlikely that a planner or administrator at the local level will be in a position to change that system, whether it is a form of capitalism or socialism.

Periodic unemployment for some and more permanent unemployment for others is a fact of life in our society. Our economy is such that (a) cycles of growth are always followed by cycles of decline, (b) inflation historically increases as unemployment declines, and (c) structural and frictional factors in our economy will produce a number of patterns, among which are higher unemployment rates in certain labor markets, regional disparities, the channeling of women and minorities into secondary labor markets with low-paying, dead-end jobs, and the exclusion of others from any labor markets, thus creating a permanent underclass.

Although these problems are "caused" by imperfections in our capitalistic system of relatively free enterprise, our "solutions" are not likely to address the capitalistic system as such but are likely to fall into one or more of the following categories: (a) training those who are unemployed, (b) providing incentives (usually tax) to employers to hire the unemployed and the underemployed, and (c) creating new jobs by attracting new industries to the community. The analysis has shifted from the "causes of unemployment" to the "factors" associated with why some people in a community are unemployed at a specific point in time.

If we were to focus on the economic system as the cause, the original hypothesis might follow this line of reasoning:

- *If* we were to modify our current economic system in such a way that cycles of growth and decline could be managed and inflation controlled,
- *then* we would be able to reduce or prevent structural and frictional factors that produce regional disparities, exclusionary employment practices, and the channeling of women and minorities into secondary labor markets, and
- *then* we could reduce the numbers of people in the permanent underclass.

Clearly, the actions implied by the above hypothesis are not within the control of a local social service agency. Recognizing, therefore, that the root problem of "imperfections in our economic system" cannot be addressed, we construct a more realistic new hypothesis:

- *If* we can identify the factors associated with an individual's unemployability, and
- *if* we can provide the necessary incentives to make currently unemployable people employable,
- *then* the unemployment rate in our community will go down.

The value of this shift in focus from large-scale national issues to local concerns is that it consciously recognizes root causes and determines them to be beyond the purview of local agency limitations, yet translates the social problem of unemployment into a framework that makes it manageable at the local level.

Example 2: The Presence of a Disabled Child as a Factor Contributing to Child Abuse

This example, one that is on a more micro level than the above, helps clarify further the issues surrounding the program hypothesis. We know from a number of studies that families caring for a severely disabled child are at greater statistical risk of abusing their children than families with children who are not disabled. A model that seeks to determine the "cause" of the problem—in this case, child abuse—would identify the cause of the problem as the presence of the disabling condition.

However, no program is likely to propose a "solution" to this problem— that is, the removal of the condition, severe mental disability. We do not have the knowledge or the technology to reverse the pathology—to increase an IQ from 50 to 100 or to reverse the physiological aspects of Down's syndrome. Therefore, we would probably conclude that, for intervention purposes, the "cause" of the problem is not simply the presence of a severely disabled child but the stress caused by that presence. Given this, the "solution" to the problem would be the reduction of the stress. The wording of the hypothesis would then shift from "if we can remove the disability" to "if we can reduce the stress associated with the care of the child who is disabled."

Example 3: Sexuality and Teenage Pregnancy

Teenage pregnancy will serve as an example of a situation in which a precondition is not addressed because it is not subject to community control or because to try to make it subject to community control would be socially or culturally unacceptable. A major problem facing families, educators, and human service professionals today is the startling increase in the incidence of pregnancy among teens. This problem has a number of subproblems. Each year, 1 in 10 teens becomes pregnant; more than a million adolescent pregnancies occur each year. Over half of these pregnancies are brought to term, and almost 40% end in abortions. One could argue that just as capitalism is the "real" cause of unemployment in the first example, and the presence of the severely disabled child is the "real" cause in the second example, the "real" cause in this example is the act of sex. The solution, then, would involve the reduction or elimination of sexual activity among adolescents. However, given the inability of society to control adolescent sexual activity, most teen pregnancy programs begin at another level, the prevention of conception. The target now is not sexual activity but conception, and interventions focus on reducing the incidence of conception by introducing effective birth control measures. The program hypothesis changes from "if we could prevent sexual activity" to "if we could prevent conception."

In all three of the examples provided, we are likely to move from higher levels of factors to an identification of a factor that we have some chance of changing. Advanced capitalism, the presence of a disabled child, or adolescent sexual activity might be the "real" causes, but they are not causes we can deal with on a practical level. Therefore, we call them *preconditions* to the presence of the problem. They help explain—they provide insight—but they are not the targets of the intervention.

The Process of Developing a Program Hypothesis

Let us return to Example 1 above. In our discussion of employment, we covered such issues as unemployment and underemployment, structural and frictional factors, and primary and secondary labor markets. We concluded that proposed interventions were likely to emphasize training and job creation and not the more basic causes of these problems.

The following section offers an example of how the problem of unemployment at the local level might be approached and takes the reader through the total process introduced and discussed up to this point.

Statement of a Condition

A recent survey carried out by the County Department of Human Services estimates that of the 10,000 families living in the Morningside neighborhood, 2,000 families had income of less than $13,000.

This statement is a statement of fact and only a statement of fact. There is no interpretation of the fact at this time, nor has a value been placed on the fact. (See Chapter 3 for a full discussion of this process of moving from condition to intervention.)

The concept of "social problem" has been discussed earlier as relative, in that individuals or groups bring a frame of reference, shaped by a value system, to a condition that allows (or forces) them to interpret it. In some cases, this interpretation results in a condition's being labeled a social problem. Furthermore, this interpretation and labeling of the condition becomes the stimulus and justification for action.

Statement of a Social Problem

There are 2,000 families in this neighborhood living in unsafe and substandard conditions below minimally acceptable levels for this community. Furthermore, this rate of 20% is almost twice as high as that for any other neighborhood or area in the county. Therefore, resources should be targeted to Morningside to raise the level of family income.

There are three parts to this statement. The first suggests that a family income of $13,000 not only is inadequate but is so low that it places a family at great risk. This is a *qualitative* statement. The second argues that the situation is problematic in its scale or size relative to other parts of the county. This is a *quantitative* statement. These two statements become the basis for the third statement: that something should be done about the situation. This is the *justification for action* statement.

Based on this labeling of the condition as a social problem, which provides a rationale for intervening in the situation, the next task is to determine who these 2,000 families are and why their family income is below $13,000. A survey is commissioned, and a series of community meetings are held over the next few months that produce the following.

Needs Assessment

Of the 2,000 families with income below $13,000,

- 1,000 (50%) are headed by single mothers who are working in marginal jobs with little chance for advancement
- 200 (10%) are headed by fathers who, because of alcohol and other substance problems, are only sporadically employed
- 500 (25%) are headed by mothers who are receiving TANF (Temporary Assistance for Needy Families; previously Aid to Families with Dependent Children, or AFDC)
- 200 (10%) are headed by fathers who are employed full time but earn slightly more than the minimum wage and mothers who cannot work because they are needed to care for their pre–school-age children
- 100 (5%) are made up of elderly persons

The needs assessment has helped us to understand why these families have incomes of less than $13,000. We now know there are at least five distinct groups of families in this neighborhood, with as many different reasons for their low income level. This type of analysis is critical as we move on in the planning process. It has provided us with the basis for the program hypothesis, or, in this instance, the five program hypotheses.

It also has provided us with *estimates of the numbers* of families in each category, information that becomes crucial when specific interventions are to be designed. The following section takes the first category (mothers in marginal jobs) and walks the reader through the assumptions that eventually become a program hypothesis. Our purpose here is only to demonstrate a line of thinking, an approach that eventually results in services. Different program hypotheses would, of course, be developed for the other four categories because each represents a different subpopulation and because the factors associated with each group's having low income are different. The first program hypothesis would not be an appropriate hypothesis for the others, nor would the services that evolve from this hypothesis be effective for the other families.

Mothers Working in Marginal Jobs

For the 1,000 families headed by single parents (mothers) earning marginal salaries, we would probably consider an intervention that included, at a minimum, the following components:

- Child support enforcement
- Job training/placement
- Child care

It is likely that for at least a percentage of these families, the father is not paying child support. This support is often ordered by a court, yet some fathers refuse to keep up with monthly child support payments. In other instances, the mother, for any number of reasons, never went to court to attempt to collect child support. It is also likely that many of these mothers are restricted to jobs in the secondary labor market because they lack marketable skills. Finally, it is likely that many of these women are restricted to less than full-time employment because of a lack of affordable, accessible child care.

Program Hypothesis: • *If* these women can acquire marketable job skills, and • *if* they are assisted in finding employment in the primary labor market, and • *if* they are relieved of their child care responsibilities by the provision of quality child care, • *then* they are likely to complete their training, secure and retain employment, and raise their standard of living to reasonable levels; and, in some instances, • *if* child support is provided to the mother, • *then* that mother will have more options open to her: Not only will she be in a position to increase her family income, but she will be able to choose between part- and full-time work outside the home and even to return to school as a first step in establishing a career.

Program Hypotheses and the Idea of Consequences

Thus far, we have discussed the concepts of primary or ultimate causes and the factors associated with primary or ultimate causes. Wherever possible, a program hypothesis should focus as clearly and consistently as possible on causes or on the factors associated with causes. There are, however, many instances in which social problems have gone far beyond primary effects and have reached a stage of secondary and tertiary consequences. One might think of this phenomenon as a series of concentric circles involving a ripple effect. In these cases, it is often necessary for program planners to shift their focus from causes to consequences and target the factors associated with consequences.

Let us continue with our example of women who have been abused. If we were concerned with preventing domestic violence, we would have to identify the cause(s) of violence in our society. While there are probably many such causes, a number of authors have argued that we learn to be violent because we were socialized into a culture of violence, or in other words, we live in a society where violence is not only accepted but also approved. David Gil has been arguing this point for over 35 years (Gil, 1970). This conclusion was also promoted by the Carnegie Council on Children (Kenniston, 1977). They discuss violence in sports, especially football; violence in the work place, especially in the military and textile towns; and violence in the media.

If we believed that the prevention of domestic violence would require strategies that would diminish violence in our society, we would be in the same predicament discussed in the political economy and periodic unemployment example discussed earlier in the chapter. We now move from primary prevention to secondary prevention or early intervention. Any Google search for *domestic violence prevention* will produce hundreds of examples of programs that describe programs that seek to identify women who are in the early stages of being abused. They can be educational programs for the general public or specialized efforts to involve human service personnel in establishing screening programs. The overall goal of these programs is early case finding and intervention before the problem becomes more serious. Another example of *secondary prevention* focuses on identifying bullying in schools where patterns of violent behavior are learned, with serious long-term negative consequences. A recent study reported that in a national sample of almost 16,000 students in grades 6 through 10, 13% self-reported being a bully, 10.6% self-reported being bullied, and 6.3% had been a bully and had been bullied (Tonja, et al., 2001).

In the same way that we developed program hypotheses around causes and factors, we can develop them around consequences and factors—*tertiary prevention*.

Following the framework of the Maternal and Child Health example introduced at the beginning of the chapter, we can now list our *assumptions* about women who have been abused. Building on the discussion of domestic violence in Chapter 2, we can generate the following assumptions and a working hypothesis guiding our intervention:

Because there are women who experience the following:

- Low self-esteem and general anxiety disorder
- Social isolation from friends, family, and community
- Lack of financial resources to meet their basic needs
- Lack of basic education and marketable skills to get and hold a steady job with a salary that meets their basic needs

The result is women who are vulnerable to becoming victims of domestic violence due to:

- A combination of personal, emotional, and psychological problems
- Isolation from social support systems and networks
- Dependence upon a partner for financial support
- Severe limitations in their ability to secure and succeed in a steady job with a career path

If the following actions are taken with a population that has been victimized by domestic violence:

- Provide individual and group counseling to address personal, emotional, and psychological problems
- Provide case management services to facilitate and support making appropriate community contacts designed to build a sustainable, steady lifestyle following treatment
- Provide financial planning services designed to manage income and meet basic expenses
- Provide employment training and placement

Then it is expected that women who participate in the program:

- Will increase self-esteem and reduce anxiety
- Will secure housing and child care and will be able to meet other needs necessary to independent living in the community
- Will be able to manage their finances effectively
- Will be employed in a job with a career path and a salary adequate to meet their financial needs

From Program Hypothesis to Service

The strength of the above transformation of conditions into problems—and eventually problems into needs—rests on our willingness and ability to propose a set of relational statements (if-then, means-ends) that explain not only what we will do but also why we are doing it. It is our rationale not only for taking action but also for the action we take. If program planners were to stop here, we would be left with a series of statements that might be logically consistent and theoretically correct, but the exercise would have produced nothing of value for clients.

The value of effectiveness-based program planning rests in the ability to create, design, and implement a relevant service that is likely to reduce or eliminate the problem. If the problem analysis and the resulting program hypothesis produce nothing of value for the clients and community, then the exercise has been a waste of time.

Incorporating Problem Analysis
Into Program Design

There are, unfortunately, numerous examples of elaborate analyses that have been carried out, often at great expense in time and resources, and have then been ignored when the program's services are developed. This is not unlike a physician ordering an elaborate series of laboratory tests and then ignoring their findings and prescribing something inconsistent with the diagnosis simply because his or her prescribed treatment is easier, more convenient, or cheaper than the "correct" prescription. Let us turn to an example of direct client service to illustrate.

A caseworker, working in a program attempting to help women achieve self-sufficiency, needs to identify all of those potential barriers standing in the way of achieving this goal. The identification of these barriers, then, should produce the prescription or case plan. What if the case plan identified only individual counseling and parent training classes? Given the assessment, we would have to question the selection of these two services. There are no relationships among problem, cause, and solution. It should be obvious that other services need to be provided.

Program planners make the same mistakes when they fail to make connections among causes, consequences, factors, and service. The introduction of an innovative planning process cannot end with "business as usual": that is, the decision to continue offering the services that have been and are being offered with the rationale that we have to offer them because we are organized to offer them. When program planners ignore the inconsistencies between cause/consequences/factors, on the one hand, and services, on the other, they are dooming a program to waste resources, to provide ineffective services, and ultimately to fail. New discoveries call for new, innovative, or redesigned services.

We address the task of designing or redesigning services in Chapter 8. But first, in the next chapter, we focus on moving from the program hypothesis to the setting of goals and objectives—statements that become, in effect, the beacons toward which we move as we develop new, innovative, or redesigned services. Goals and objectives succinctly summarize the problem analysis, needs assessment, and program hypothesis components of the plan and guide the design of the service.

References

Gil, D. (1970). *Violence against children: Physical child abuse in the United States.* Cambridge, MA: Harvard University Press.

Kenniston, K. (1977). *All our children: The American family under pressure.* New York: Harcourt Brace Jovanovich.

Tonja, R., Overpaek, M., Pilla, R., Ruan, J., Simons-Mortin, B., Scheidt, P., (2001). Bullying behavior among US youths: Prevalence and association with psychological adjustment. *Journal of the American Medical Association, 285,* 2094–2100.

Chapter 7

Setting Goals and Objectives

CHAPTER OVERVIEW

The purpose of this chapter is to explain:

- The benefits of the program hypothesis
- The purpose of and criteria for a complete mission statement
- The relationship between agency mission and program goals and objectives
- The purpose of and criteria for a goal statement
- The parts of a complete objective
- The components of an outcome
- The purpose of an outcome objective
- The ways in which outcome objectives fit with goals and with process objectives
- The ways in which process objectives and activities work together

The following topics are covered in this chapter:

- Goals and Objectives: A Framework for Action
- From Program Hypothesis to Goals and Objectives

- The function of a mission statement
- The formulation of goals
- The formulation of objectives
- Requirements for all objectives
    Clarity
    Time frames
    Target of change
    Results
    Criteria for measurement
    Responsibility
- Outcome objectives
- Process objectives and activities
    Time frames
    Target and result
    Criteria for measurement or documentation
    Responsibility
- Integrating outcome objectives, process objectives, and activities
    Activities
    Is it worth the effort?

Goals and Objectives: A Framework for Action

Up to this point in the effectiveness-based program planning process, activities have focused on the first three steps in the process: problem analysis, needs assessment, and establishing the program hypothesis. These steps involve gathering data and information about the problem and thinking creatively about cause-and-effect relationships. The fourth step in the process is setting goals and objectives.

Goals and objectives provide a framework for action. Goals establish a general direction for a program. Objectives establish precise expectations of what the program is attempting to achieve. Activities specify detailed tasks to be carried out. Objectives and activities also provide a framework for monitoring, performance measurement, and evaluation.

From Program Hypothesis to Goals and Objectives

In Chapter 6, we introduced the idea that the design of a relevant and effective program or service is dependent on the development of a clear and logical hypothesis based on knowledge about the problem and the population. The program hypothesis is made up of two sets of sub-hypotheses: a *hypothesis of etiology* and a *working intervention hypothesis*. Determining etiology involves examining all the information accumulated about the problem and the population and distilling it into a concise statement of cause-and-effect relationships. The intervention hypothesis addresses the ways in which causes will be addressed.

Earlier we introduced an example of efforts to deal with domestic violence. In the discussion of problem analysis, we identified barriers to self-sufficiency supported by research as including depression, social isolation, general anxiety disorder, low self-esteem, substance abuse, poor health, financial need, lack of education, and few marketable skills. From this list, program planners would select certain barriers to be addressed by the program. In this instance, the following statements could act as a hypothesis of etiology, which would then lead to a working intervention hypothesis.

Because there are women who experience the following:

- Low self-esteem and general anxiety disorder
- Social isolation from friends, family, and community
- Lack of financial resources to meet their basic needs
- Lack of basic education and marketable skills to get and hold a steady job with a salary that meets their basic needs

The result is women who are vulnerable to becoming victims of domestic violence due to:

- A combination of personal, emotional, and psychological problems
- Isolation from social support systems and networks
- Dependence upon a partner for financial support
- Severe limitations in their ability to secure and succeed in a steady job with a career path

If the following actions are taken with a population that has been victimized by domestic violence:

- Provide individual and group counseling to address personal, emotional, and psychological problems
- Provide case management services to facilitate and support making appropriate community contacts designed to build a sustainable, steady lifestyle following treatment
- Provide financial planning services designed to manage income and meet basic expenses
- Provide employment training and placement

Then it is expected that women who participate in the program:

- Will increase their self-esteem and reduce anxiety
- Will secure housing and child care and will be able to meet other needs necessary to independent living in the community
- Will be able to manage their finances effectively
- Will be employed in a job with a career path and a salary adequate to meet their financial needs

The *hypothesis of etiology* explains our current understanding of cause-and-effect relationships. The *working intervention hypothesis* then focuses its activities (interventions) on the "causes," with an expectation that, if successful, it will have a positive impact on the "effects." Taken together, these two sets of statements or subhypotheses make up the *program hypothesis*. We will assume for the sake of this example that the state is providing the funding to test this hypothesis, and is calling its initiative the "Victims to Victors" program. We will also assume that a portion of this program is being delivered through Safe Haven, a domestic violence shelter.

Benefits of the Program Hypothesis

The above approach—beginning with problem analysis, moving to needs assessment, developing a program hypothesis, and developing a hierarchical set of goals and objectives—will produce a number of benefits that cannot be produced from any other process. These benefits are listed below, and each is discussed in turn.

The Program Hypothesis Helps Focus
Programs on Problems Rather Than on Activities

In his discussion of the current landscape of social welfare management, Patti (2000) emphasizes the increasing expectations that managers will measure organizational performance in a way that is responsive to funding and policy bodies, while taking into consideration available resources, technology, and the needs and preferences of the consumer. Meeting the expectations of these widely varying constituents means that organizations and programs must be structured around understanding and resolving problems, and not solely on the activities of staff.

In the Victims to Victors Program, the problem analysis, program hypothesis, and eventually goals and objectives are all focused on ways (the "how") to protect women and children who have been victims of domestic violence, and to provide the kind of support needed by the target population for long-term self-sufficiency (the "what"). Because the program hypothesis is problem directed, it forces us to think first about the purpose of our program and not about the details of the actual services.

A traditional approach would tend to focus on the services provided by workers—services that eventually take on purposes and lives of their own. In this example, in the absence of problem-oriented goals and objectives based on a program hypothesis, a plan might be developed focused on the provision of casework services, leaving the decision about what the participants need to the judgment of many different caseworkers. This approach could very well result in trial and error and ignore all the research and evaluation findings that point to specific factors that, in combination, increase the risk of subjecting vulnerable women to continued physical and emotional violence.

The Program Hypothesis Can Link Program Activities to Outcomes

In discussing the importance of client outcomes, Poertner (2000) points out that the bottom line for the social service administrator is the result of transactions between workers and clients. "Information on client outcomes," he says, "is important to managers to judge program performance, motivate and direct staff, and acquire resources from the environment" (p. 270).

This linkage between means and ends specified in the working intervention hypothesis is critical in that it allows the administrator to determine whether a program is working. This sentence is deceptive in its apparent simplicity. There are, however, two distinct questions involved, both of which are the essence of program evaluation:

1. Did we actually implement the program we designed?

2. To what extent did we achieve the proposed results?

If a working intervention hypothesis is a series of statements that includes, at a minimal level, a relationship between identified programs and anticipated results, we need to determine two things: (1) whether the intervention was implemented as designed (e.g., case management services, counseling, financial management training, and employment training and placement provided), and (2) the extent to which the expected results (e.g., increase in self-esteem, reduction in anxiety, strengthening of social support networks, ability to manage finances effectively, employability, and self-sufficiency) were achieved. This, then, forms the basis for ever-increasing precision in matching programs to problem and need and ultimately for supporting, rejecting, or modifying the program hypothesis.

The Program Hypothesis Can Provide a Basis for Long-Range Planning

The system we are outlining requires that the planner think beyond the present, or, more accurately, beyond a single year. By planning programs around problems and by linking activities to identified results or outcomes, we are encouraged to focus efforts on long-term effects. Austin and Solomon (2000) describe long-range planning as involving "a profound shift in management philosophy from reactive crisis management to proactive strategic management" (p. 342).

Most of the problems we are concerned with are complex. Many cannot be successfully dealt with in a single year's time frame. Many are of such a scale that only a portion of the people in need can be served—or a portion of the services to be provided can be completed—in a single year. We need, then, to identify multiple-year objectives and to generate multiple-year estimates of resources needed to achieve these objectives.

For example, a needs assessment might provide an estimate of 180 young women within a particular geographical boundary at any given time who meet the definition of being at high risk of domestic violence. In program planning, those knowledgeable about domestic violence services might calculate that during the first year only about 30 women can be served, given the capacity and the resources to be made available in this program. Planners would still want to develop, during the second and subsequent years, the capacity to serve a greater number and secure the resources needed to accomplish this. The planning process would also identify other shelters within the community that may participate in this program and serve different groups of women.

*The Program Hypothesis Can Provide a Framework for Continuous
Monitoring and Evaluation of the Service Provision Process*

The system we are describing is one that will have different levels of outcomes. One set can be described as the ultimate results expected from the program. Another can be described as intermediate results. In the Victims to Victors Program, the ultimate result expected is the reduction of domestic violence in the community by reducing recidivism. Realistically, we should not expect to observe meaningful changes in the impact of this program on the community within the first year in which the program was initiated, especially in view of the program's attempt to somehow change lifestyles and attitudes of women who have become dependent on abusers. However, this does not mean that we should ignore evaluation until the end of the second year. We should take intermediate measures such as successful completion of an Individual Rehab Plan and mastery of certain knowledge and skills, so that, if all is not going according to plan, we can be in a position to take corrective action when it can make a difference (i.e., early in the program's life).

Again, our program hypothesis and accompanying goals and objectives allow us to begin our evaluation at an early date. We have posited a relationship between the variables of (1) low self-esteem (Kirkwood, 1993), (2) high anxiety (Tolman and Rosen, 2001), (3) lack of independent living skills (Johnson and Ferraro, 1998), (4) poor financial management skills, and (5) lack of employable skills (McCauley, Kern, Koladron, and Dill, 1995). Are we finding that the program is having success in its attempt to increase self-esteem? reduce anxiety? Are there measurable improvements in knowledge about managing finances? Are independent living skills being mastered? Are training courses being successfully completed, and if so, are these newly mastered skills resulting in steady jobs that can lead to successful careers? If the program hypothesis is correct, and if the interventions are effective, these are some of the factors that can be measured early in the life of the program, and we can plan to measure reductions in the incidence of domestic violence in the community at a later time. The relationships between program hypothesis, intermediate outcomes, and final outcomes are illustrated in Table 7.1.

*The Program Hypothesis Can Provide a Database
for Cost-Benefit and Cost-Effectiveness Studies*

The final contribution of this system is that it gives us the ability to tie cost data to program data. The program hypothesis provides a framework

Table 7.1   The Relationship Between Working Intervention Hypothesis, Intermediate Outcomes, and Final Outcomes

Working Intervention Hypothesis	Intermediate Outcomes	Final Outcomes
If women who are victims of domestic violence are able to: improve self-esteem, reduce social anxiety, establish ties to community resources leading to self-sufficiency, develop financial management skills, learn job skills, and be placed in a job with a career path Then abuse victims will demonstrate: an improvement in self-esteem, a reduction in social anxiety, mastery of financial management skills, employment in a job with a career path, self-sufficiency, and a reduced incidence of returning to the same or another abuser	Improvement in self-esteem Reduction in social anxiety Knowledge and skill in using community resources for independent living Demonstrated ability to manage finances Demonstration of ability to perform critical job skills Placement in a job for which the client was trained	Reduction in the incidence of program participants returning to the same or another abuser

for linking resources to outcomes. The effectiveness of a financial management system should be judged, at least in part, on the basis of how well it contributes to services effectiveness (Ezell, 2000). Cost data allow us to take the next step, which is the assessment of how much these outcomes have cost. This allows the administrator to address the following questions:

1. Is the program cost-effective (are the results worth the cost)?

2. Could we achieve the same results at a lower cost?

This issue is the focus of later chapters dealing with budgeting.

In summary, the program hypothesis provides an important transition statement. It is crafted from the earlier study and analysis of the problem and the need, and it establishes a foundation on which subsequent components of the plan are built. Goals and objectives will establish the direction of planning from this point on, so it is critical that goals and objectives be written in a way that is consistent with the program hypothesis. Planners must also be cognizant of the purpose and direction of the host agency. Purpose and direction are established in the agency's mission statement.

The Function of a Mission Statement

Every organization needs a sense of direction. Without a clear focus on its reason for existence, an organization can easily become distracted by whatever happens to be the dominating problems or issues of the day. An agency's mission statement provides direction and continuity to keep an organization on track (Andringa and Engstrom, 2002; Kettner, Daley, and Nichols, 1985). A good mission statement is lofty, inspiring, concise, and understandable (Brody, 2005).

A mission statement is formally approved and sanctioned by designated officials in public agencies and by boards of directors in private agencies. Another way of describing the purpose of a mission statement is that it establishes broad and relatively permanent parameters within which goals are developed and specific programs designed. A mission statement includes, at minimum, a target population and a statement of the agency's vision for what ideally might be achieved in collaboration between the agency and the target population. A good, clear mission statement is usually limited to just a few sentences. Some examples follow.

Type of Organization	Sample Mission Statement
Domestic violence shelter	To ensure a safe environment for women and children who have been victims of physical and emotional violence, while strengthening their abilities to

	function independently in a positive lifestyle free of violence
Family service agency	To promote family strength and stability in a manner that allows each individual to achieve his or her potential while, at the same time, supporting strong and productive interrelationships among family members
Drug and alcohol counseling	To promote and support the achievement of a positive and productive lifestyle, including steady employment and stable relationships, for those formerly addicted to chemical substances

The key is that a mission statement should focus on what lies ahead for its clients or consumers if the agency is successful in addressing their problems and meeting their needs. Some mission statements make the mistake of *describing* their services (a key to this is when the mission statement uses the term *provide*). It is perfectly acceptable to have follow-up statements about services or agency values, but the mission statement itself should be brief, clear, and stated in outcome terms.

Mission statements are intended to be visionary and should be reevaluated when societal conditions are altered or when the problems that the agency was established to resolve are no longer present (e.g., a health clinic may decide to focus exclusively on the treatment of patients with AIDS).

As Brody (2005) points out, the mission statement should be the most enduring part of the organization. When an agency continually changes or modifies its mission statement, that agency is usually found to be experiencing profound and pervasive internal problems. Implicit in the relative permanence of a mission statement is an understanding that the problems or conditions of concern to the agency are broad enough in scope and scale that they are unlikely to be achieved in the near future. Just as the mission statements "to strengthen independent functioning," "to promote family stability," and "to promote and protect a chemical dependency-free lifestyle" are legitimate statements in the year 2008, so they are likely to be relevant in 2025. Even though the concepts of independent functioning or family stability might be operationalized differently in the future, the concept will continue to have validity.

The Formulation of Goals

Program goals are intended to be compatible with the agency's mission. Goals are statements of expected outcomes dealing with the problem that the program is attempting to prevent, eradicate, or ameliorate. They are responsive to problems and needs, and represent an ideal or hoped-for outcome (Coley and Scheinberg, 2000). Goals need not be measurable or achievable. They tend to be more general and provide a sense of programmatic direction. Time frames are not established for goal achievement. In some cases goals may be specified by funding sources, and the agency or program will be expected to work within these limits. In these instances the mission statement should be reviewed to ensure a fit between organizational mission and program goals.

In the Victims to Victors Program, we hope to reduce the incidence of violence and promote self-sufficiency among the at-risk population. A goal statement for a special program designed for women who have repeatedly returned to their abusers after treatment might read as follows:

To ensure that women in Franklin County who have repeatedly been abused by a spouse or partner are able to become self-sufficient and capable of avoiding future relationships with abusers.

A goal statement should fit within a system: it should flow logically from the agency's mission statement, while providing a framework and sense of direction for the objectives which are to follow. In working toward the program goal of preventing a return to abusers and promoting independent functioning, we move a few small steps in the direction of furthering the mission of the total organization, understanding that the mission is something that is never fully achieved.

Goal statements provide a beacon that serves as a constant focal point and lends a sense of direction to the program. They are the reasons for which the program is funded and implemented. They are statements of preferences or values. Goals statements are also political statements and are written in such a way that they tend to build consensus. Who can be opposed to "reducing the incidence of drug use among 8- to 12-year-olds in Canyon City" or "increasing the employment rate of TANF recipients in Springfield"? Goal statements become rallying causes around which we attempt to gather support for a program. Disagreement will inevitably arise when we attempt to set out the best *means* to resolve the presenting problem(s), but at this point we are looking for consensus around the quality of life we hope will be achieved by those we serve.

The Formulation of Objectives

In effectiveness-based program planning, one should be able to make explicit two things about a program: (1) the results that are to be achieved and (2) the manner in which these results will be achieved.

The specification of results is a statement of the "ends" or expectations of the program, and in the program planning literature these ends are referred to as *outcome objectives* (Brody, 2005, Coley and Scheinberg, 2000, Poertner, 2000). The specification of service provision is an articulation of the "means" that will be used to achieve the ends, and these are referred to as *process objectives*. Finally, under process objectives, we find listings of specific *activities* that represent a further breakdown or refinement of the details of program implementation.

Throughout the literature, a variety of terms are used by planners to distinguish these three different levels, including *strategies, milestones, operational objectives,* and *program objectives.* In the following discussion, we will use the program planning terms *outcome objectives, process objectives,* and *activities.* The hierarchy is similar to that depicted in Figure 7.1.

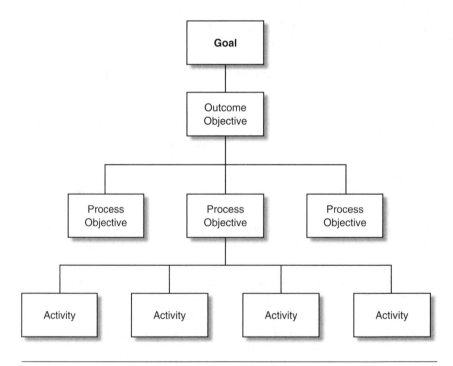

Figure 7.1   Hierarchy of Goals, Objectives, and Activities

Requirements for All Objectives

All objectives have a number of elements in common. A good objective is *clear, specific, measurable, time limited,* and *realistic* and represents a *commitment.* These elements can be addressed through the following questions:

- *Use of Clear, Unambiguous Terms.* Is the objective clear? Does it mean the same thing to anyone who reads the statement?
- *Expected Results.* Does the objective specify results to be achieved (expected improvements in quality of life of clients or consumers)?
- *Measurable Results.* Is the objective written in such a way that it can be measured? Are measurement (numerical) criteria incorporated into the objective?
- *Time Frame.* Does the statement indicate a clearly defined time limit within which the objective will be achieved?
- *Achievability.* Is the objective realistic given our technology and knowledge as well as available resources?
- *Accountability.* Does the objective identify who has responsibility for ensuring that the objective is achieved?

More specifically, in writing objectives, the following five components should be included:

1. Time frame

2. Target of the change

3. Products (process) or results (outcomes) to be achieved

4. Criteria by which the products or results will be documented, monitored, or measured

5. Responsibility for implementing and measuring achievement of the objective

The issue of clarity as well as these five components will be discussed in the following paragraphs. In order to emphasize the chronology of the objective-setting process, we will first discuss *outcome* objectives, and following that we will discuss the construction of *process* objectives. Outcome objectives should always be developed first (even though they appear last as depicted in the logic model in Chapter 1), because it is from the specification of desired outcomes that the remainder of the program planning process flows.

Clarity

The critical test of an objective is that anyone who reads it will understand it. There should be a minimum of ambiguity. Adjectives should be minimized or eliminated in favor of straightforward phrases made up primarily of verbs and nouns. Brody (2005) advises those who write objectives to use action verbs that describe an observable change in a condition, such as to *reduce, improve, strengthen,* or *enhance.* Everyone who works with the objective should interpret it in essentially the same way. For example, a statement such as "to improve the quality of interaction between spouses" could have many interpretations. It is vague and uncertain without further modifiers and descriptors. Better, more measurable statements would be "to reduce the number of arguments each week in at least 80% of participating families" or "to increase the number of days in each month for 75% of participating families when there are no arguments." Even here, the term *arguments* would probably need further definition and clarification.

Precision becomes extremely important as the program goes through its implementation stage. By the time of implementation, the initial authors of the objectives may not be available for interpretation, nor should they have to be if the objectives have been crafted correctly.

One way to ensure clarity (and, later, measurability) is to develop objectives that have behavioral aspects. Examples of these would include statements that begin with verbs such as *write, list, increase, reduce, terminate,* or *demonstrate.* Examples that use vague and nonbehavioral (i.e., not observable) referents might include statements that begin with verbs such as *understand, know, realize, feel, believe,* or *enable.*

Time Frames

The time frame specified is the date when it is expected that the objective will have been achieved. The United Way of America (1996) describes three levels of outcomes:

1. *Initial outcomes:* the first benefits or changes that participants experience (e.g., changes in knowledge, attitudes, or skills). They are not the end in themselves, but they are necessary steps toward the desired end and therefore are important indicators of participants' progress toward those ends.

2. *Intermediate outcomes:* often the changes in behavior that result from new knowledge, attitudes, and skills.

3. *Longer term outcomes:* the ultimate outcomes that a program desires to achieve for its participants. They represent meaningful changes for participants, often in their condition or status (p. 32).

Using the United Way framework, initial and possibly intermediate outcomes may be the focus of the first year. Longer term outcomes would involve multiyear efforts. Wherever possible, time frames should be stated as specific dates, including month, day, and year. These, then, become the dates on which readings are taken to monitor progress and review performance measures that indicate whether the program is meeting its objectives. One-year time frames are usually stated as follows:

- By June 30, 20XX (with a specific year, one year from the start date, inserted)
- By the end of the first year (when the start date is not known)

Multiple-year planning may be necessary, given the complexity of most social service program outcome expectations. When multiple-year outcome objectives are developed, they may be stated as follows:

- By September 30, 20XX (when the start and completion dates are known)
- By the end of the third year (when the start and completion dates are not known)

Specific dates are always preferable because they are so much more useful for monitoring purposes, but when a program is faced with an uncertain start date, objectives may have to use flexible time frames that can later be translated into specific dates.

Target of Change

Objectives also specify the population or the elements that are expected to be changed if the objective is achieved. *Outcome objectives* focus on populations. The following are client populations that might be specified in an outcome objective:

- 30 women who have been victims of physical and/or emotional violence
- 75 low-income families
- 90 parents who have been cited for child neglect

Results

Client outcomes identify what positive changes should have been achieved by clients by the time they have completed the program. For example:

- 50 families will report at least a 25% increase in incidences of healthy communication

- 24 graduates of the trainee program will secure employment in the area in which they were trained
- 20 preschool children will demonstrate mastery of at least 6 skills needed for kindergarten readiness

Deciding how much to promise in terms of client outcomes is a critical decision in program planning. Occasionally, program planners think that the more they promise, the more likely it is that they will obtain funding for their programs. In most instances, this strategy backfires. Funding source personnel are very savvy and can recognize when the projected results are unrealistic and the program is "overpromising." And in those instances where the program has overpromised but gets funded anyway, program planners often find that they have put themselves and the implementers of the program in the untenable position of attempting to achieve unachievable outcomes and, eventually, of attempting to explain why they did not.

This type of behavior begins to affect an agency's credibility. A program's goals and objectives should be seen as a contract. If requested resources are made available, then stated outcomes will be achieved. An objective that is well written technically (one that meets the above criteria) but that cannot possibly be accomplished can be a serious waste of time, energy, and resources. It is better in the long run not to get such a program funded than to waste valuable resources that might have been used more effectively in another program with realistic objectives.

Criteria for Measurement

If the objective cannot be measured, the program cannot be evaluated— or at least we will never be able to know whether the objective has been achieved. The corollary of this is that we need to state in the planning phase not only what we hope to achieve (such as a reduction in child abuse or an increase in job placements) but also the criteria of acceptable performance: for example,

- To reduce incidents of child abuse in District 1 by 15% as measured by referrals recorded in the Child Abuse Central Registry
- To increase awareness of the warning signs of a potential abuser as measured by the Straus Conflict Tactic (CT) Scales (Straus, 1990).
- To increase self-esteem as measured by the Hudson Self-Esteem Scale (Hudson, 1982).

To ensure that measurement criteria have been included, one should always look for the phrase "as measured by" (or something similar) in a complete outcome objective. This part of the objective allows the writer of the objective to state an outcome that may not be completely and precisely understood in the same way by all, with the understanding that its meaning will be further clarified and defined when stating the measurement criteria. For example, "improving healthy communication" may not be understood in the same way by all, but when the criterion for measurement—"as measured by the Flynn Compatibility Scale"—is added, ambiguity is removed.

Responsibility

The final issue is that of accountability for implementation of the objective. Up to this point our concern has been that objectives be clear, specific, measurable, time based, and realistic. The last necessary component is the ability to fix responsibility for carrying out and reporting on the objective's attainment. The statement should include an identification of a title (e.g., supervisor, program administrator) or a person, by name, and a simple additional phrase or sentence such as, "The person responsible shall be the child care program manager."

Not all writers of objectives include the name or title of the person responsible in the objective itself. Nevertheless, the principle of identifying the person(s) responsible is an important one. In the same manner that we identify a specific date of completion for the objective so that we will know *when* the objective is to be completed, we identify a person or title so that we will know *who* is to be held responsible for monitoring. When the plan is fully fleshed out, it will include a list of objectives to be achieved and activities to be accomplished. If no one is assigned to track progress and monitor due dates, much of the carefully crafted plan could be ignored and the plan could fail. The person identified is usually considered to be responsible for managing implementation, not for carrying out the work.

Outcome Objectives

Outcome objectives are extremely important parts of a program plan in that they explain the reason for the existence of the program as well as project measurable results. Outcome objectives flow directly from the problem analysis phase in a number of ways. First and foremost, an outcome objective is a statement that is intended to reflect a reduction in the incidence or prevalence of the problem. Outcome objectives should state clearly what effect the intervention is expected to have on the target population—for example,

- To increase the graduation rate among high-risk adolescents
- To prevent the reoccurrence of child abuse or neglect in 25 families
- To return 100 children in foster care to their natural parents

The problem analysis section will provide the numbers necessary to meet the criteria of measurability and specificity discussed above. By identifying the numbers of individuals or families with a particular problem, we have established the outside limits for the program. Given agency, personnel, and resource constraints, we identify the number of clients that we realistically expect to be able to serve during a given period of time. Now the task is to *predict* our success rate. The following are examples of outcome objectives (N.B. the wording may seem awkward, but the phrase "it is the objective of this program" is not included in each statement for the purpose of brevity):

- By June 30, 20XX, to graduate at least 50 of 100 participating high-risk students in the Roosevelt School District as documented in school records. The Dropout Prevention Supervisor is responsible for monitoring.

- By December 31, 20XX, to prevent the reoccurrence of child neglect in 75% of the families participating in this program, as documented by referrals to the Child Abuse Central Registry. Responsible person will be the Child Abuse Supervisor.

- By August 1, 20XX, to improve the relationship between 50 adolescents and their natural parents as measured by at least a 50% improvement on the Parent/Adolescent Communication Scale. Counseling Supervisor will be responsible for implementation and monitoring.

To restate, outcome objectives flow from the problem analysis phase and focus on a reduction of the problem or an improvement in the quality of life of the program's target population. They are statements that translate a program goal into precise and measurable language. Once the outcome objectives are clearly conceptualized and stated, their companion process objectives should begin to become clear. These are addressed in the next section.

Given the complexity of the problems that we are attempting to resolve, it is often necessary to think of outcome objectives in hierarchical terms, as with the United Way of America's use of initial, intermediate, and long-term outcomes (United Way of America, 1996). Invariably, we will have more than one level of outcomes, and all deal with a positive change in the quality of life of the clients. In effectiveness-based program planning we deal with only two levels: intermediate and final. The highest level or longest term outcome reflects the reason for existence of the program, as in the following examples:

- To reduce the incidence of physical violence against women
- To increase the number of homeless who become self-sufficient and secure a permanent residence
- To reduce the number of adolescents who participate in street gangs

Most programs designed to achieve these outcomes would require a mix of interventions. The hierarchy with family violence would be as follows:

Final or ultimate objective:
- Reduce the reoccurrence of domestic violence in at least 80% of participating families

Intermediate objectives:
- Resolution of emotional and psychological issues that act as barriers to self-esteem and self-confidence
- Achievement of a certificate for successful completion of employment training
- Placement in a job for which the client was trained
- Mastery of independent living skills

With the homeless, it could be a combination of learning basic job-finding skills (such as resume preparation and interviewing), learning a skill (such as short-order cooking or construction skills), and finding affordable housing. With potential high school dropouts, it could be a combination of developing a relationship with a mentor, participating in after-school activities, and improving academic performance.

In each instance, it is expected that if clients improve in the areas specified, they will achieve the stated overall expected outcome or result. We know (or believe) this because our research done during the problem analysis phase supports this hypothesis.

What must be recognized, however, is that each of the interventions designed to achieve the final or long-term outcome objective also has expected outcomes. If one phase of the family violence intervention is designed to ensure the development of independent living skills, then there must be a measurable outcome for that phase. In this instance it would mean that clients were able to secure permanent housing, make acceptable child care arrangements, and build a social support network. The expected outcome might read as follows:

- To achieve all objectives in the Individual Rehab Plan (IRP) related to self-sufficiency and independent community living (N.B. this would assume that housing, child care, and social supports were included in IRP objectives)

Likewise, there must be measurable outcomes for increasing self-esteem, lowering anxiety, managing finances, and for employment training and placement. It is these outcomes *in combination* that we believe will enable a woman at risk to achieve a violence-free life, self-sufficiency, and independence. So to understand all the necessary components of the program, we must understand whether each individual client (as well as all clients aggregated) achieved expected outcomes. Once we know that these lower level outcomes have been achieved, and whether or not there have been subsequent incidents of violence, we can begin to support or reject the intervention hypothesis that states that achievement of these lower level outcomes will lead to a reduction in family violence. The two levels of outcomes used in effectiveness-based program planning are referred to as *final* (i.e., reduction in reoccurrence of domestic violence) and *intermediate* (i.e., self-esteem, low anxiety, independent living skills, social supports, financial management skills, and employable skills). Table 7.2 depicts the relationships between and among final and intermediate outcomes.

Table 7.2   Relationship Between Intermediate and Final Outcomes

Final or Ultimate Outcome	Reduce the incidence of reoccurrence of domestic violence in at least 80% of participating families
Intermediate Outcomes	Increase in self-esteem Lower social anxiety Mastery of independent living skills Mastery of financial management skills Mastery of job skills Placement in a job for which the client was trained

Process Objectives and Activities

Once the ends (outcome objectives) have been developed, we are in a position to specify the means (process objectives) by which we hope to achieve the stated results. Again, we return to the program hypothesis, which explains the assumed relationships between means and ends (if the following actions are taken, then the following results can be expected). The "if' statements in the hypothesis become the basis for the process objectives, just as the "then" statements dealing with the ends formed the basis for the outcome objectives.

In the Victims to Victors Program, we identified four intermediate outcome objectives. Process objectives are the tools we use to describe how these outcomes will be achieved. Process objectives are always related to the lowest level of outcome objectives which, in most cases, will be the intermediate outcome objectives. We assume that highest level outcome objectives (final outcomes) will be achieved through the attainment of the lower level outcome objectives (i.e., the reoccurrence of family violence will be reduced through victims learning independent living skills and securing a steady job).

Process objectives, then, are intended to spell out the milestones necessary to achieve the intermediate outcome objectives. Like all objectives, well-written process objectives require the five basic parts: (a) time frame, (b) target (population or product), (c) result (the tangible expectation of this process), (d) criterion (how the result will be measured or documented), and (e) responsibility (who is responsible for ensuring the completion of this process objective). Just as with outcome objectives, we find that process objectives have their own set of verbs and descriptors–for example:

- To increase the level of services or number of cases . . .
- To provide case management . . .
- To serve hot meals . . .
- To recruit program participants . . .
- To train volunteers . . .
- To make home visits . . .

Time Frames

Time frames are expressed in process objectives in the same manner as outcome objectives. A date is specified when it is expected that the objective will have been achieved. Time frames should be stated as specific dates, including month, day, and year. One-year time frames are usually stated as follows:

- By September 30, 20XX (with a specific year, one year from the start date, inserted)

When multiple-year outcome objectives are developed, the year will reflect the longer time required.

Target and Result

Targets of change in *outcome objectives* focus on the population in need of change. *Process objectives* focus on the completion of products or milestones or other elements needed in order to implement the program. The purpose of a program-planning effort is the accomplishment of changes that are achievable within stated time frames. To get to the point of successfully achieving client changes, certain processes must first be implemented and followed through to completion. In order that processes not be allowed to continue on indefinitely without concrete, measurable achievement, milestones should be identified that can be used to mark the completion of the process.

The question to be answered in identifying the target and result of a process objective is: "What processes must be completed and/or products produced in order for the program to be implemented and monitored?" The answer to this question can vary from preparation of a training program to hiring of personnel to producing reports.

The following are examples of milestones to be achieved or products to be produced that might be specified in a process objective. Note that target and result are both contained within these milestones.

- Case managers will be hired.
- An interim report will be produced.
- A screening system will be designed.

Criteria for Measurement or Documentation

If a process objective cannot be measured or documented, difficulties will arise in monitoring (keeping track of) the program once it is under way. The issue here is to ensure that everyone who expects to be guided by a process objective must agree on how all will know when it has been achieved. Sometimes completion of a process objective is obvious, as in the hiring of a staff member. Either the position is filled or it isn't. But just to be sure there is no uncertainty, the process objective would state " . . . as documented by an offer and acceptance signed by the designated authority and the candidate," or something to that effect. Sometimes completion of a milestone is not as obvious. If a process objective target was "development of a training program," for example, the terms "development" and "training program" could mean many different things. To one person training program may mean a one-page, skeleton outline of topics to be covered. To another it may mean complete lesson plans, workbooks, audiovisual aids, evaluation forms, and more. Likewise, development could mean that the person preparing the program says it is complete, or it could mean that all components defined in a contract must meet the approval of the training director. In order to prevent conflicting opinions to the greatest extent possible, it is useful to specify a criterion for documentation in the process objective.

To ensure that measurement or documentation criteria have been included, one should always look for the phrase *as measured (or documented) by* in a complete process objective. This allows the writer of the objective to clarify and define precisely how one will know when the target and result have been achieved.

Responsibility

As with outcome objectives, the designating of a responsible party ensures that all will know who is expected to implement and monitor the process objective. The statement should include an identification of a title (e.g., supervisor, program administrator) or a person, by name. For example, in the following process objective, the supervisor is designated as the responsible person: "By June 1, 20XX, to complete the outreach, screening, and assessment phases of the program for 30 women who have been identified as 'high risk,' as documented in a report written by the social work supervisor."

Just as with outcome objectives, we find that process objectives have their own set of verbs and descriptors—for example:

- To *recruit* at least 30 potential program participants . . .
- To *complete the screening process* with all potential program participants . . .
- To *complete the assessment process* with all who have been accepted into the program . . .

Integrating Outcome Objectives, Process Objectives, and Activities

The Victims to Victors Program will be used to illustrate the relationship between outcome and process. The numbering system proposed here is merely a suggestion. There are no hard-and-fast rules that make one numbering or lettering system superior to another. Use of any system is a matter of choice. The intent is simply that goals, objectives, and activities be coded in some way that makes for easy identification of interrelationships. With the numbering scheme used below, those working with Process Objective 1.1.1, for example, will always know that this objective relates to Goal #1, to Final Outcome Objective 1.0, to Intermediate Outcome Objective 1.1.

Note also that we have used figures between 75 and 90% in our projections for intermediate outcome objectives. This represents about 22 to 27 out of the 30 participants selected for the program. This avoids the unrealistic expectation that the program will achieve 100% success, and makes it more likely that the objective will be achieved.

Assume that the following program has been funded and begins on July 1, 20XX.

Outcome Objective (Final)

1.0. By June 30, 20XX (probably at least 2 years from inception of the program), there will be no reoccurrence of domestic violence for at least 80% of program participants

Outcome Objectives (Intermediate)

1.1. By April 1, 20XX (prior to final outcome), at least 75% of program participants will demonstrate at least a 25% increase in self-esteem scores as measured by the Hudson Self-Esteem Scale. Counselors are responsible for monitoring.

1.2. By May 31, 20XX (prior to final outcome), at least 85% of women who have participated in the program will have secured the community resources (housing, child care, and other resources included in the Individual Rehab Plan) necessary to establish independent living. The case manager is responsible for monitoring and evaluation.

1.3. By March 15, 20XX (during the first year of the program), the knowledge and skill necessary to managing their finances will mastered by at least 90% of women who have participated in the program, as measured by the Martin Assessment of Financial Management Skills. The trainer is responsible for monitoring and evaluation.

1.4. By December 31, 20XX (probably during the second year of the program), at least 85% of women who have participated in the program will master employable skills as defined in the training curriculum, as measured by receiving a GPA of 3.0 or better in the curriculum in which they participated, and receive a certificate for successful completion. The employment training contractor will monitor and evaluate.

Examples of process objectives for Intermediate Outcome Objective 1.1 might include the following:

Process Objectives

1.1.1. By August 1, 20XX, to recruit at least 30 victims of domestic violence into the program . . .

1.1.2. By September 1, 20XX, to provide at least one individual session and one group session with a counselor each week . . .

1.1.3. By November 1, 20XX, to prepare an Individual Rehab Plan . . .

A second example illustrates objectives related to the incidence of child abuse:

Outcome Objective (Final)

1.0. By December 31, 20XX, to reduce the incidence of child abuse in 75% of the high-risk families who participate in the program, as measured by reports from the child abuse registry

Outcome Objective (Intermediate)

1.1. By June 30, 20XX, to demonstrate reduction in stress in at least 90% of client families on those stress factors that cause a family to be at risk; success to be measured by a family's moving at least two points in a positive direction on the Sullivan Stress Scale

Process Objectives

1.1.1. By September 1, 20XX, to develop a screening process for all families referred to the program, as documented by the completion and approval of a screening instrument and a flowchart of the process

1.1.2. By December 1, 20XX, to develop a stress profile on at least 100 families using the Sullivan Stress Scale, as documented in case records and monthly project report

1.1.3. By March 1, 20XX, to provide stress reduction counseling services to at least 85 families, as documented in the case records

In establishing dates for outcome and process objectives, remember that the processes must be completed *before* you can measure the achievement of the expected outcome. This means that services to individual clients and families must be planned and coordinated so that services are completed prior to the dates specified in process objectives.

Activities

The next and final task in structuring the plan is to take each process objective and break it down into specific tasks that must be completed to achieve the process objectives. These we refer to as *activities* in the classification system suggested earlier in this chapter. In the above example, we might find the recruitment process objective (Process Objective 1.1.1) to include the following activities:

Process Objective 1.1.1 By August 1, 20XX, to recruit at least 30 victims of domestic violence into the program . . .

Activities:

a. Convene a task force to develop or refine a screening instrument specific to the Victims to Victors Program. Due date: July 1.
b. Interview at least 20 women who are on the shelter's waiting list. Due date: July 22.
c. Select the top 10 candidates and rank order at least 5 additional candidates. Due date: July 25. (The program will eventually have 30 participants. The shelter will phase them in over the course of the first year.)
d. Have the first 10 participants in the Victims to Victors Program move into the shelter. Due date: July 29.

Is It Worth the Effort?

When all of the above elements have been fully developed, the complete document represents a plan ready for implementation. A major criticism of this management-by-objectives technology is that it is extremely time consuming, taking staff time away from an already full schedule. This is a valid criticism. In actual practice, however, social work program planning and social work practice have moved to the point where performance measurement is an expectation and not an option, as pointed out in Chapter 1.

Effectiveness-based program planning offers the conceptual tools to set up services as ongoing, in vivo, program hypothesis-testing experiments designed to inform practitioners, administrators, and funding sources about the extent to which a program is achieving its objectives. Further, it spells out staff activities in precise language, thereby permitting a proactive approach to ensuring program success. So while the system does require an initial investment, there are clearly benefits on many levels that make the investment worth the effort. The United Way of America (2006) identifies just a few of the benefits of outcome measurement, including improving services to clients, providing feedback to staff, enabling board members to understand program issues, identify training and technical assistance needs, comparing alternative strategies, pinpointing areas of need, greater precision in allocating resources, and many other benefits.

In describing major administrative trends in social work, Martin (2000) cites several trends that support the value of effectiveness-based program planning. He anticipates more emphasis on *results,* including performance measurement, performance budgeting, and performance contracting. He also predicts more *strategic planning,* including "a systematic approach to the ongoing assessment and evaluation of environmental forces and their potential client, program, and agency impacts" (p. 64). And he expects that there will be more emphasis on managing the *quality of services,* requiring precise definitions of quality and the capacity to measure its effects on clients. Agencies that fail to bring precision to their expected program outcomes, outputs, and activities will be risking their futures as they move into increasingly competitive environments.

References

Andringa, R., & Engstrom, T. (2002). *Nonprofit board answer book.* Washington, DC: Boardsource.

Austin, M., & Solomon, J. (2000). Managing the planning process. In R. Patti (Ed.), *The handbook of social welfare management* (pp. 341–359). Thousand Oaks, CA: Sage.

Brody, R. (2005). *Effectively managing human service organizations* (3rd ed.). Thousand Oaks, CA: Sage.

Coley, S., & Scheinberg, C. (2000). *Proposal writing* (2nd ed.). Thousand Oaks, CA: Sage.

Ezell, M. (2000). Financial management. In R. Patti (Ed.), *The handbook of social welfare management* (pp. 377–394). Thousand Oaks, CA: Sage.

Hudson, W. (1982). *The clinical measurement package.* Homewood, IL: Dorsey.

Johnson, M., & Ferraro, K (1998). Research on domestic violence in the 1990's. *Journal of Marriage and the Family, 62*, 948–960.

Kettner, P., Daley, J., & Nichols, A. (1985). *Initiating change in organizations and communities.* Monterey, CA: Brooks/Cole.

Kirkwood, C. (1993*). Leaving abusive partners: From the scare of survival to the wisdom of change.* Thousand Oaks, CA: Sage.

Martin, L. L. (2000). The environmental context of social welfare administration. In R. Patti (Ed.), *The handbook of social welfare management* (pp. 55–67). Thousand Oaks, CA: Sage.

McCauley, J., Kern, J., Koladron, D., & Dill, L. (1995). The battering syndrome: Prevalence and clinical characteristics of domestic violence in primary care. *Annals of Internal Medicine, 123*, 737–745.

Patti, R. (2000). The landscape of social welfare management. In R. Patti (Ed.), *The handbook of social welfare management* (pp. 3–25). Thousand Oaks, CA: Sage.

Poertner, J. (2000). Managing for service outcomes: The critical role of information. In R. Patti (Ed.), *The handbook of social welfare management* (pp. 267–281). Thousand Oaks, CA: Sage.

Straus, M. (1990). Measuring intrafamily conflict and violence: The conflict tactic (CT) scales. In M. A. Straus & R. J. Gelles (Eds.), *Physical violence in American families: Risk factors and adaptations to violence in 8,145 families* (pp. 29–47). New Brunswick, NJ: Transaction.

Tolman, R., & Rosen, D. (2001). Domestic violence in the lives of women receiving welfare. *Violence Against Women, 7*, 141–158.

United Way of America. (1996). *Measuring program outcomes: A practical approach* (4th ed.). Alexandria, VA: Author.

United Way of America. (2006). *Outcome measurement: Showing results in the nonprofit sector.* Outcome Measurement Resources Network. http://national .unitedway.org/outcomes/resources.

Chapter 8

Designing Effective Programs

The purpose of this chapter is to explain:

- The rationale for breaking programs down into elements
- The need for a precise definition for each element
- The systems model and the ways in which it provides a framework for program design
- How the program hypothesis and program objectives fit together with the elements of program design

The following topics are covered in this chapter:

- The significance of program design
- Designing the elements of a system
- Defining the elements of a program
    Inputs
    Throughputs
    Outputs
    Outcomes
- The relationship between objectives and system components
- Specifying the program hypothesis

The Significance of Program Design

Like the earlier phases of effectiveness-based program planning discussed in the previous chapters, program design is an activity that requires careful analysis and attention to detail. As used here *program design* refers to identifying and defining the elements that go into the delivery of a service. In some ways the concept of program design is similar to protocols as used in research and treatment practice. Protocols are formal sets of procedures to be followed during the conduct of research or treatment.

For many years, the whole notion of program design was all but overlooked or taken for granted in planning programs. For the vast majority of social service programs, program design involved simply hiring caseworkers, assigning clients, and instructing the workers to provide casework services. Although this approach is simple in its design and allows maximum flexibility for practitioners, it fails to deal with critical questions of relevance of services provided, accountability, and measurement of effectiveness, and fails to take advantage of research knowledge and best practices.

Let us explore these issues by contrasting two programs for elderly, isolated seniors. Program A has five caseworkers, each of whom carries 30 cases. Caseworkers decide how often to meet with clients. When they meet, they attempt to determine needs and to find resources in the community to meet those needs. After each session, caseworkers write narrative recordings of case activity in the case record.

Program B is structured differently. Program B has an intake and screening worker, two case managers, a meal coordinator, a transportation coordinator, and a socialization and recreation specialist. Program B staff identify at-risk seniors in the community, transport them to the senior center, screen and assess to determine unmet needs using scaled instruments, and build a case plan designed to meet unmet needs to the greatest extent possible, including (at a minimum) a daily noon meal and transportation to and from the center.

When a client completes Program A, a caseworker writes a narrative explanation of why the client is no longer in the program and describes the client's progress and status as of the point of termination. On completion of Program B, a case manager administers a posttest on nutrition, social isolation, and general mobility and secures agreement from the client to participate in a 6-month follow-up evaluation. In Program B's case records, case managers record test scores, itemize barriers, and code the special units from which each client receives services. The case manager then enters all data into the computer. Aggregated data reveal monthly patterns of participation and improvement on the part of clients.

Which is the better program? The answer to that question depends on your perspective on the purpose of social service programs. Program A clearly provides for a stronger and more comprehensive relationship between caseworker and client. Program B, however, is clearly superior when effectiveness and accountability are the issues. Program B's design is based on a hypothesis that the major barriers to full participation for isolated elderly include transportation and socialization and recreation opportunities, including congregate meals. Regular analysis of their data will enable Program B's staff to discover whether this hypothesis is correct and to make adjustments as needed to make the program more effective.

The major differences between these programs are differences of precision, specificity, and detail. Program A caseworkers may also discover that socialization, recreation, and congregate meals are important factors in success for isolated elderly, but each caseworker would have to make this discovery independently and decide to act on it. For Program B, the *problem analysis* produced the findings, and the *goals and objectives* established the direction. Let us examine how planners, using effectiveness-based program planning principles, move from goals and objectives to program design.

Designing the Elements of a System

Bringing precision and understanding to a phenomenon involves breaking it down into some basic elements. One analytic framework that has proved very useful to business and industry as well as to the social sciences is the systems framework. Organizations such as General Electric, IBM, and Microsoft have been able to achieve a greater understanding of their programs (and therefore a greater capacity to make positive changes) by breaking them down into elements using systems concepts.

Drawing on logic model concepts, the United Way of America refers to the four program elements as inputs, activities, outputs, and outcomes (United Way of America, 2006; Hatry, van Houten, Plantz, and Greenway, 1996). The more traditional systems theory language uses the term *throughputs* in place of *activities*. Throughout this book we will use the term *throughputs*, for two reasons. First, the term incorporates the slightly broader concept of a conversion process, where raw materials (inputs) are converted to outputs and outcomes (Katz and Kahn, 1966; Thompson, 1967). Second, we use the term *activities* to define the tasks associated with process objectives (see Chapter 7), and using the same term for two different purposes may be confusing to the reader. Nevertheless, in most instances the reader should understand that the terms *throughputs* and *activities* (as used in the logic model) are more or less synonymous. *Inputs* are defined as resources and raw materials. *Throughputs* are defined as the series of tasks or processes necessary to convert raw materials to successful outputs and outcomes. *Outputs* are products produced or services completed. *Outcomes* are planned, measurable changes in the life situation or circumstances of clients or consumers as a result of services provided.

Defining the Elements of a Program

This systems model can be applied to a social service program by breaking the system down into its inputs, throughputs, outputs, and outcomes.

Inputs

Inputs in a program include five elements representing an agency's resources and raw materials: (1) clients or consumers, (2) staff, (3) material resources, (4) facilities, and (5) equipment. Clients represent the "raw materials" in a human service system; the other four elements represent the resources that will be used to perform the activities needed to "convert" the clients from persons with problems and needs to persons who have been able to resolve problems and meet needs.

Each element needs to be further defined, and we provide examples of how they might be defined in Table 8.1. As each element is defined, it is important to remember that at some point we will have to put in place a data collection system for use in monitoring, performance measurement, and evaluation. For this reason, it is useful to define each of the above elements in terms that will be useful for analytical and reporting purposes. For example, what breakdown of such factors as age, ethnicity, or income will be useful later on when it is necessary to analyze the population served? When dealing with the variable of age, one option often used is to categorize in 5-year increments (e.g., 21 to 25, 26 to 30, and so on). However, with software available for data collection and aggregation and

Table 8.1 Variables Related to Program Inputs

Variable	Example	Purpose
Client-Related Variables Eligibility	Age, residence, income	To ensure that those served are eligible for the program
Demographic or descriptive variables	Race, gender, income, education, employment, census tract	To record elements that may later prove helpful in describing population served, to ensure that the targeted population is being served, and to identify those client characteristics that seem to be assoicated with success or failure in the program
Social history factors	History of substance abuse, mental health history, violence, etc.—whatever is considered to be relevant	To identify factors that may later be useful in evaluating the types of clients for whom the program is effective or not effective
Client problem and strength profile	Alcohol abuse, drug abuse, parenting skills, money management skills	To identify areas of concern that will become the focus of intervention. Problems are scaled so that assessment will reveal those areas where problems are significant, but also those areas where there are strengths.
Staff-Related Variables Demographic or descriptive variables	Gender, ethnicity, education, experience	To identify staff variables that might later be useful in determining what types of workers seem to be most effective with what types of clients or problems

(Continued)

Table 8.1　(Continued)

Variable	Example	Purpose
Accreditation or licensing	Licenses, certificates, degrees	To collect data that will be readily available when called for by accrediting or licensing bodies
Physical Resources Material resources	Food, clothing, toys, or cash provided directly to clients	To collect data that will be helpful in defining what resources seem to affect client change or improvement
Facilities	Residences used to house clients; office facilities used for client treatment	To collect data that may help to understand whether a facility, such as a particular type of residential treatment setting, affects client improvement when compared to other treatment settings
Equipment	Vehicles, computers, medical or other equipment used in direct client service	To collect data about equipment used by or in direct service to clients that may affect the helping process. Data would not be collected on equipment used by staff, only on equipment used directly with and by clients.

the simplicity of data entry, interval data (exact age rather than categories) is superior for analysis and evaluation. It is always possible to aggregate data, but not possible to disaggregate. Again, we emphasize that these categories are defined with future data and information needs in mind. Table 8.1 may be used as a guide in defining elements specific to a program. Not all elements listed in Table 8.1 will be used in every program.

Throughputs

Throughputs (or activities as used in the logic model) refer to the procedures that will be implemented in order to carry out the program. It is during the service provision process that resources, including staff, material resources, facilities, and equipment, are used to help clients so that they may complete the service process (output) and, it is hoped, resolve their problems (outcome).

Throughputs in social service programs usually involve such treatment, rehabilitation, or support methods as counseling; job training; provision of day care, residential treatment, and shelter; dispensing of food baskets; and provision of information and referral (Hatry, van Houten, Plantz, and Greenway, 1996). To bring some degree of uniformity to the process, it is necessary to identify and define data elements that make up throughputs. These elements include service definition, service tasks, and method of intervention.

Service Definition

The *service definition* is usually a simple one- or two-sentence definition of services to be provided. Its function is to narrow down the service from something that might cover a whole range of client problems and needs to something that is focused on a specific aspect of client problems and needs. For example, the broad category "drug treatment" can include the following: detoxification; inpatient or outpatient medical treatment; individual, group, or family counseling; job training and placement; and follow-up supportive services.

Simply describing a program as a drug treatment program does not sufficiently narrow its scope in a way that informs relevant parties what the program is intended to accomplish. A definition such as "This program or service is intended to provide outpatient detoxification to cocaine addicts ages 18 and older" helps those who need to know whom and what the program is for.

A comprehensive listing of service definitions has been developed by the United Way of America (1976) in a volume titled *UWASIS II: A Taxonomy of Social Goals and Human Service Programs,* in which more than 230 services are labeled and defined. An example from the UWASIS directory is the definition of pre-job guidance: "Pre-job guidance is a program designed to help individuals who need to learn the basic tools of obtaining employment to suit their particular skills and talents" (p. 208). Another listing of service definitions is the *Arizona Dictionary and Taxonomy of Human Services* (Department of Economic Security, 1995). The service of "adoption placement" is defined as follows: "This service provides the selection of a family and placement, and supervision of a child until the adoption is finalized." "Shelter services" may be defined as "the provision of temporary care in a safe environment available on a 24 hour basis." "Case management" may be defined as "a process in which an individual who is determined to be in need of and eligible for services works with a professional staff person to identify needs, plan for services, obtain services, collect data on the service process, monitor and evaluate services, terminate the process, and follow up as needed."

Service Tasks

Service tasks help to define the activities that go into the provision of the service. If, for example, a program or service is intended to increase independence and self-sufficiency for single mothers by training them in job finding skills, what tasks might make up the service? Such tasks as screening and assessment, resume preparation, interviewing skills, work habits, job training, job placement, and follow-up might be considered to be part of a complete package. Payne (1997) summarizes the social work process into eight phases, each phase having its own associated activities or tasks. For example, the first phase, Assessing Problems, includes the tasks of: stating the problem, analyzing the system, setting goals, setting strategy, and stabilizing the change effort. To ensure some degree of comparability in what clients receive, it is important that some thought be given to identifying and defining service tasks.

In most cases service tasks tend to follow a chronological order of services to a client. In such cases, it is helpful in the planning and design phases for program planners to develop a client flowchart that tracks a client from entry to exit. Figure 8.1 illustrates a client flow through the Victims to Victors Program at the Safe Haven Shelter.

Specifying tasks in this way and bringing increasing degrees of precision to their definition helps to introduce at least some degree of uniformity to what helping professionals provide and can serve a similar function to that of protocols in medicine. Tasks serve to bring a clearer focus to the question of who does what with clients, for what purpose, and under what conditions. Tasks not only address the accountability question but also permit ongoing evaluation of effectiveness. If a particular approach is effective, the treatment can be repeated. If it is not, problem

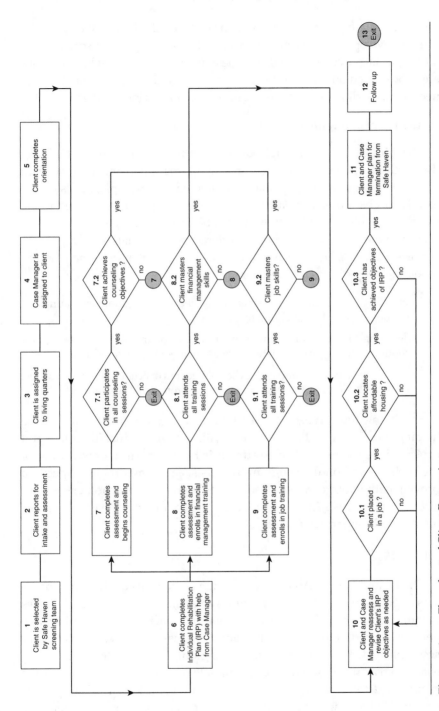

Figure 8.1   Flowchart of Client Processing

149

areas can be pinpointed and the treatment modified. A service protocol can be developed by beginning with the flowchart of client services and adding a narrative chart that includes an explanation of what activities are to be carried out at each step in the process and what documentation is necessary. An illustration of such a narrative chart is included as Table 8.2.

Method of Intervention

The third element of throughput is the method of intervention. Defining the method of intervention requires that program planners specify in advance the ways the service may be delivered. For example, meals for the elderly can be provided in a congregate setting or can be delivered to the elderly person's home. Job training can be carried out in a classroom setting or on the job. Counseling can be offered to individuals, in groups, or in families. Payne (1997) describes three roles for social workers when the aim is helping people to make transitions:

1. Enabling (for example, strengthening the client's motivation, validating and supporting the client, helping to manage feelings);
2. Teaching (like helping clients learn problem-solving skills, clarifying perceptions, offering appropriate information, modeling behavior);
3. Facilitating (such as maintaining clients' freedom of action from unreasonable constraints, defining the task, mobilizing environmental supports). (p. 148)

Specifying these types of roles helps guide the worker through the helping process rather than leave everything to individual judgment and choice. Since the method of treatment is based on an understanding of the problem and on the program hypothesis, it is important to specify a proven method of treatment or service delivery (e.g., psychotherapy, cognitive therapy, crisis intervention, etc.) if such a method exists. Table 8.3 illustrates throughput elements.

Outputs

The United Way of America (1996) defines outputs as the direct products of program activities, and provides as examples the number of classes taught, the number of counseling sessions conducted, or hours of service delivered. Brody (2005) adds that outputs measure the volume of work accomplished. The purpose of measuring output is to determine (a) *how much* of an available service a client actually received and (b) whether the client *completed treatment* or received the full complement of services as specified in the program design. The "how much" question is answered by

(*Text continued on p. 154*)

Table 8.2   Narrative Chart

Process Number	Title	Procedures	Documents
1	Client is selected by Safe Haven Shelter screening team	Appointment is made for client to meet with team. Team determines eligibility and makes selection	Screening form
2	Client reports for intake and assessment	Client meets with Intake Worker to complete all intake forms and to complete an assessment	Intake Form Social History Data Entry Forms Strengths and Needs Profile
3	Client is assigned to living quarters	Client is assigned to a room and given a tour of the facility	Residential Assignment Form Resident Responsibilities Form
4	Case manager is assigned to client	Case manager meets with client	Data entry form Case notes
5	Client completes orientation	Client attends the next scheduled orientation session	Orientation log Pretest and posttest
6	Client completes Individual Rehabilitation Plan (IRP) with help from case manager	Case manager meets with client to assist in developing a plan to meet individual and program objectives	IRP Form
7	Client completes assessment and begins counseling	Client meets with counselor to set up a schedule for individual and group counseling sessions. Initial assessment is completed and counseling objectives are established	Data Entry Form Counseling Plan Case Notes

(Continued)

Table 8.2   (Continued)

Process Number	Title	Procedures	Documents
7.1	Client participates in all counseling sessions?	Counselor tracks attendance and evaluates quality of participation. Failure to participate can lead to exit from the program	Attendance Form Case Notes
7.2	Client achieves counseling objectives?	As client continues, progress is evaluated against objectives in the counseling plan. Work continues until objectives are achieved. Reassessments completed as needed.	Attendance Form Data Entry Form Case Notes
8	Client completes assessment and enrolls in financial management training	Client completes assessment of financial management skills and enrolls in the next available class	Financial Management Skills Assessment Form Training Enrollment Form
8.1	Client attends all training sessions?	Trainer tracks attendance and evaluates quality of participation. Failure to attend or participate can lead to exit from the program	Attendance Form Trainer Evaluation Form
8.2	Client masters financial management skills?	Mastery of skills is measured by testing. When client receives a passing grade on all units of the course she receives a certificate of completion. Reassessment is completed as needed	Record of Progress and Completion Form

Process Number	Title	Procedures	Documents
9	Client completes assessment and enrolls in job training	Client meets with Job Counselor to assess job skills. Training referral is made. Client meets with trainer	Job Skills Assessment Form Training Enrollment Form
9.1	Client attends all training sessions?	Trainer tracks attendance and evaluates quality of participation. Failure to attend or participate can lead to exit from the program	Attendance Form Trainer Evaluation Form
9.2	Client masters job skills?	Mastery of skills is measured by testing. When client receives a passing grade on all units of the course she receives a certificate of completion. Reassessments are completed as needed	Record of Progress and Completion Form
10	Client and case manager reassess and revise client's IRP objectives as needed	When all activities of the IRP have been completed, client and case manager assess achievement and begin to prepare for termination if client is determined to be ready	Individual Rehab Plan (IRP) Case Notes Data Entry Form
10.1	Client is placed in a job?	Client meets with job placement counselor to identify available job slots that fit with training. Job opportunities are continually explored until a job is secured	Job Placement Referral Form

(Continued)

Table 8.2   (Continued)

Process Number	Title	Procedures	Documents
10.2	Client locates affordable housing?	Client meets with housing placement counselor to identify available housing and continues until housing is secured	Housing Placement Referral Form
10.3	Client has achieved objectives of IRP?	Client and case manager review objectives of IRP and assess level of success	IRP Assessment Form Strength and Needs Profile Data Entry Form
11	Client and case manager plan for termination from Safe Haven	Client and case manager assess client's readiness to function independently in the community and make plans for follow up contacts as needed	Victims to Victors Termination Form Safe Haven Termination Form Data Entry Form
12	Follow Up	Case manager makes telephone contacts at the agreed-upon times and otherwise follows up according to plan	Case Notes Data Entry Form
13	Exit	Follow up contacts end by mutual agreement	Case Closure Form Case Notes Data Entry Form

defining *units of service,* and the answer is referred to as an *intermediate output.* The "service completion" question is answered by defining what we mean by completion, and the answer is referred to as a *final output.* For example, if a training program consists of 10 sessions, one unit of service would be one session. Calculating intermediate outputs would require taking attendance and recording how many sessions each trainee actually completed. The purpose of this type of tracking is to learn whether

Table 8.3   Throughput Elements

Element	Examples	Purpose
Service definition	This program is intended to provide counseling to women who have been victims of domestic violence to enable them to increase self-esteem and self-confidence, and to reduce social anxiety	To provide a formal definition as a basis for common understanding and agreement about the services to be provided
Service tasks	1. Screening and assessment 2. Developing a treatment plan 3. Validating and supporting the client 4. Teaching problem solving skills 5. Etc. . . .	To ensure some degree of uniformity in services received by similar clients with similar problems; to tie services to what has been learned from research on this population and problem
Method of intervention	Client will participate in weekly individual counseling sessions and weekly group sessions	To ensure uniformity in the way counseling services are provided for the same types of clients within the same program

those who drop out or are spotty in their attendance achieve the same results as those who are regular in their attendance.

Final output in this example refers to completion of the course. Participants are divided into completers and dropouts. Final output is the rate of completion (a percentage) for all the trainees in a given class. Isolating the group of completers allows program planners to determine whether or not the training made a difference in achieving the outcome projected in the program hypothesis and the outcome objectives. If dropouts and completers are equally successful, then the training cannot be said to have made a difference.

A third focus—quality of service provided—also emerges in current discussions of output measures. Quality performance measures are discussed in one of the following sections in this chapter.

Units of Service

Units of service can be measured in three different ways: (a) as episodes or contact units, (b) as material units, or (c) as time units (Martin and Kettner, 1996). An *episode* or *contact* unit is defined as one contact between a worker and a client. It is used when the recording of client contact information is important but when the actual duration (time) of the contact is not considered important. Information and referral services often use a contact unit, simply counting the number of requests for information they receive.

A *material* unit of service is a tangible resource provided to a client and can include such items as a meal, a food basket, a trip, an article of clothing, cash, or a prescription. Material units are generally considered to be the least precise of the three types of units of service because variation may or may not exist between individual units. For example, the number and types of items in two food baskets or two boxes of clothing can vary widely, but each basket or box is still counted as one unit of service. However, with cash or a trip (measured in miles) the units are precise and comparable.

A *time* unit can be expressed in minutes, hours, days, weeks, or months, depending on the information needs of individual human service programs. Minutes might be used to measure the length of a phone call. An hour is often the unit used for a counseling session. Days might be used to measure the length of a stay in foster care. Weeks or months could be used for residential care. A time unit is the most precise of the three types of units of service because it is expressed in standardized increments. When time is used as a unit of service, it is important to state whether the time refers only to direct client contact time or whether support activity time (e.g., completing paperwork, attending client staffings, etc.) is also included. Ultimately, units of service are used for a number of purposes, including a determination of cost per unit of service, so decisions about defining units of service should be made with a good deal of care and attention to their purpose.

The ways in which units of service may be used become evident when we calculate how many units a program can provide in 1 year. Let us assume that there are five counselors and that each one can see 20 clients per week at 48 weeks per year (allowing for 2 weeks for vacation and 10 paid holidays for each counselor in a year). Each counselor, then, has a capacity to provide 48×20, or 960, units of counseling per year. The entire program, with five counselors, can provide 4,800 units per year. (In a later chapter we will discuss how a unit cost is calculated.) In the same manner for any given program, examination of resources provides a basis for calculating the number of units to be provided in a given year.

Episode units, even though they are not exact measures, help provide a degree of comparability from program to program. For example, a "child care day" usually runs from 6:00 A.M. to 6:00 P.M., and even though some children may be in child care for 6 hours, some for 8 hours, and some for 12 hours, for the purpose of measuring volume, all are considered to have received an episode of one child care day of services. It may simply not be worth the time and effort involved to calculate the hours and minutes for the purposes for which the measure is used.

Material units may be precise and comparable, or may vary. One newborn care kit may consist of exactly one package of diapers, two blankets, assorted soaps and lotions, and other necessities, with all being exactly the same. One food basket, on the other hand, might consist of a mix of canned and other nonperishable goods, but there could be wide variation from basket to basket, depending on the needs of the family. The rule of thumb is that the degree of precision and comparability in using episode and material units should be guided by the ways in which the information will be used. Table 8.4 illustrates time, episode, and material units of service.

Service Completion

The second data element involved in defining output is that of service completion and is referred to as a final output. The question that must be answered is: When is a client finished with a service? Service completion is defined at the time the program is designed. For some services, final output is easily and clearly defined; for others, it is problematic. In most training programs, for example (or even in a university setting, for that matter), a number of training sessions or class sessions are required for successful completion of the course. One intermediate output unit might be attendance at one class, and a final output might be defined as one client's completing all the requirements of an automobile mechanics training course. A prenatal care program might consist of at least six monthly prenatal visits with a physician, and successful completion of a detoxification program might be defined as completion of a 60-day stay in an inpatient detox unit. Table 8.5 provides examples of intermediate and final outputs.

Table 8.4   Calculating Units of Service

Type of Unit	Design Elements Needed to Calculate	How to Calculate a Program's Capacity to Provide Units for the Entire Program for One Year
Time	1. Staff time with a client for one week 2. Service type	1. Calculate how many units one staff member can provide in one week 2. Multiply by 52 weeks 3. Multiply the result of #2 by the number of FTE* staff
Episode	1. Staff-client encounters for one week 2. Service type	1. Calculate how many encounters one staff member can complete in one week 2. Multiply by 52 weeks** 3. Multiply the result of #2 by the number of FTE staff
Material	1. Material resources (e.g. food, clothing, cash) provided to a client in one year	1. Calculate the material resource provided to one client in one week (e.g. $100 cash stipend, 1 food basket)*** 2. Multiply by the number of clients receiving this resource each week. 3. Multiply the result of #2 by 52 weeks

*Full-time equivalent
**Weeks can be adjusted for holidays and vacations
***If material resources are provided irregularly, adjustments will need to be made to this formula

For some services, final outputs can be difficult to define. In ongoing services such as day care or long-term residential care for the elderly, it is not useful to define final outputs in terms of exit or completion of a program because these programs are not designed to move clients in and out at a steady and predictable pace. Clients in these types of long-term programs may remain for many years, and effective monitoring and evaluation cannot occur if measurements are taken only after an extended period of years. Effective monitoring and evaluation requires much more frequent examination.

Table 8.5   Output as an Element of Service Design

Element	Examples	Purpose
Intermediate output	One unit equals attendance at one family counseling session (*episode unit*)	To measure the volume or quantity of service provided to each consumer, using a uniform definition for all participants
Final output	One unit equals completion of 12 family counseling sessions with no absences	To ensure agreement among program personnel and clients as to what constitutes full participation, and to ensure that, in evaluating outcomes, distinctions are made between completers and dropouts

In these types of instances, the program designers should define the final output in terms of completion of a fixed-term treatment plan. For example, one might define a final output as "completion of an individual care plan" for day care or "completion of the prescribed service plan for a 3-month period" in the case of long-term residential care for the elderly. Here we are dealing with the equivalent of achieving *milestones* as required in *individual education plans*.

Building milestones into long-term service designs permits measures to be taken at certain selected points to determine whether the treatment plan is having the desired effects. Its purpose is to ensure that the full service mix, as intended by the designers of the program, has been received by a client.

Defining output prior to implementation of a program also enables evaluators to distinguish between someone who completes the program and someone who drops out. These two groups need to be evaluated separately, but if output is defined simply as an exit from the program, it is impossible to distinguish completers from dropouts for evaluation purposes. Table 8.6 illustrates calculation of intermediate and final outputs.

Quality

As units of service have become more clearly conceptualized and defined, there has been a tendency to base contracts and reimbursement plans on the number of intermediate output units actually delivered

Table 8.6   Calculating Output Units

Type of Unit	Design Elements Needed to Calculate	How to Calculate a Program's Capacity to Provide Units for the Entire Program for One Year	Example
Intermediate output	1. Staff time with a client for one week 2. Service type	1. Calculate how many units one staff member can provide in one week 2. Multiply by 52 weeks 3. Multiply the result of #2 by the number of FTE staff	25 hours of counseling $\times 52 = 1300$ hours $\times 2.5$ FTE $= 3250$ hours
Final output	1. Definition of a service completion 2. Number of intermediate output units needed for one client to meet the requirements specified in the definition	1. Calculate the number of intermediate output units needed for one client to complete the service as defined. 2. Calculate how many of those blocks of time (e.g., 10 training sessions) can be provided in one year by one counselor or trainer. 3. Multiply the result of #2 by the number of FTE staff available for this function.	1. 10 training sessions of two hours each 2. One trainer can provide 5 sessions per week or 260 per year 3. .5 FTE available for training $= 130$ training sessions per year or 13 complete training courses

(e.g., the number of counseling hours provided). This emphasis has, in turn, led to a concern about what is often referred to as "bean counting," an exclusive focus on quantity to the exclusion of quality.

It is easy to see how this emphasis can come about. If an agency is reimbursed and rewarded for the number of interviews its staff conducts, a program manager for the agency may be tempted to cut down on the time of an interview and squeeze in 10 or 12 interviews per worker per day, regardless of the quality of those interviews. On the other hand, if an agency is held responsible for meeting certain standards of quality in its services, and is reimbursed on the basis of both efficiency (the number of units) and quality (meeting the standards), then the agency must find a way to balance both of these factors. This is the principle behind measuring quality.

However, quality, unlike quantity (units of service), tends to be somewhat elusive and is defined differently depending on one's perspective. In business and industry, customers have tended to be the final arbiters of what constitutes quality (Crosby, 1980, 1985; Deming, 1986; Juran, 1988, 1989). In human services, customer (client) perspectives are important but are not the sole criteria for determination of quality. Other perspectives, including professionals, board members, and funding sources, may also have important input to offer in determining what constitutes quality. If quality dimensions are to be a part of the program design it is necessary that they be defined, that quality data be collected, and that service quality be monitored and evaluated on a regular basis.

Quality is frequently addressed through the use of standards. A standard is a specification accepted by recognized authorities that is regularly and widely used and has a recognized and permanent status (Kettner and Martin, 1987). For many of the elements of program design, standards will be imposed by outside sources. For example, wherever licensing, certification, or accreditation is a concern, standards must be identified and incorporated as a part of the program. If food is served, standards will be imposed by the health department. If medical services and facilities are a part of the program, the Joint Commission on Accreditation of Healthcare Organizations will impose standards.

In most instances, it is necessary to identify and operationalize standards. In some instances, however, it will be necessary to develop them. It is often a judgment call, for example, what credentials casework or counseling staff should have. Some drug treatment programs operate exclusively with ex-addicts, regardless of educational background. Some programs insist on a staff member's having at least a master's degree and prefer a Ph.D. Some positions require bilingual staff, and defining a qualification such as bilingual depends on preestablished standards for the ability to speak two languages. In many ways, standards serve as protection for clients or consumers in that they affect the services provided. Martin (1993) made an important contribution to the measurement of quality by identifying 14 generally recognized quality dimensions (see Table 8.7).

Working from this table, program planners (in conjunction with clients and other stakeholders) can determine which of the quality dimensions listed in Table 8.7 are the most important for a given program. Quality dimensions to be used in the program must then be operationally defined. For example, the quality dimension of "accessibility" could be defined as having services within a 15 minute drive for at least 80% of clients. The quality dimension of "responsiveness" could be defined as ensuring that at least 75% of clients who come to the agency for services are seen within 10 minutes of their scheduled appointment time.

Once the quality dimensions are selected and defined, they must be melded with units of service (intermediate outputs) and tracked. For example, in tracking responsiveness, each time a client comes to the agency for services, it will be necessary to record whether that client was seen within 10 minutes of the scheduled appointment time. Or if the quality dimension of "competency" is used and defined in terms of having an MSW and 3 years of counseling experience, it will be necessary to record the number of client counseling sessions that met this standard and the number that did not.

In measuring quality over the course of a year, two different sets of units will be recorded and tracked: (1) the number of units of a given service provided to clients, and (2) of those units provided, the number that met the preestablished standard. Following this format, any quality standard established within a field can be used in conjunction with outputs to determine the extent to which quality dimensions are being achieved within a program.

In instances in which quality dimensions are too difficult, time consuming, or cumbersome to track, the client satisfaction approach may be used. When this option is selected, it is still necessary to select quality dimensions, but they are measured by translating them into questions to be asked of clients: for example, "Did your home-delivered meals arrive

Table 8.7   Dimensions of Quality

Dimension	Definition
Accessibility	The product or service is easy to access or acquire
Assurance	The staff are friendly, polite, considerate, and knowledgeable
Communication	Customers are kept informed, in language they can understand, about the product or service and any changes thereto
Competence	Staff possess the requisite knowledge and skills to provide the product or service
Conformity	The product or service meets standards
Deficiency	Any quality characteristic not otherwise identified that adversely affects customer satisfaction
Durability	The performance, result, or outcome does not dissipate quickly
Empathy	Staff demonstrate an understanding of and provide individualized attention to customers
Humaneness	The product or service is provided in a manner that protects the dignity and self-worth of the customer
Performance	The product or service does what it is supposed to do
Reliability	The ability to provide the product or service in a dependable and consistent manner with minimal variation over time or between customers
Responisveness	The timeliness of employees in providing products and services
Security	The product or service is provided in a safe setting and is free from risk or danger
Tangibles	The physical appearance of facilities, equipment, personnel, and published materials

SOURCE: Adapted from Martin, L. (1993). *Total quality management in human service organizations.* Thousand Oaks, CA: Sage Publications, Inc. Reprinted with permission.

on time (within 10 minutes of scheduled delivery time)?" and "Do your home-delivered meals arrive hot?" The findings are then turned into percentages of clients who answer "yes" to determine whether the quality standard has been achieved.

Outcomes

In the human service literature, a great deal of attention has increasingly been devoted to the topic of outcome evaluation. For many funding sources, it has become the sine qua non for program planning and proposal writing. The questions that must be answered are: (1) Do clients improve as a result of services? and (2) How do you define and measure improvement?

An *outcome* is defined as a measurable change in quality of life achieved by a client between entry into and exit from a program. Outcome measures can be placed into one of four categories: numerical counts, standardized measures, level of functioning scales, or client satisfaction (Kuechler, Velasquez, and White, 1988; Martin, 1988).

Numeric Counts

Numeric counts are nominal measures related to client flow. They require yes or no answers to specific questions, such as the following: Was the client placed in a job on completion of training? Did the child return home following residential treatment? Was another crime committed by the juvenile subsequent to treatment? The answers are then converted into percentages to determine the extent to which the expected outcome was achieved. Numeric counts are relatively easy to define and interpret, and many programs already collect these data. Calculating the number of families in the Child Abuse Prevention Program who are reported for child abuse in each of the next 5 years is an example of how numeric counts might be used. Recidivism is also a commonly used numeric count.

Standardized Measures

Standardized measures are objective instruments that have been validated and are widely used by practitioners. Examples include the Minnesota Multiphasic Personality Inventory (MMPI) and standardized intelligence tests such as the Stanford-Binet. Several volumes have been devoted to standardized measures of quality-of-life factors. For example, Kane and

Kane (1981) developed measures for the elderly, and Fischer and Corcoran (1994) developed measures for families and children. Martin and Kettner (1996) identified a variety of different perspectives from which standardized measures have been developed, including population, problem, behavior, attitude, intrapersonal functioning, interpersonal functioning, development personality traits, achievement, knowledge, aptitude, and services (see Table 8.8)

The following is an illustration of a question from a Generalized Contentment Scale developed by Hudson (1982):

I feel that I am appreciated by others:

1 = rarely or none of the time

2 = a little of the time

3 = some of the time

4 = a good part of the time

5 = most or all of the time

Level-of-Functioning Scales

Level-of-functioning scales are instruments developed by staff and other local experts familiar with a particular population and problem and are specific to a program or service. They require that practitioners rate their clients on several aspects of functioning. For example, persons who are chronically mentally ill may be rated on such factors as self-care, decision-making ability, and interpersonal interaction. Persons with developmental disabilities may be rated on activities of daily living, functional communication, interaction skills, and other factors. For each scale, indicators are specified and clients are rated at intake, at intervals during their participation in the program, and at exit from a program on a multipoint scale ranging from low to high functioning on each item. The following is an illustration of a level-of-functioning measure for the safety of a person at risk of domestic violence:

1	2	3	4	5
Residence/ work is not safe/lethality is high	Safety threatened/ temporary safety available	Minimally adequate/ ongoing safety planning	Environment currently safe/ future uncertain	Environment apparently safe and stable

Table 8.8   Focus of Standardized Measures

Focus	Example
Population	Young Children's Social Desirability Scale (YCSD)
	A 26-item scale for measuring young children's need for social approval
Problem	Child Abuse Potential (CAP) Inventory
	A 160-item scale for measuring potential for child abuse in parents and prospective parents
Behavior	Preschool Behavior Rating Scale
	A set of 20 scales rating preschool devlopment on several different dimensions
Attitude	Maryland Parent Attitude Survey (MPAS)
	A 95-item scale for measuring attitudes of parents toward child rearing
Intrapersonal functioning	Generalized Expectancy for Success Scale
	Measures an individual's belief in abillity to attain goals
Interpersonal functioning	Index of Family Relations
	A 25-item scale for measuring family relationships
Development	Developmental Profile II
	A 186-item scale for measuring child development up to age 9
Personality traits	Liking People Scale
	Measures whether an individual approaches or avoids social interaction
Achievement	Career Skills Assessment Program
	Measures student competency in areas important to career development
Knowledge	Knowledge Scale
	A 73-item scale for measuring a parent's knowledge of appropriate growth and behavior in children up to age 2

Focus	Example
Aptitude	Differential Aptitude Tests
	An integrated series of measures for assessing verbal reasoning, spelling, need for education, and vocational guidance
Services	Seattle/King County Four C's Evaluation Checklist for
	In home Care, Day Care Homes, and Day care Centers Measures child health and nutrition and staff-child interactions

SOURCE: From Martin, L. & Kettner, P. (1996). *Measuring the performance of human service programs*. Thousand Oaks, CA: Sage Publications, Inc. Reprinted with permission.

For a given client a program would most likely develop a complete battery of scales like this, rating such factors as housing, transportation, education, employment, and others. Completion of all scales at intake then presents a profile that helps in determining priorities for case management, and allows for tracking of progress throughout the helping process.

Client Satisfaction

The fourth measure is *client satisfaction*. Several studies have demonstrated a significant correlation between satisfaction and other, more tangible positive outcomes (Martin, 1988; Millar, Hatry, and Koss, 1977). Martin's research with services such as transportation and ambulance services has demonstrated that although it is possible to measure such factors as response time, arrival at destination time, cost per trip, and cost per mile, client satisfaction proves to be a much less costly and equally valid and reliable measure and therefore would be indicated for these services. This does not mean, however, that client satisfaction should be considered the preferred measure across the board.

In response to early demands for program evaluation, many service providers have opted for client satisfaction, apparently because it appears to be the easiest information to collect. However, correlations have not been established in all services between client satisfaction and improved quality of life, and program planners need to be cautious about overuse and unrealistically high expectations for this measure.

Measuring client satisfaction requires the development of questions with responses ranging from "very satisfied" to "very dissatisfied" and options in between. The following is an example of a client satisfaction question:

How satisfied were you in terms of resolving the problem that brought you to this agency in the first place?

1 = very satisfied
2 = somewhat satisfied
3 = neither satisfied nor dissatisfied
4 = somewhat dissatisfied
5 = very dissatisfied

Intermediate Outcomes and Final Outcomes

As with objectives and outputs, there are two types of outcomes: intermediate outcomes and final outcomes. Intermediate outcomes are those changes in quality of life for the client (such as improved skills or placement in a job) that can be measured at the point of completion of the services provided—that is, at the point of final output. Final outcomes are those changes in quality of life for the client (such as self-sufficiency or stabilization in a job and a career path) that are measured at a designated follow-up point. Table 8.9 illustrates outcomes as an element of service design.

Intermediate and final outcomes may be the same or they may be different. For example, to continue with the domestic violence example, in

Table 8.9   Outcomes as Elements of Service Design

Element	Examples	Purpose
Intermediate outcome	Demonstrated ability to complete the steps taught in training to ensure protection from violence inflicted on self and children	To identify and define what a client should be able to do or should have accomplished at the point of termination from the program or episode of service
Final outcome	To remain free of any episodes of violence inflicted on self and children for at least one year following termination from treatment	To identify and define outcome expectations for a client after a specified period of postservice time has elapsed to determine whether there is carryover of results achieved in treatment

measuring intermediate outcomes, we would want to know if a victim: (1) was able to make all contacts with community resources necessary to live independently (e.g., housing, legal, transportation, child care, etc.), (2) was capable of taking steps necessary to ensure safety for herself and her children, (3) was trained to qualify for a job with a career path, and (4) was placed in a job for which she was trained. If all of these things happened, then we would expect that the final outcome of "no further incidents of violence perpetrated against the victim or her children" would be achieved.

Intermediate outcomes can be documented by using any of the four measures: numerical counts, standardized measures, level-of-functioning scales, or client satisfaction instruments. Numerical counts would involve calculating percentages using outcome indicators (e.g., reduction in depression for a counseling program or reduction in recidivism for a program working with first-time juvenile offenders). With standardized measures or level-of-functioning scales, pre- and post-assessments are required. The difference between the pre- and post-scores represents an indicator of intermediate outcome. These scores may indicate such factors as improvement in self-esteem, improvement in intrafamily communication, or an acceptable level of performance in activities of daily living. Client satisfaction scores provide a one-time statement of a client's perception of the usefulness of the services provided. The percentage of positive responses is used as an indicator of an outcome, with high satisfaction indicating a positive outcome and low satisfaction indicating a negative outcome.

Likewise, in determining final outcomes, it is possible to use any of the four measures. Numerical counts or level-of-functioning scales, however, are the more likely candidates for final outcomes. This is because final outcome expectations are likely to be broader and more ambitious than intermediate outcome expectations and therefore need measures that are broader than a single standardized test or a client satisfaction score can provide. Final outcome measures typically focus on factors such as long-term stability in areas such as family relationships, employment, education, self-sufficiency, and other major life activities and achievements. Many of these domains have standardized numerical count indicators such as employment status, income adequate to meet daily needs, grade in school, and grade point average. These tend to be more useful measures of final outcome expectations. Table 8.10 illustrates how outcomes indicators are used to calculate outcome units.

Table 8.10   Calculating Outcome Units

Type of Unit	Design Elements Needed to Calculate	How to Calculate Units	Example
Intermediate outcome unit	1. A definition of an intermediate outcome 2. The number of clients who enrolled in the program 3. The number of clients who achieve *intermediate outcomes*	1. Calculate the number of possible completions (*final outputs*) 2. Calculate the number that achieve the *intermediate outcome,* as defined 3. Divide the number of those who achieve the *intermediate outcome* by the *total possible completions* 4. The result is the success rate for *intermediate outcomes*	1. Intermediate outcome is defined as demonstrating an acceptable level of skill on completion of training 2. Total enrolled in the training program is 30 3. Of those 30, 26 demonstrated an acceptable level of skill upon completion of the training program 4. 26 divided by 30, or 86.7% is the success rate for *intermediate outcomes*
Final outcome unit	1. A definition of a final outcome 2. The number of clients who achieve *intermediate outcomes* 3. The number of clients who achieve *final outcomes*	1. Calculate the number of clients who achieved *intermediate outcomes* 2. Calculate the number who achieve *final outcomes* 3. Divide the number who achieve final outcomes by the number who achieve *intermediate outcomes* 4. The result is the success rate for *final outcomes*	1. Final outcome is defined as being violence free for at least one year 2. There were 26 clients who demonstrated an acceptable level of skill upon completion of the training program 3. Of those 26, 19 were free of any acts of violence against them or their children for one year 4. 19 divided by 26, or 73.1% is the success rate for final outcomes*

* It is also possible that various stakeholders, including funding sources, may want to know the success rate as calculated using the total number of enrollees in the program. In this case that would be 19 successes divided by 30 enrollees or 63.3%

The Relationship Between Objectives and System Components

In Chapter 7, we discussed in some detail the importance of distinguishing between process objectives and outcome objectives. At this point, it should be evident that there are some relationships between *objectives* and the *input, throughput, output,* and *outcome* components of a program or system. *Throughputs* and *outputs* are related to *process objectives* in that they are the activities or means we are introducing to achieve the program's ends. *Intermediate* and *final outcome objectives* have a direct relationship to *intermediate and final outcomes* as elements of design. Table 8.11 depicts the relationship.

Table 8.11   Relationship Between Objectives and System Components

Type of Objective	*Purpose*	*Related System Component*	*Purpose*
Process objective	To define the services to be provided within the program	Throughput	To achieve consensus on a formal service definition, service tasks, and methodology
		Final output	To specify what combination of services must have been received by a client to constitute a completion of services
Intermediate outcome objective	To define results to be expected on completion of service	Intermediate outcomes	To specify what indicators will be used and how they will be measured
Final outcome objective	To define results to be achieved after a specified period of post-service time has elapsed	Final outcomes	To specify what indicators will be used and how they will be measured

In summary, we have focused in this section on the input, throughput, output, and outcome components of a system. This framework is used to identify and define each element of program design.

- *Inputs* include client, staff, and physical resource elements
- *Throughputs* include service delivery elements
- *Outputs* include service completion elements

Intermediate outputs are completions of units of service

Final outputs are completions of the full complement of services prescribed

- *Outcomes* include measures of life changes for clients

Intermediate outcomes are changes at the point of completion of services

Final outcomes are changes achieved or maintained as of a specified point in the follow-up process after services have been completed

Specifying the Program Hypothesis

Program hypothesis, as discussed in Chapter 6, is a term used to sum up the assumptions and expectations of a program. It is probably fair to say that every program has one, whether or not it is made explicit. Simply providing a service to deal with a problem implies hypothetical thinking (e.g., *if* we provide counseling to couples contemplating divorce, *then* we may be able to prevent divorce).

For example, when a law or policy change mandates that welfare benefits be terminated after a set period of time and recipients be required to go to work, there is an implied hypothesis that terminating welfare benefits will act as a motivator to become employed which, in turn, will lead to self-sufficiency. When the law requires termination of parental rights under certain conditions of abuse and neglect, there is an implied hypothesis that the children affected will turn out to be physically and emotionally healthier if they are raised in an environment where they are free from abuse and neglect.

In Chapter 6, we introduced the example of a program hypothesis related to the problem of domestic violence. The purpose then was to lay the foundation for the development of goals and objectives. As part of that process, we reviewed the various theories of why people commit violent acts against others within a family or household (etiology). From that we developed a hypothesis of etiology and a working intervention hypothesis. Continuing this line of reasoning, we argued that if a program is designed to teach parenting skills, it should be made clear that the intent is to deal only with those parents who lack knowledge and skill in parenting. For those who need extensive counseling to deal with their own abused childhoods, for those who need jobs, or for those who need social contacts or help with child care, parent training alone will probably not be effective.

The program hypothesis guides the definition and selection of the elements of program design, including client characteristics, staff characteristics, service definition, tasks, and methodology, as well as output and outcome definitions. It establishes the framework that brings internal consistency and integrity to the program.

In sum, the following questions might be asked as they relate to each system component:

Inputs

• What types of clients (in terms of demographic, descriptive, or diagnostic characteristics) do we expect will benefit from this program, given our assumptions and our program hypothesis?

• What types of staff should be employed in this program to provide the expected services and serve the clientele we have defined? Is gender, ethnicity, or age a consideration? What degrees, certification, or experience should staff members have?

• What resources, facilities, or equipment will be needed to carry out the services and meet the needs of clients?

Throughputs

• What kinds of services, service tasks, and methods of intervention are most relevant to address the problems and work with the client population as defined in the program design?

Outputs

• Given program expectations, what mix of services represents a full complement of services, and what is the minimum volume or quantity of these services that could be expected to produce a measurable result?

Outcomes

• Given the program hypothesis, what outcomes can we expect to achieve, and, by implication, what outcomes do we not expect to achieve, given the limitations of the program?

This list is not intended to be exhaustive, but it illustrates the types of questions that, if answered in a manner consistent with the program hypothesis, will help to ensure program consistency and integrity. As program planners think through and define these elements, the fit between client need and service or program design should be greatly enhanced.

Defining the elements of program design is a critical step in effectiveness-based program planning. It is the step that lays the groundwork for practitioners to discover what interventions are most likely to produce positive results, given a target population and a problem, and what interventions are not effective. In the place of a hit-or-miss human service technology, definitions of the elements of program design provide for a more precise assessment of client problems and needs, together with a prescription for the mix of services most likely to alleviate the problems and meet the needs. Using these definitions, data collection systems can increasingly inform program planners, managers, and practitioners of the success or failure of a wide range of intervention technologies.

In summary, we have pointed out in this section that a program hypothesis

1. helps make explicit assumptions about program expectations;

2. establishes a framework that can be used to bring internal consistency to the program; and

3. should be used to examine inputs, throughputs, outputs, and outcomes for their internal consistency.

By attending to the elements of program design as described in this chapter, program planners can ensure that a program has been designed in a manner that is comprehensive, that attends to detail, and that can demonstrate internal consistency and integrity. By establishing the relationships between and among (a) resources and raw materials (inputs), (b) the processing system (throughputs), (c) the completion of an episode of service (output), and (d) a change in the quality of life of the client served (outcome), program planners can feel confident that the program is logical, can be implemented, and can be evaluated.

References

Brody, R. (2005). *Effectively managing human service organizations* (3rd ed.). Thousand Oaks, CA: Sage.

Crosby, P. (1980). *Quality is free.* New York: Mentor.

Crosby, P. (1985). *Quality without tears: The art of hassle-free management.* New York: McGraw-Hill.

Deming, W. (1986). *Out of the crisis.* Cambridge: MIT Center for Advanced Engineering Study.

Department of Economic Security. (1995). *Arizona dictionary and taxonomy of human services.* Phoenix, AZ: Author.

Fischer, J., & Corcoran, K. (1994). *Measures for clinical practice: Vol. 1. Couples, families, and children.* New York: Free Press.

Hatry, H., van Houten, T., Plantz, M., & Greenway, M. (1996). *Measuring program outcomes: A practical approach.* Alexandria, VA: United Way of America.

Hudson, W. W. (1982). *The clinical measurement package: A field manual.* Chicago: Dorsey.

Juran, J. (1988). *Juran's quality control handbook* (4th ed.). New York: McGraw-Hill.

Juran, J. (1989). *Juran on leadership for quality: An executive handbook.* New York: Free Press.

Kane, R., & Kane, R. (1981). *Assessing the elderly: A practical guide to measurement.* Lexington, MA: Lexington Books.

Katz, D., & Kahn, R. L. (1966). *The social psychology of organizations.* New York: John Wiley.

Kettner, P., & Martin, L. (1987). *Purchase of service contracting.* Newbury Park, CA: Sage.

Kuechler, C., Velasquez , J., & White, M. (1988). An assessment of human services program outcome measures: Are they credible, feasible, useful? *Administration in Social Work, 12,* 71–89.

Martin, L. (1988). *Consumer satisfaction surveys: Are they valid measures of program performance?* Paper presented at the Eleventh National Conference on Specialized Transportation, Sarasota, FL.

Martin, L. (1993). *Total quality management in human service organizations.* Newbury Park, CA: Sage.

Martin, L., & Kettner, P. (1996). *Measuring the performance of human service programs.* Newbury Park, CA: Sage

Millar, A., Hatry, H., & Koss, M. (1977). *Monitoring the outcomes of social services: Vol. I. Preliminary suggestions.* Washington, DC: Urban Institute.

Payne, M. (1997). *Modern social work theory* (2nd ed.). Chicago: Lyceum Books.

Thompson, J. (1967). *Organizations in action.* New York: McGraw-Hill.

United Way of America. (1976). *UWASIS II: A taxonomy of social goals and human service programs.* Alexandria, VA: Author.

United Way of America. (1996). *Measuring program outcomes: A practical approach* (4th ed.). United Way of America, 701 N. Fairfax Street, Alexandria, VA 22314.

United Way of America. (2006). *Outcome measurement: Showing results in the nonprofit sector.* Outcome Measurement Resources Network. http://www .unitedway.org/outcomes.

Chapter 9

Using Management Information

CHAPTER OVERVIEW

The purpose of this chapter is to explain:

- Why documentation is important in program implementation
- The ways in which computerized data can be used to measure performance
- The relationship between program evaluation and data collection
- How a data collection system can be designed to ensure that necessary information will be provided to stakeholders

The following topics are covered in this chapter:

- Documentation practices in social services
- Designing a data collection system for a program
    - Step 1: Consider the evaluation context of data collection and aggregation
    - Step 2: Identify the programmatic questions to be answered
    - Step 3: Identify data elements
    - Step 4: Develop a strategy for analysis
    - Step 5: Prepare format for monthly reports

Documentation Practices in Social Services

Beginning with the earliest case records, documentation has always been a very important part of social work practice. Early efforts, however, were focused more on the orderly, systematic management of cases, and ensuring that a permanent record of activities was kept. Over the past few decades expectations have changed where government, United Way, foundation, and other funding is involved. There are now expectations for precision in matching service to need, for performance measurement, for overall program cost-efficiency and cost-effectiveness, for transparency, and for reporting of results. Data collection and recording on individual cases play a part in all of these.

In Chapter 1 we discussed documentation and reporting requirements established at the federal level in the Government Performance & Results Act, in the performance contracting requirements of the Federal Acquisition Regulation (FAR), at the state and local government level, the reporting initiative of the Governmental Accounting Standards Board, and the performance measurement requirements imposed by governors and state legislatures. Private sector funding organizations, such as foundations and the United Way, have also adopted performance accountability systems. Very few social service agencies and programs in the early 21st century are left untouched by expectations of data collection for the purpose of performance measurement, yet some research suggests that management information is underutilized in social service agencies (Carrilio, 2005).

Because of funding source requirements and because of the advances in information technology, data collection and data entry procedures have changed dramatically over the past decade. Social service agencies and programs today have a variety of computerized data collection and entry options available to them. Relatively inexpensive hardware and software allow social service agencies and programs to computerize their client, program, financial, and performance files. Management information systems can be built on a basic spreadsheet program such as Microsoft Excel or a database program like Microsoft Access. Some states use templates and data entry screens where data are entered directly into the database. These screens can be constructed in a way that if the wrong type of response is entered, the screen will not accept the data and will not process the transaction until every data field is complete and determined to be accurate. Eligibility can be determined by completing a template (a series of data entry screens) on their personal computers. When completed, the social worker logs onto the Internet, connects with the state database, and uploads the completed application directly to the department database. The principle today is "enter once, use multiple times."

Even more sophisticated technology is available in the form of "dashboards" and "scorecards." Eckerson (2005) describes them as follows:

> In many ways, dashboards and scorecards represent the culmination of business intelligence. A dashboard or scorecard interface finally makes it easy for the majority of users to quickly find, analyze and explore the information they need to perform their jobs on a daily basis. To borrow a term from the telecommunications industry, dashboards and scorecards represent the "last mile" of wiring that connects users to the data warehousing and analytical infrastructure that organizations have created during the past decade.

These tools can produce charts and graphs to guide program managers and supervisors through the analytical processes of determining whether programs are on track to achieve objectives, among other functions.

Regardless of the type of management information system utilized, a program manager is confronted with three issues: (1) What questions do I need the system to answer? (2) What data elements must be included in the system in order to answer the questions? and (3) What types of routine reports do I want the system to generate? The role of the program planner is to ensure that these three issues are resolved satisfactorily so that the management information system will provide the necessary data to manage, monitor, and evaluate the program. The actual work of setting up the management information system to address these three needs is best left to the information technology professionals.

Effectiveness-based program planning requires that data be generated that will support decision making based on what is in the best interests of clients—on information about what services are most effective with what types of clients and what types of problems. The remainder of this chapter focuses on understanding conceptually how the elements of the data collection and reporting system are created, aggregated, and reported. Our assumption is that issues related to technology will be addressed by professionals in that field. It should further be noted that what we are proposing here is the development of a data collection system designed to measure performance, to monitor, and to evaluate a *program*. In dealing with the more complex issues surrounding the development of an Information Technology (IT) application for an entire agency, the reader is referred to the work of Schoech (1999, 2000).

Designing a Data Collection System for a Program

A major assumption of effectiveness-based program planning is that each activity is shaped by the completion of previous activities and, in turn, each activity will shape future activities. The process, of course, is not actually linear. Earlier decisions may have to be modified as later activities are addressed. Still, the overall process needs to be guided by commitment to internal consistency between the parts. With these considerations in mind, the design of a data collection system becomes totally dependent on the processes described in the previous chapters. The development of goals and objectives is an articulation of the hypothesis in different terminology; the development of inputs, throughputs, outputs, and outcomes is a reformulation of the goals and objectives section, and the development of a data collection system builds on all of these.

Each system component has implications for data collection, and we will examine them later in this chapter. But before we deal with data elements, it is important to ensure that thought has been given to the ultimate purposes for which the system is being created. To accomplish this we propose establishing a context in which planners first think through the *evaluation function* of program planning, and second, revisit the *problem analysis* completed at the beginning of the program planning process.

It may seem counterintuitive to "begin at the end," so to speak, but these steps will help to make the data collection more efficient, and will ensure a more useful database once the system is up and running. The approach proposed here is more likely to lead to an *understanding* of the many ways in which inputs, throughputs, outputs, and outcomes interact with each other to help in solving client and community problems.

The steps involved in designing and implementing such a system are these:

1. Consider the evaluation context of data collection and aggregation.

2. Identify the programmatic questions to be answered.

3. Identify the data elements needed.

4. Develop a strategy for analysis.

5. Prepare a format for monthly reports.

The details involved in carrying out each of these steps are covered in the following sections.

Step 1: Consider the Evaluation Context of Data Collection and Aggregation

While evaluation design will be addressed in greater detail in Chapter 13, it is important that the program planner think conceptually about selected evaluation principles before beginning the work of designing the data collection system. In the human services it is common practice to begin thinking about program evaluation after everything else is finished. This is one of the major reasons evaluations so often fail to provide the type of information needed for program improvement. Well-planned evaluations begin very early in the program planning process. We have attempted to reinforce this notion by laying the groundwork from the very first chapter.

As program planners prepare the evaluation strategy, they are attempting to accomplish two purposes: to assess the relative success of programs in meeting their stated objectives and to identify potential sources of program improvement in current program operations. Measures of program activity and outcome are compared with normative standards, empirical tests and knowledge, or the experience of others. The central question is: What happened as a result of this particular intervention strategy that would not have happened in its absence? The intent of program evaluation is to assist managers in solving problems through the determination of what program strategies work best under what conditions.

There are two categories of evaluation of concern to program planners: formative evaluation and summative evaluation. These concepts will be developed at greater length in later chapters dealing specifically with program evaluation. *Formative* evaluation is conducted during the actual operation of the program. It attempts to provide information during the implementation of the program to help in determining the extent to which the program is being implemented according to the program's design. Formative evaluation answers questions such as: Is the program doing what it is supposed to be doing? Are the program participants representative of the program's target population? Are the services provided appropriate to the client's needs? Based on answers to these and other questions, the manager is able to determine whether modifications should be made to program operations. Formative evaluation focuses on *process objectives* as discussed in earlier chapters.

Summative evaluation, as the name implies, is carried out at either the end of a program cycle or component (e.g., the budget cycle, the completion of a training unit) or at the conclusion of a program. Summative evaluation is designed to provide an assessment of program accomplishments (the relative successes and failures of the program), and focuses on *outcome objectives.*

Types of Evaluation

Program evaluation may take many forms and may examine a variety of program aspects. The type of evaluation that is undertaken should be based on a realistic assessment of both feasibility and the needs of decision makers for information regarding program operations.

Five general types of evaluation can be identified, each capable of providing different kinds of information about program functioning: (a) evaluation of effort, (b) evaluation of cost-efficiency, (c) evaluation of outcome, (d) evaluation of impact, and (e) evaluation of cost-effectiveness (Suchman, 1967). Each category is briefly defined below. This is followed by a more detailed discussion in a later chapter.

- *Effort evaluation* is concerned exclusively with documenting the characteristics of the program participants and the quantity of activity that takes place within a program—how much and what type of service is being provided. An assessment of effort may be viewed as a reflection of service provision, including both *inputs and throughputs.*

- *Efficiency evaluation* looks at the costs of providing a unit of service. More specifically, cost-efficiency looks at the costs in terms of time, episode, or material units—the costs of the *outputs.*

- *Outcome evaluation* examines the results achieved with clients and seeks to identify the extent to which the program's *outcome objectives* have been achieved.

- *Impact evaluation* is concerned with the extent to which the community's needs, as determined in the planning process, have been met by the program.

- *Cost-effectiveness* looks at the costs of achieving the results—the cost per successful *outcome*.

These five categories, in sum, address all of the information needs a program manager will use to evaluate a program. They can be summarized by the following general questions:

- What kinds of clients? (Effort)
- Experiencing what types of problems? (Effort)
- Receiving what type and volume of services? (Effort)
- Get what results? (Outcome)
- At what costs? (Cost-efficiency and cost-effectiveness)

With these questions as a road map, we are now in a position to build a responsive management system.

Step 2: Identify the Programmatic Questions to Be Answered

If the program planning process proposed in this book has been followed from the beginning, an efficient way to generate questions to be answered is to revisit the problem analysis and the working intervention hypothesis. The objective here is to reexamine the reasons for developing the program in the first place, and to ensure that it is on track to address the problems it is intended to alleviate or resolve.

For the sake of illustration, we turn once again to the Victims to Victors program to address domestic violence (DV). The program hypothesis reads as follows:

Because there are women who experience the following:

- Low self-esteem and general anxiety disorder
- Social isolation from friends, family, and community

- Lack of financial resources to meet their basic needs
- Lack of basic education and marketable skills to get and hold a steady job with a salary that meets their basic needs

The result is women who are vulnerable to becoming victims of domestic violence due to:

- A combination of personal, emotional, and psychological problems
- Isolation from social support systems and networks
- Dependence upon a partner for financial support
- Severe limitations in their ability to secure and succeed in a steady job with a career path

If the following actions are taken with a population that has been victimized by domestic violence:

- Provide individual and group counseling to address personal, emotional, and psychological problems
- Provide case management services to facilitate and support making appropriate community contacts designed to build a sustainable, steady lifestyle following treatment
- Provide financial planning services designed to manage income and meet basic expenses
- Provide employment training and placement

Then it is expected that women who participate in the program:

- Will increase their self-esteem and reduce anxiety
- Will secure housing and child care and will be able to meet other needs necessary to independent living in the community
- Will be able to manage their finances effectively
- Will be employed in a job with a career path and a salary adequate to meet their financial needs

As we examine this program hypothesis, a number of questions should come to mind.

- We have designed a program to deal with a specific problem profile. This particular program is not equipped to deal with certain problems, such as drug addiction, or with a client who is determined to return to her abuser upon completion of the program. How can we be sure the participants we recruit will fit the intended profile? (Input question)

- Do members of the at-risk population reveal the same characteristics as those identified in the literature: namely, low self-esteem, generalized social anxiety, limited independent living skills, limited financial management skills, limited job skills? If the population recruited to participate in this program does not match this profile, then the relevance of the intervention as designed is questionable. (Input question)

- If members of the at-risk population do have some of the same characteristics as those identified in the literature, does it appear that these characteristics have contributed to their becoming victims of domestic violence? These are the feelings and behaviors we are attempting to change or eliminate. We must be certain that if the intervention is successful it will lead to an independent, violence-free future to test the intervention hypothesis. (Input question)

- Are members of the at-risk population participating in the case management, counseling, and training activities on a regular basis as intended? (Throughput question)

- Are program participants completing all the services that are a part of their Individual Rehab Plans (IRPs)? (Output question)

- Do program participants, after spending time in the planned activities, demonstrate improved self-esteem, lower social anxiety, mastery of independent living skills, mastery of financial management skills, and mastery of job skills? (Outcome question)

These types of questions will prove to be very useful in identifying data elements to be collected as well as in developing a strategy for analysis.

Step 3: Identify Data Elements

Data elements are bits of information about clients, services, and performance that, when aggregated, present a profile of the program in terms of the client population being served, the services being provided, and the results being achieved. Data elements should be organized around program inputs, throughputs, outputs, and outcomes. They can be further organized around the following headings and subheadings. Each of these will be discussed in detail below.

Program Inputs

- Client demographic and descriptive characteristics
- Quantified client social history data
- Client problem/strength profile
- Material resources provided to clients
- Facilities used by clients
- Equipment used by clients
- Staff demographic and descriptive characteristics

Program Throughputs

- Services provided
- Service tasks
- Method of intervention

Program Outputs

- Intermediate outputs (units of service provided)
- Final outputs (service completions)

Program Outcomes

- Intermediate outcomes (change at the point of service completion)
- Final outcomes (change at the designated point of follow-up)

Program Inputs

Client demographic and descriptive characteristics. As discussed in Chapter 8, one of the first data elements to be considered is that of client demographic and descriptive characteristics. The task at this point is not one of developing data collection forms but one of identifying and justifying what data are to be collected. Only when this task is completed can we turn to the task of instrument development. Demographic and descriptive characteristics typically include such elements as:

- Age
- Number of children
- Ethnicity
- Education
- Income
- Marital status

Considering the questions to be answered in the program to prevent domestic violence, in addition to the above characteristics, we might also want to know something about the domestic partner, housing arrangements, transportation availability, the number of social contacts per week, distance from nuclear family members or other support system, employment status, and other such characteristics. These factors, to a large extent, will help us to determine whether we are actually working with the intended population and what factors may play a part in a client's transition back to the community.

Client social history data. Like client demographic data, social history data may help provide clues to factors in clients' backgrounds that are related to their current situations. It is usually an expectation of caseworkers that they take a social history on their clients at the point of intake so that they can determine patterns of behavior and behavioral changes over time, as well as documenting legal considerations.

To be useful for performance measurement, monitoring, and evaluation purposes, social history data must have a "research" focus. In other words, there must be a reason, based on the problem analysis, to believe that a particular variable may have some relevance to the program, its clients, and the outcomes achieved.

With the domestic violence program, for example, we know that factors such as low self-esteem and high social anxiety can lead to victimization. We may, therefore, want to explore factors in the client's history that have diminished her self-confidence. This topic could be explored by asking questions about the number of current friends and associates, about the nature of relationships, about substance abuse history, and other such factors. Any data to be used for performance measurement, monitoring, or evaluation purposes will have to be quantified and formatted for data entry.

Client problem/strength profile. Clients who come to social service agencies for help typically present a profile that includes both problems and strengths. One may have a steady job but poor financial management skills. Another may have poor transportation and a spotty attendance record at work, but good parenting skills. These factors are important to the case management process. In fact, approaches to casework have been built around the concepts of problems and strengths (Reid, 1992; Saleeby, 1992). In the aggregate these profiles are important to the program planner as well. As discussed in Chapter 7, these become the *intermediate outcome objectives* the program will attempt to achieve. In collecting data for performance measurement it is important to know for later program analysis purposes the number and percentage of clients during the course of a year that are identified as having a particular problem or strength. This information can be drawn from assessment tools completed at the point of intake by the intake and screening person, by the client, by a third party, or by some combination of these.

By using a simple scaling device on which the scale ranges from "a serious problem" at the low end of the scale to "an area of strength" at the high end, a problem and strength profile can be developed for individual clients as well as for all program participants. These assessment tools, either purchased from the author of a standardized scale or developed by staff, can be designed to determine (a) problems being experienced by clients, (b) level of severity, (c) areas of strength, and (d) degree of strength. A simple 1 to 5 scale could be used, where 1 = Severe problem, 2 = Problem, 3 = Neither a problem nor a strength, 4 = Strength, and 5 = Major strength. Other scales have used the terms 1 = In crisis, 2 = Vulnerable, 3 = Stable, 4 = Safe, and 5 = Thriving, or 1 = Profound need, 2 = High need, 3 = Moderate need, 4 = Low need, and 5 = Minimal need. Many types of measurement scales are available, and most are designed in a way that will yield useful information about problems and strengths. (See, for example, Fischer and Corcoran, 1994; Hudson, 1982.)

The following scale might be used with a target group of women who have experienced domestic violence where 1 = a severe problem and 5 = an area of strength:

1. Quality and stability of housing	1	2	3	4	5
2. Reliability of transportation	1	2	3	4	5
3. Stability of employment	1	2	3	4	5
4. Level of job skills for career advancement	1	2	3	4	5
5. Income and budgeting skills	1	2	3	4	5
6. Level of safety in relation to abuser	1	2	3	4	5
7. Sense of self-confidence/self-esteem	1	2	3	4	5
8. DV education and awareness	1	2	3	4	5

Some of the questions to be answered by these data might include these:

- What problems are most prevalent (items most often rated 1 or 2)?
- What strengths are most prevalent (items most often rated 4 or 5)?
- Do any problems (e.g., housing or employment) appear to be associated with any demographic or social history factors (e.g., age or education)?

- Are there any predominant "problem profiles" or problems that tend to cluster together (e.g., income and budgeting with housing and/or transportation)? Are there any common profiles that seem to be associated with abuse?
- Are there any apparent "strength profiles" that might help in predicting success in overcoming victimization and developing a violence-free lifestyle?

Material resources. When material resources such as cash, food, or clothing are provided for clients, it is important that these items be tracked so that it can be determined what contribution they make to achieving positive outcomes. Some of the items that might be made available to a client on an "as needed" basis might include:

- Transportation for job interviews or to secure housing, provided by a volunteer
- Articles of clothing for client for job interviews
- Articles of clothing for client's child(ren)
- First and last month's rent for an apartment

Amount and frequency of receipt of each of these and other such data need to be tracked on a data collection form. Questions to be answered by tracking material resources might include:

- Do resources like clothing and transportation increase the likelihood that clients will have a successful job interview?
- Does assistance with rent increase stability of housing after clients leave the shelter?

Facilities. In a way, facilities can also be considered resources used for the benefit of clients. Agencies that have more than one branch office may discover that certain locations or settings are more conducive than others to success. Success may be influenced by convenience of location for clients. In the case of residential treatment, it may be valuable to learn whether factors associated with the facility such as rooms, meals, or opportunities for privacy have any influence over whether or not a client remains for the full duration of treatment. (See Chapter 8 for a related discussion of *qualitative* dimensions of outputs.) If use of facilities is included in a data collection system, categories might include one or more of the following:

- Office visit, main office
- Office visit, branch office
- Home visit, client's home
- Home visit, relative or friend's home

- School
- Other community facility

Some of the questions to be explored are these:

- Is there a relationship between facility location and keeping appointments?
- Does it appear that certain clients make better progress when there are home visits?
- Does it appear that there is any relationship between location and client outcomes?

Equipment. The importance of equipment will vary by program. Programs that provide transportation need to have vehicles in good working condition. Some residential treatment centers may make computers available to residents for e-mail and for searching the Internet. Training programs may have the option of using several different software packages, and it is helpful to know which ones achieve the best results with trainees. Providing cell phones to domestic violence victims has made an important contribution to safety and security for some DV programs. In some instances there may be a correlation between the provision of equipment and social participation. Some of the equipment-related questions to be answered might include these:

- Does provision of transportation contribute to keeping appointments?
- What types of equipment contribute to successful client outcomes?
- What is the unit cost of equipment currently used by clients? How would costs compare to contracting with another provider for use of this equipment?

Staff descriptive characteristics. Descriptive characteristics about staff are not likely to be entered into a management information system for a *program*, but it may be useful to record them elsewhere (perhaps in a *personnel or human resources management information system*). Typically, in a system designed to record program and service data, there will be some mechanism for connecting clients to workers (e.g., through a worker identification number).

At some point program evaluators may want to look at successful cases to determine if any particular staff characteristics are correlated with client success. Capturing staff descriptive characteristics will make it possible to identify what factors about staff, if any, make a difference in terms of client outcomes. Keep in mind, we are making a distinction here between *criteria for hiring staff* (e.g., all case mangers will be bilingual) and *staff characteristics* that may influence outcome (e.g., the language skills of the case manager). It may also be important to record staff demographic information if accrediting organizations need to know about such factors as ethnicity, gender, education, and experience. Some of the staff descriptive characteristics that might be useful include the following:

- Education
- License or certification
- Number of years of experience
- Type(s) of professional experience
- Ethnicity
- Sex

Some of the questions to be explored might include these:

- How do education and/or experience correlate with client satisfaction and client outcomes?
- When worker demographics are matched up with client demographics, what are the relationships, if any, to completion of the service plan and to outcomes?

Program Throughputs

Service tasks. The concept of service tasks, introduced in Chapter 8, is used to define the helping process and to break it down into a series of stages or phases. This breakdown is important because, by tying tasks to units of service, the management information system can help to identify what tasks were provided in what volume over what period of time. In the absence of service tasks, the service process defaults to just one, simple, undifferentiated task called casework. By defining service tasks, it is possible, for example, to determine how many units of service (either in the aggregate or by a particular worker) are devoted to each task. A program evaluator may learn that the more time spent in intake and screening, the better the eventual outcome of service. Services provided in a program to serve domestic violence victims might include:

1. Case management, broken down into the following tasks:
   - Intake
   - Screening
   - Case planning
   - Implementation of the case plan
   - Completion of the case plan

- Termination
- Follow up

2. Counseling, broken down into the following tasks:
   - Assessment
   - Stating the problem
   - Analyzing the system
   - Setting goals
   - Implementing the plan
   - Stabilizing the change effort
   - Completing the plan
   - Termination
   - Follow-up

These data elements could help to answer such questions as the following:

- How much time is being spent on each service task?
- Do patterns vary by worker and type of client?
- What correlations exist between time spent on service tasks and outcomes?

Method of intervention. Defining the method of intervention will help evaluators and program staff to learn whether one particular method is more effective than others with certain types of clients. If, for example, a program's intent is to maintain or improve nutritional levels for seniors, meals can be provided in a congregate setting or can be home delivered. It may be that one method is more effective than the other for certain types of clients. This discovery can lead to adjustments in the method of meal provision prescribed, depending on the likelihood of success, based on findings. Methods of counseling might include individual, group, or family and some may work better than others, depending on the presenting problems. Over the years as research has been conducted on social work practice, certain types of interventions have been found to work better with certain types of clients (See, for example, Bennett, Stoops, and Flett, 2007; Chen, Jordan, and Thompson, 2006). Tracking method of intervention provides an opportunity to discover whether the method being used currently works best. The program evaluator is interested in any possible relationship between method of intervention and rates of success.

Questions that might be answered by collecting data on method of intervention might include these:

- With what methods of intervention are clients most likely to complete the service plan?

- What methods of intervention lead to the most successful client outcomes with what types of clients?

Program Outputs

Intermediate outputs. Intermediate outputs are defined as *units of service* and can be measured in any one of three different ways: (a) a time unit, (b) an episode or contact unit, or (c) a material unit. Each service included as part of service tasks must define an accompanying unit of service. For counseling, one hour is a commonly used time unit. For information and referral services, one inquiry about service availability might be used as an episode or contact unit. One trip provided to a job interview is an example of a material unit.

The evaluator is interested in the number of units per week/month/ year. If a center typically serves a noon meal to 50 seniors per day, that will be defined as 50 units of service per day or 250 units during a normal 5-day week. If a case manager spends one hour per week in a counseling session with each resident in a shelter, the evaluator will be interested in the total number of units (hours) of counseling provided each week/month/year. Units of service provided is a measure of productivity and can be useful in answering such questions as:

- What is the mean number and range of units provided by case managers each week?
- What is the mean number and range of units of each type provided to clients each week?
- Are there correlations between types of units provided and client outcomes?

Final outputs. Final outputs are defined as service completions and require that each service provided have a definition of what is meant by "completion." For example, the Safe Haven shelter might define completion of the job training module as a client's participation in at least 90% of training sessions, two of which must be the first and last sessions. Detailed attendance records must be kept to make a distinction as to whether the client actually completed the program or whether she should be considered a "dropout" from the program. The following items illustrate the type of data that would be collected to measure service completions for each client and, in the aggregate, for an entire program:

- Number of training sessions prescribed
- Number of training sessions attended

- Number of counseling sessions prescribed
- Number of counseling sessions attended
- Number of job referrals made
- Number of job interviews completed

This information helps to determine whether clients are actually carrying out the treatment plans prescribed and, if not, to probe for reasons why not. Some of the questions to be answered include these:

- What percentage of clients complete the prescribed treatment plan?
- What factors influence completion and dropout?
- Are there any significant relationships between completing a plan and positive client outcomes?

Program Outcomes

Intermediate client outcomes. Intermediate client outcomes are defined as those client changes achieved at the point of termination from a program. Client outcomes are calculated by conducting an assessment at the point of intake and producing a score that can be used as a baseline or starting point for measurement purposes. Assessments may be done in terms of numeric counts, standardized measures, level-of-functioning scales or client satisfaction (see Chapter 8).

When standardized measures or level-of-functioning scales are used, intermediate outcomes are calculated by administering the same measurement device at the completion of service as was used at intake (a pre-post assessment). The purpose is to determine whether there has been progress in solving the problems presented at intake, whether they have remained the same, or whether they have gotten worse. Safe Haven case managers and clients would revisit the eight factors assessed at intake and once again rate each on a scale from 1 to 5, with 1 representing a serious problem and 5 representing a strength, assuming that each point on the scale would be operationally defined for each item.

1. Quality and stability of housing	1	2	3	4	5
2. Reliability of transportation	1	2	3	4	5
3. Stability of employment	1	2	3	4	5
4. Level of job skills for career advancement	1	2	3	4	5
5. Income and budgeting skills	1	2	3	4	5

6. Level of safety in relation to abuser	1	2	3	4	5
7. Sense of self-confidence/self-esteem	1	2	3	4	5
8. DV education and awareness	1	2	3	4	5

These types of measurements emphasize the central issues of effectiveness-based program planning. If all has gone according to plan, the initial assessment will reveal problems and strengths. The treatment plan will focus on dealing with the problems and capitalizing on the strengths. If the treatment plan has been implemented, if the client has completed all the services prescribed, and if the plan has worked, the problem areas should show some improvement. If case managers have collected all needed data during the process, these data can now be aggregated and can begin to inform staff about overall program effectiveness. Questions to be addressed include these:

- What types of problems seem most often to be resolved?
- Which types seem most resistant to change?
- Are there any patterns in the types of clients who seem to be most successful and least successful with certain problems?

Final outcomes. Final outcomes are identified and defined by returning to the purpose for which the program was created, or what we have in Chapter 7 called *final objectives.* The Victims to Victors program was created to enable women who have been abused by their partners to become self-sufficient and live violence-free lives. Final outcome measurements are always taken in a follow-up contact with clients, using numerical counts, standardized measures, level-of-functioning scales, or client satisfaction measures (see Chapter 8).

The period of time that should elapse between the end of the program and the follow-up is a judgment that must be made by those familiar with the program and depends on the results to be achieved. An outcome such as "no further incidents of violence" would require follow-up for at least a year, and perhaps longer. If the final outcome required that we measure whether the at-risk population has improved in self-esteem or decreased in social anxiety, a standardized scale would be administered periodically for as long as the client remains in the program, and a follow-up measurement would be taken between 6 months and 1 year after termination if the client is willing to continue to participate. It should be recognized that in some programs, such as long-term care for the elderly, formal, planned termination may never happen. Clients may remain until death. In cases such as these, periodic measurements may be taken after an episode of service (such as a quarterly or annual completion of a treatment plan) to determine whether the effects of treatment are being sustained over time.

Questions to be addressed in analyzing these data would include:

- What types of clients seem to be having the most success in this program? What are their characteristics?
- For what types of clients does this program seem to be least effective? What are their characteristics?
- What services seem to contribute to success?
- What elements of the program seem to have no impact, and should be considered for redesign?
- What mix of services, given to which types of clients in what volume, has the highest probability of leading to successful outcomes?

Step 4: Develop a Strategy for Analysis

The fourth step in designing a data collection system involves examining the data elements identified in Step 3 and determining how variables will be used for performance measurement, monitoring, and program evaluation. As mentioned earlier, some data systems will be structured so that agency level inputs can be uploaded directly into a larger system in order to track data needed at the county or state level. Alternatively, funding source requirements may dictate that certain elements be tracked and reported. For example, program planners at the Safe Haven shelter would be expected to collect data as required by the Victims to Victors program funded by the state.

In addition to these considerations, program managers, administrators, board members, and other stakeholders will undoubtedly have a need for information at the agency and/or program levels. Using data and information for performance measurement, monitoring, and evaluation purposes completes the cycle of effectiveness-based program planning phases.

When developing a strategy for analysis, it is important to maintain a focus on the program hypothesis as the overall framework, so that analysis does not get sidetracked into becoming an exercise in exploring what seem to be interesting issues but are peripheral to the intent of the program. One approach to help keep the data collection system on track is to structure data collection around program objectives, listing each objective and using the following format:

- Outcome Objective 1.1: By April 1, 20XX (prior to final outcome), at least 75% of program participants will demonstrate at least a 25% increase in self-esteem scores as measured by the Hudson Self-Esteem Scale. Counselors are responsible for monitoring.
- Data Elements Required: Client identification number; pretest score; posttest score
- Data Source: Counselors' tracking system on client
- Data Display/Analysis: Table listing client identification numbers, pretest scores, posttest scores, and percentage difference

This approach helps to keep the focus on objectives and makes clear how data will be used to support the findings in relation to the objective.

In addition to the questions generated by the funding source and the program hypothesis, our recurring, compound question will always need to be addressed, as illustrated in Table 9.1.

Table 9.1   Considerations in Developing a Strategy for Data Analysis

Question	System Component	Example
What types of clients?	Input question	Demographic, descriptive or social history data
Receiving what types of services?	Throughput question	Counseling, job training
Receiving what volume of services?	Output question	Units of service received such as number of counseling or training sessions
Get what results?	Outcome question	Demonstrate an increase in self-esteem; demonstrate an improvement in financial management skills
At what cost?	Output question	Cost per training session; cost per "trained client"
At what cost?	Outcome question	Cost per "success" at the point of follow-up

Each of these subsets of data elements makes up a part of a comprehensive list of all variables that will form the basis for the data collection and performance measurement system. Once all variables to be incorporated into the system have been identified, variables to be aggregated need to be selected. It is important to remember that, while information technology professionals are able to develop the necessary computer programs, they will rely on program planners to make clear what data and information it is that they would like to display for performance measurement, monitoring, and evaluation purposes. The aggregation and cross-tabulation of selected data elements begins to reveal relationships between services and client progress that will help answer the questions identified in Step 2 and will shape future program modifications.

Preparing Output Tables

An output table is a display of columns and rows that is used as a basic document in compiling management information. Where the columns and rows intersect, *cells* are formed, and the numbers or values calculated (for example, the number African American, Asian American, Latino, Native American, and Caucasian clients for each age grouping) are entered into the cells. (The term *output,* in this context, does not in any way refer to output as a part of the program design discussed in Chapter 8 and in this chapter. Rather, the term *output table* in Step 4 is used in a data-processing context as the format for data aggregation. We need to think, at this point, in terms of computer output.)

Output tables take the data collection and performance measurement system from a simple listing and calculating of discrete elements like age, education, and income, to the next level of data aggregation. Tables should be designed to answer the questions that were generated in Steps 1, 2, and 3. A spreadsheet such as Excel may be used to produce output tables, as illustrated in Figure 9.1.

An output table designed to assess program throughputs, outputs, or outcomes might use one or more of the following variables:

Participation

1. Number and percentage of clients who attended at least 80% of the financial management training sessions

2. Number and percentage of clients who developed an Individual Rehab Plan (IRP) within 60 days of admission to the program

	% of Women Who Complete Their IRPs	% of Women Living Independently for 1 Year	% of Women Holding Same/Better Job for 1 Year	% of Women with No Reports of Violence for 1 Year
AGE				
Under 20	15%	8%	16%	17%
20-24	18%	13%	11%	20%
25-29	24%	22%	31%	33%
30-34	32%	35%	21%	14%
Over 34	11%	22%	21%	16%
EDUCATION				
Less than HS	18%	16%	20%	11%
HS	22%	23%	25%	19%
Some College	25%	29%	31%	29%
College Grad	35%	32%	24%	41%
ETHNICITY				
African American	12%	26%	10%	18%
Asian American	8%	12%	18%	9%
Caucasian	43%	30%	36%	42%
Hispanic	29%	16%	30%	24%
Native American	8%	13%	6%	7%

Figure 9.1   Excel Screen

Knowledge and Skill

3. Number and percentage demonstrating an increase in knowledge and awareness of domestic violence issues

4. Number and percentage demonstrating mastery of entry-level skills in the job category for which they were trained

Creating output tables should be an inclusive process. While program planners may develop a first draft of questions to be asked and output tables designed to answer them, review and comment should be solicited from key agency personnel, board members, or others stakeholders. Individuals who are familiar with the problem, the population, and the program from different perspectives (e.g., case managers, supervisors, budget personnel) will invariably identify different sets of questions and create different output tables because their interests and need for information differ. Final drafts of output tables should be produced in consultation with information technology professionals to ensure that they are compatible with the software to be used and will produce the desired reports.

Step 5: Prepare Format for Monthly Reports

The Commonwealth of Australia has made extensive use of performance measurement principles, and based on their experiences to date their program planners have identified five guiding principles in collecting performance information that may also be useful in tracking program progress:

1. *A focus on outcomes* - indicators should reflect whether service objectives have been met

2. *Comprehensiveness* - performance should be assessed against all important objectives

3. *Comparability* - data should be comparable across jurisdictions whenever possible

4. *Progressive data availability* - since progress may vary, data are reported for those jurisdictions that are prepared to report

5. *Timeliness* - data reported need to be as recent as possible to retain relevance for decision makers (SCRGSP, 2006, pp. 1.9–1.10)

Their experience has demonstrated that it is necessary to make the system as accurate and as timely as possible while recognizing that there will be imperfections during developmental phases. If all of the important cross-tabulations have been identified in the previous step, the tables produced should be able to provide information for monthly tracking of progress. Data displays can include cross-sectional analysis, time-series comparisons, and comparisons with other data units (Netting, Kettner, and McMurtry, 2008). Cross-sectional analysis examines the same population from a number of different perspectives at a particular point in time. Table 9.2 illustrates a cross-sectional analysis.

A time-series comparison illustrates repeated observations over time and displays trends. Time-series comparisons are especially important in monthly reporting in order to track progress toward achievement of outcome and process objectives. Figure 9.2 illustrates a time-series comparison.

Table 9.2   Cross-Sectional Analysis of Safe Haven Clients at Entry

	In Crisis	Vulnerable	Stable	Safe	Thriving
Quality and stability of housing	25%	33%	18%	14%	10%
Reliability of transportation	10%	27%	33%	15%	15%
Stability of employment	27%	39%	18%	9%	7%
Level of job skills for career advancement	44%	30%	11%	7%	8%
Income and budgeting skills	17%	28%	25%	21%	9%
Level of safety in relation to abuser	38%	41%	16%	5%	0%
Sense of self-confidence/ self-esteem	21%	32%	34%	16%	7%
DV education and awareness	19%	25%	32%	10%	14%

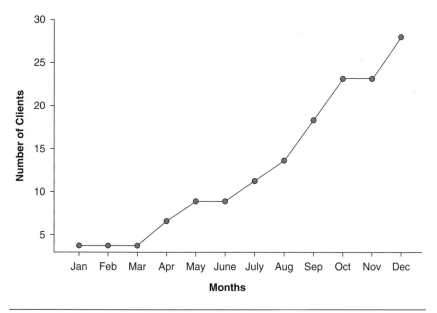

Figure 9.2   Time-Series Comparison of Completions in Job Training

Comparison to other data units depicts data from one program side by side with a similar program in another jurisdiction. Some organizations use a technique called "benchmarking," which involves a search of comparable programs for best practices. If data and information are available from these agencies, they can be used for comparative purposes. When statewide programs are delivered by a number of agencies, comparisons can be made across agencies to determine how well each agency is performing in relation to established milestones. Table 9.3 illustrates comparison to other data units.

Rapp and Poertner (1992) propose five principles for report design. They suggest that reports: (1) provide standards for comparison; (2) be kept simple and not attempt to provide too much information; (3) be amply illustrated with charts and graphs; (4) include labels on graphs and charts in simple, nontechnical language; and (5) present data aggregation at a level that matches the recipient's place in the organization.

Chapters 10 through 13 present approaches to calculating the cost and value of the intervention and provide the tools needed to complete the analysis of the program from a variety of perspectives.

Table 9.3 Comparison to Other Data Units on Safety at Entry and Follow-Up

	Safe Haven	The Open Door	Family Care Center	Transitional Living, Inc.
Number of clients served	30	22	36	48
Percentage in crisis or vulnerable on safety at entry into program	79%	72%	84%	92%
Percentage safe or thriving in one-year follow-up after termination from program	82%	88%	76%	61%

References

Bennett, L., Stoops, C., & Flett, H. (2007). Program completion and re-arrest in a batterer intervention system. *Research on Social Work Practice,* 17(1), 42–54.

Carrilio, T. (2005). Management information systems: Why are they underutilized in the social services? *Administration in Social Work,* 29(2), 43–61.

Chen, S., Jordan, C., & Thompson, S. (2006). The effect of cognitive behavioral therapy (CBT) on depression: The role of problem-solving appraisal. *Research on Social Work Practice,* 16(5), 500–510.

Eckerson, W. (2005). *Scoreboards and dashboards.* www.visualmining.com/products/ executive-dashboards.

Fischer, J., & Corcoran, K. (1994). *Measures for clinical practice: Vol. 1. Couples, families and children.* New York: Free Press.

Hudson, W. (1982). *The clinical measurement package: A field manual.* Chicago: Dorsey.

Netting, F., Kettner, P., & McMurtry, S. (2008). *Social work macro practice* (4th ed). Boston: Allyn & Bacon.

Rapp, C., & Poertner, J. (1992). *Social administration: A client-centered approach.* New York: Longman.

Reid, W. (1992). *Task strategies: An Empirical Approach to Clinical Social Work.* New York: Columbia University Press.

Saleeby, D. (1992). *The strengths perspective in social work practice.* New York: Longman.

Schoech, D. (1999). *Human services technology: Understanding, designing, and implementing computer and Internet applications in the social services.* New York: Haworth Press.

Schoech, D. (2000). Managing information for decision making. In R. Patti (Ed.), *The handbook of social welfare management* (pp. 321–339). Thousand Oaks, CA: Sage.

SCRGSP (Steering Committee for the Review of Government Service Provision). (2006). *Report on government services 2006.* Canberra, Australia: Productivity Commission.

Suchman, E. (1967). *Evaluative research.* New York: Russell Sage Foundation.

PART IV

Calculating the Costs and Value of the Intervention

Chapter 10

Budgeting for Control, Management, and Planning

CHAPTER OVERVIEW

The purpose of this chapter is to introduce:

- The principal purposes of budgeting
- The major models of budgeting
- The major types of budgeting systems

The following topics are covered in this chapter:

- The differences between budgeting and accounting
- The principal purposes of budgeting
  The control purposes
  The management purposes
  The planning purposes
- Budgeting and the systems framework

- Models of the budgetary process
- Major budgeting systems
- Dealing with revenue increases and decreases
- Budgeting in social service agencies today

The Differences Between Budgeting and Accounting

The terms *accounting* and *budgeting* are unfortunately often used interchangeably, but budgeting and accounting are not the same thing. Accounting is a financial activity, whereas budgeting is both a programmatic and a financial activity. Accounting and accounting systems are retrospective: They are concerned with the past and present condition of a social service agency and its various programs. Budgeting systems and budget formats are prospective: They are concerned with the present and future condition of a social service agency and its various programs.

The Principal Purposes of Budgeting

Historically, the principal purposes of budgeting have long been acknowledged to be threefold: *control, management,* and *planning* (Lohmann, 1980; Martin, 2001; Schick, 1966). Seldom, however, does the budgeting system (or systems) of most social service agencies fulfill all three purposes. Even in those rare instances when all three purposes are included, the control purposes tend to overshadow the management and planning purposes. The tensions among the three principal purposes of budgeting are attributable to the dual programmatic/financial nature of budgeting. Only when a social service agency is consciously aware of this dual nature are the control, management, and planning purposes all given relatively equal consideration.

For a social service agency to derive the maximum benefit from its budgeting system, the control, management, and planning purposes of budgeting should all be included and assigned relatively equal importance.

The Control Purposes

The control purposes of budgeting deal with ensuring that agency and program expenses do not exceed agency and program revenues and that both are properly accounted for and documented. The control purposes of budgeting come into play in the policies and processes used to bind an agency's organizational elements and staff to its plans, goals, and objectives. In an era of increased demands for accountability, the maintenance of control over agency and program resources is essential. It is through the budget and the budgeting system that the resources of a social service agency are controlled. Resources are committed and spent only when they conform to the approved agency budget and only when their expenditure works toward the accomplishment of the agency's plans, goals, and objectives. For these reasons, the budget is formally adopted by the governing board in the case of nonprofit organizations and by the appropriate legal authority in the case of government organizations. It is through the formal adoption of the budget and its management that the leadership and top management of social service agencies discharge their control responsibilities as required by federal, state, and local government laws and regulations.

The Management Purposes

The management purposes of budgeting deal with the policies and procedures used to ensure that agency and program revenues are expended in an efficient manner to provide as much service as possible and to serve as many clients as possible. Consequently, an agency's budget needs to be managed. A budget is not a self-implementing document.

The management purposes of budgeting include ensuring that the budget is implemented as adopted while also ensuring that budget revisions are requested and approved before being implemented. Just as a social service agency or program may need to alter its plans due to unforeseen circumstances, a social service agency's budget may also require some adjustments. The budgets of some programs may need to be cut back, while others may need to be expanded. The ability of a social service agency and its programs to operate efficiently in a dynamic and constantly changing environment is highly dependent on how well the budget is managed.

The Planning Purposes

The planning purposes of budgeting deal with the determination of what revenues will be used to achieve what goals and objectives. In this context, a budgeting system is seen not as a stand-alone activity, but rather as an integral component of a social service agency's planning system. For example, issues such as where additional revenues should be allocated or where funding reductions should be made are first and foremost planning decisions. Consequently, the direction—or redirection—of resources should be determined in accordance with a social service agency's priorities as articulated in its plans, goals, and objectives. To allocate resources otherwise can lead to situations where the agency's budgeting system actually hinders, rather than facilitates, achievement of agency and program plans, goals, and objectives.

Budgeting and the Systems Framework

To more fully appreciate the distinctions between the control, management, and planning purposes of budgeting, Figure 10.1 depicts the relationship to the systems framework.

As Figure 10.1 graphically illustrates,

1. The *control* purposes of budgeting deal with the relationship between revenues (inputs) and expenditures (activities) and address the question: What is the financial condition of the agency and its programs?

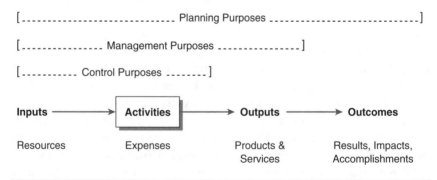

Figure 10.1   The Systems Framework and the Principal Purposes of Budgeting

2. The *management* purposes of budgeting deal with the relationship between revenues (inputs) and outputs (intermediate outputs, quality outputs, and service completions) and address the question: How efficient, or productive, is the agency and its programs?

3. The *planning* purposes of budgeting deal with the relationship between revenues (inputs) and the accomplishment of agency and program goals and objectives (outcomes) and address the question: How effective is the agency and its programs?

Collectively, the three principal purposes of budgeting combine to provide a comprehensive picture of the functioning of a social service agency that none is capable of providing separately.

In summary:

- Budgeting and accounting are not the same thing.
- Budgeting has three principal purposes: control, management, and planning.
- The control functions of budgeting deal with keeping agency and program revenues (inputs) in balance with agency and program expenditures (activities).
- The management purposes of budgeting deal with the utilization of revenues (inputs) to maximize agency and program efficiency or productivity (outputs).
- The planning purposes of budgeting deal with the utilization of revenues (inputs) to accomplish agency and program goals and objectives (outcomes).

Models of the Budgetary Process

The creation and adoption of the budget is one of the most important activities that take place in a social service agency. A social service agency and its programs need adequate resources in order to provide efficient, effective, and high quality services. Because resources generally tend to be scarce, considerable competition can take place during the budget process. Over the years, several different models have been proposed to explain how the budget process actually works. Three of the more commonly referenced models are: the *incremental model,* the *political model* and the *rational planning model.*

The *incremental model* views the budgetary process and budget decisions as largely extensions of past budgetary processes and decisions.

In this model, social service programs are seen as being allocated a share of agency resources based primarily on what each received in previous years, often with a marginal (or incremental) increase or decrease. In this model, an agency's programs are all considered to have merit or they would not have been funded in previous years. Thus, in good financial years, programs usually receive some sort of across-the-board incremental increase. During bad financial years, programs experience some sort of across-the-board incremental decrease.

The *political model* is frequently seen as a major alternative to the incremental model. The political model views the budgetary process as primarily one of negotiation. According to the political model, budgeting decisions are seen as end products of conflict and compromise between competing interests. In this model, agency administrators and staff as well as clients, advocacy groups, and other stakeholders attempt to mobilize political pressure (both within and without the agency) to support their preferred programs and to ensure that they receive an equitable allocation of resources. In this model, increases in resources generally go to those agencies and programs that generate the most political support. Conversely, those agencies and programs that generate the least amount of political support are more likely to experience resource decreases.

The *rational planning model* views the budgetary process as a set of logical steps tied to the agency's planning process that results in budgeting decisions based on needs, priorities, plans, goals, and objectives. The rational planning model uses data and information as the basis for decision making and is in keeping with the concept of "data driven" decision making. Following this model, a social service agency goes through a planning process (such as effectiveness-based program planning) that includes a needs assessment, the establishment of agency and program goals and objectives, and the linking of agency resources to those identified goals and objectives. The rational planning model thus ensures that the budget process is tied to, and supports, the agency's planning process.

Social service agencies that pursue the incremental or political models of budgeting tend to use budgeting systems that focus only on revenues (inputs) and expenditures (activities). These agencies seldom gather, analyze, and present budgetary data and information dealing with agency products or services (outputs) or the accomplishment of agency and program goals and objectives (outcomes). A budgeting system concerned only with revenues and expenditures seldom challenges the organizational status quo. Questions about the efficiency or productivity (outputs) and effectiveness (outcomes) of programs—questions that might challenge the organizational status quo—are usually not raised, or if raised, are not answered because the budgetary information needed to address such questions is simply not available.

From a social service perspective, the major criticism of both the incremental and political models of budgeting is that the needs of clients are considered of secondary importance. The only factors that really matter are the amount of funding received in previous years and the amount of political pressure that can be generated. From a social services perspective, there is frequently an inverse relationship between previous funding levels and need and between political power and need. A new social service program, which by definition has little or no funding history, is placed at a considerable disadvantage in the incremental model. In the same vein, client groups with the least political power, such as the homeless, children, and the chronically mentally ill, are frequently the ones most in need, but may possess the least political power.

The rational planning model is not without its drawbacks. Critics point out that this model is time consuming and utilizes scarce resources that could otherwise be used to provide more services and to serve more clients. These critics also argue that in the end, budgeting decisions are still heavily influenced by incremental and political considerations. Information and analysis, these critics argue, are seldom considered by decision makers except when it happens to coincide with their own preconceived ideas.

A social service agency concerned about the needs of clients would probably not want to make budgeting decisions based primarily on incrementalism or politics, but rather would prefer instead to be guided by rational planning. As discussed in Chapter 2, the rational planning model is the *only* model that is compatible with and that supports effectiveness-based planning.

In pursuing the rational planning model, however, it is likely that incrementalism and politics will continue to play a major role in shaping a social service agency's budgeting decisions. Nevertheless, when the rational planning model is pursued, the level of budgetary debate is raised. If the level of debate is not raised, and if an alternative decision-making framework is not provided, then the incremental and political models win by default.

To summarize:

- There are three models of the budgetary process: the incremental model, the political model, and the rational planning model.
- The incremental model is driven by history and past budgeting decisions.
- The political model is driven by political power and stakeholder support.
- The rational planning model is driven by data and information.
- The rational planning model is preferable because it raises the level of debate to a discussion of client needs, agency goals and objectives, and agency and program outputs and outcomes.

Major Budgeting Systems

Just as there are three principal purposes of budgeting (control, management, planning), there are three corresponding major budgeting systems. These major budgeting systems are *line-item, functional,* and *program.*[1] As Figure 10.2 shows, the three major budgeting systems represent the way in which the three principal purposes of budgeting are operationalized.

As Figure 10.2 illustrates, a line-item budgeting system deals with inputs (resources) and activities (expenditures) and has *control* as its principal purpose. A functional budgeting system deals with inputs (resources) and outputs (intermediate outputs, quality outputs, and service completions) and has *management* as its principal purpose. And a program budgeting system deals with inputs (resources) and the accomplishment of goals and objectives (outcomes) and has *planning* as its principal purpose.

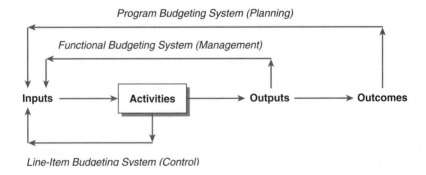

Figure 10.2   The Systems Framework and the Three Major Types of Budgeting Systems

Social service agencies desiring to pursue the rational planning model of budgeting cannot rely solely on a line-item budgeting system that deals only with revenues (inputs) and expenditures (activities). An effectiveness based approach to budgeting requires that the analysis and debate be raised to at least the level of agency and program products and services (functional budgeting system) and preferably to the level of the accomplishment of agency and program goals and objectives (program budgeting system).

Dealing With Revenue Increases and Decreases

Dealing with fluctuating budget increases and decreases is an everyday fact of life for social service agencies today. Revenue increases provide opportunities for expansion, provided social service agencies and programs can demonstrate their efficiency and effectiveness. Revenue shortfalls force social service agencies and programs to justify their current funding levels or face budget reductions. The three budgeting systems (line-item, functional, and program) provide differing perspectives on the implications of revenue increases and shortfalls. The following example demonstrates these differing perspectives.

Suppose, for example, that a social service agency operating an early learning program for 4-year-olds is faced with the task of decreasing its budget by $50,000. Table 10.1 demonstrates how the level of debate changes due to the different types of information provided by line-item, functional, and program budgeting systems.

Table 10.1　　Budgeting Systems, Revenue Shortfalls, and the Level of Debate

Issue: The Implications of a $50,000 Budget Reduction	
Line-Item Budgeting System	Reduce by 1.5 FTEs (full-time equivalent positions) the number of staff.
Functional Budgeting System	Reduce by 2,000 the number of days of service.
Program Budgeting System	Reduce by 25 the number of children who are school ready (educationally prepared to enter kindergarten).

As Table 10.1 points out, in a line-item budgeting system the debate surrounding a $50,000 budget reduction primarily involves a discussion about what items of cost should be reduced. In this case, the decision might be to reduce the number of staff by 1.5 FTEs (full-time equivalent positions) to bring revenues and expenditures into balance. In this type of analysis, nothing is said about the effect of a $50,000 budget reduction on the amount of service (outputs) that can be provided or the effect of the budget reduction on the number of client outcomes that can be achieved.

In a functional budgeting system, the debate shifts to a discussion about the effect on the amount of service (outputs) that can be provided. In this example, a $50,000 budget reduction might result in a decrease of some 2,000 days of service. In a program budgeting system, the debate shifts to a discussion about decreases in the number of client outcomes that can be achieved. In this instance, a $50,000 budget reduction might mean that 25 fewer children would be school ready (i.e., educationally prepared to enter kindergarten).

As the analysis moves from a line-item budgeting system to a functional budgeting system to a program budgeting system, the level of debate is raised from a discussion of items of cost to service considerations to client outcome considerations. The process also works in reverse. A budget increase of $50,000 might mean that an additional 1.5 FTE staff could be hired, an additional 2,000 days of service could be provided, and 25 more children could be made school ready.

While the information provided by line-item budgeting systems is important for social service agencies and programs, it is incomplete. From an effectiveness-based planning perspective the type of information provided by functional and program budgeting systems is needed to assess the impact of revenue increases and decreases on the amount of service that can be provided as well as the number of clients that can be served. Knowledge of the implications for service delivery and for clients of budget increases and decreases raises the level of debate and informs decision makers about the real life implications of their choices. All too frequently, decision makers really do not know the actual implications of their budgeting decisions. This type of information also enables staff of social service agencies to begin planning for orderly increases or reductions in the provision of services and the numbers of clients served. For example, actions that could be taken in response to a budget reduction might include closing intake so that no new children are accepted. In terms of advocacy, information about the service delivery and client effects of budget increases and decreases also can be used to inform and educate clients, advocacy groups, and other stakeholders.

Budgeting in Social Service Agencies Today

Most social service agencies still rely primarily on line-item budgeting systems. However, research suggests (Martin, 2001, 2002a) that the trend today is towards more use of functional and program budgeting systems. This trend can be attributed to the need to generate performance and cost data to satisfy performance and accountability requirements and to operate under performance-based contracts and grants.

To make their own rational budgeting decisions concerning the awarding of contracts and grants, governments, the United Way, private foundations, and other funders necessarily make comparisons between agency and program requests. For valid comparisons to be made, a complete financial picture of each competing agency and program is required including a line-item budget as well as performance data (outputs, quality, and outcomes) and cost data (cost per output, cost per outcome). Once a social service agency or program has been selected for funding, the resulting financial arrangement is likely to be a performance-based contract or grant. A performance-based contract or grant generally pays a social service agency or program a fixed price per output (or unit of service) provided or outcome achieved (Martin, 2002b, 2005). Only functional and program budgeting systems can deal with higher order considerations such as cost per output and cost per outcome.

In the final analysis, it is really only convention that separates line-item, functional, and program budgeting systems. These three budgeting systems can just as easily be seen as components of one comprehensive budgeting system, with the parts building on and complementing one another. Functional and program budgeting systems both build on line-item budgeting. Extending a line-item budgeting system to incorporate the concepts needed for functional and program budgeting is well worth the effort and supports an effectiveness-based approach to social services.

To summarize:

- There are three major types of budgeting systems: line-item, functional, and program.
- Line-item budgeting systems have control as their primary purpose.
- Functional budgeting systems have management as their primary purpose.

- Program budgeting systems have planning as their primary purpose.
- Only functional and program budgeting systems can deal with such higher order considerations as performance data (outputs, quality, and outcomes) and cost data (cost per output and cost per outcome).
- Today's accountability and funding environments necessitate the use of all three budgeting systems (line-item, functional, and program).

The following chapter provides a more in-depth discussion and analysis of line-item, functional, and program budgeting systems and addresses implementation issues such as: What do these three budgeting systems look like? How are they created? And how are they utilized in the day-to-day operations of social service agencies and programs?

Note

1. Considerable disagreement exists in the literature as to the number of separately identifiable budgeting systems and the names that should be given to each. "Line-item," "program," "performance," "program-planning and budgeting" or "PPB," "zero-base" and "outcome" are all budgeting systems identified in the literature (Martin, 1997, 2001, 2002a). Some authors make a distinction between performance and program budgeting; others use the terms interchangeably. The term *functional budgeting* is used to describe many different budgeting systems and is often used interchangeably with both *performance budgeting* and *program budgeting*. Despite the passage of time, little has been done to resolve the confusion. Any attempt to classify budgeting systems therefore must be somewhat arbitrary. The approach taken here continues to utilize the taxonomy first proposed by Gundersdorf (1977) and employed in the first two editions of this text.

References

Gundersdorf, J. (1977). Management and financial controls. In W. Anderson, B. Frieden, & M. Murphy (Eds.), *Managing human services*. Washington, DC: International City Management Association.

Lohmann, R. (1980*). Breaking even: Financial management in human service organizations*. Philadelphia: Temple University Press.

Martin, L. (1997). Outcome budgeting: A new entrepreneurial approach to budgeting. *Journal of Public Budgeting, Accounting and Financial Management, 9*, 108–126.

Martin, L. (2001). *Financial management for human service administrators*. Boston: Allyn & Bacon.

Martin, L. (2002a). Budgeting for outcomes. In A. Khan & W. Hildreth (Eds.), *Budget theory in the public sector* (pp. 246–260). Westport, CT: Quorum Books.

Martin, L. (2002b). Performance-based contracting for human services: Lessons for public procurement. *Journal of Public Procurement, 2*, 55–71.

Martin, L. (2005). Performance-based contracting: Does it work? *Administration in Social Work, 29,* 63–77.

Schick, A. (1966). The road to PPB: The stages of budget reform. *Public Administration Review,* 26, 243–258.

Chapter 11

Line-Item, Functional, and Program Budgeting Systems

CHAPTER OVERVIEW

The purpose of this chapter is to illustrate:

- How a line-item budgeting system is created
- How a functional budgeting system is created
- How a program budgeting system is created

The following topics are covered in this chapter:

- The focus of major budgeting systems
- Line-item budgeting systems
  Designing the line-item budget format
  Developing common budget definitions and terms
  Identifying all revenues and expenses
  Balancing the budget
- The link between line-item budgeting and functional and program budgeting
  Developing the line-item budget
  Determining the agency's program structure
  Creating the cost allocation plan format

Identifying direct and indirect costs

Assigning direct costs to programs and indirect costs to the indirect cost pool

Allocating indirect costs to programs and determining total program costs

    Total direct cost methodology

    Direct labor costs methodology

    Direct labor hours methodology

    Direct costing methodology

    Which cost allocation methodology is best?

    Is cost allocation worth the effort?

- Functional budgeting systems

    Selecting the program's intermediate output (unit of service) measure

    Determining the program's intermediate output (unit of service) objective

    Computing the program's cost per intermediate output (unit of service)

    Selecting the program's final output (service completion) measure

    Determining the program's final output (service completion) objective

    Computing the program's cost per final output (service completion)

- Program budgeting systems

    Selecting the program's intermediate outcome measure

    Selecting the program's intermediate outcome objective

    Computing the program's cost per intermediate outcome

    Selecting the program's final outcome measure

    Determining the program's final outcome objective

    Computing the program's cost per final outcome

- A comprehensive budgeting system

The Focus of Major Budgeting Systems

Each of the three budgeting systems discussed in this chapter has a different focus.

Line-item budgeting systems (see Figure 11.1) focus on expenses (activities) and relate expenses to revenues (inputs). For this reason, line-item budgeting systems can also be thought of as "activity budgeting" or "expense budgeting."

Functional budgeting systems (see Figure 11.2) focus on outputs, including program products and services (intermediate outputs), quality

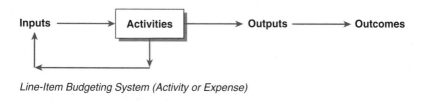

Figure 11.1   Line-Item Budgeting System

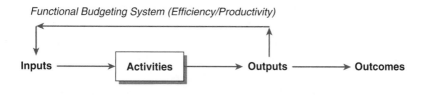

Figure 11.2   Functional Budgeting System

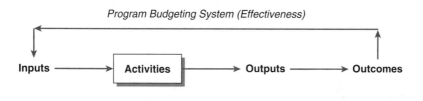

Figure 11.3   Program Budgeting System

products and services (quality outputs), and service completions (final outputs), and relate these outputs to revenues (inputs). Consequently, functional budgeting systems can be thought of as: "output budgeting," "efficiency budgeting," or "productivity budgeting." The classical definition of efficiency or productivity is the ratio of outputs to inputs.

Program budgeting systems (see Figure 11.3) focus on: results, accomplishments, or impacts (outcomes) and relate these outcomes to revenues (inputs). Program budgeting systems can be thought of as: "outcome budgeting" or "effectiveness budgeting."

As a social service agency moves from a line-item budgeting system to a functional budgeting system and finally to a program budgeting system, the financial side of a social service agency becomes more closely linked to the planning function.

Line-Item Budgeting Systems

Line-item budgeting systems are characterized by the use of standardized budget formats, common budget definitions, and a structured budgetary process. Line-item budgeting systems seek to bring consistency to the budgetary process and to provide a financial overview of a social service agency and its various programs.

The time covered by line-item budgeting systems is usually 12 months, a period called a *fiscal year*. A fiscal year tends to follow one of three time frames: (a) January 1 to December 31 (used by many nonprofit social service agencies), (b) July 1 to June 30 (used by many state and local government social service agencies), and (c) October 1 to September 30 (used by the federal government). Regardless of the fiscal year utilized, all agency budgeting systems are tied to that time frame.

The creation of a line-item budgeting system in a social service agency involves the following steps:

1. Designing a standardized line-item budget format

2. Developing common budget definitions and terms

3. Identifying all revenues and expenses

4. Balancing the budget

Designing the Line-Item Budget Format

A line-item budget format derives its name from the categories (or line-items) utilized in its design. The categories of revenues and expenses in a line-item budgeting system are designed to be mutually exclusive and exhaustive. This means that all revenue and expense items should fit into one, and only one, category. The number of categories created in a line-item budget must be sufficient to cover all major items of revenue and expense. The inclusion of a miscellaneous category for both revenues and expenses ensures that the line-item budget format will accommodate all budget items. Table 11.1 illustrates the line-item budget utilized by Safe Haven, our ongoing case example. The Safe Haven budget is typical of the type of line-item budget format that would be utilized by most social service agencies.

Developing Common Budget Definitions and Terms

In a line-item budgeting system, each category of revenue and expense is operationally defined to provide guidance and ensure uniformity in the

Table 11.1   Safe Haven Line-Item Budgeting System

Revenues

1. United Way	$350,000.00
2. Government Contracts & Grants	356,000.00
3. Third Party Payments	84,750.00
4. Contributions	35,000.00
5. Special Events	100,000.00
6. Program Income	45,000.00
7. Endowment (Income)	50,000.00
8. Other (Miscellaneous)	25,000.00
Total Revenues	$1,045,750.00

Expenses

1. Salaries & Wages		$ 655,000.00
Executive Director @ $75,000.00	$75,000.00	
Business Manager @ $65,000.00	65,000.00	
Accountant @ $42,000.00	42,000.00	
Case Managers 2 @ $42,000.00	84,000.00	
Counselors 3 @ $47,000.00	141,000.00	
Job Training Specialists 2 @ $47,000.00	94,000.00	
Support Services Supervisor @ $42,000.00	42,000.00	
Support Services Staff 4 @ $28,000.00	112,000.00	
Total Salaries & Wages	$655,000.00	

2. ERE @ 25%	$163,750.00
3. Rent	40,000.00
4. Utilities	17,000.00
5. Equipment	42,000.00
6. Supplies	25,000.00
7. Telephone	12,000.00
8. Travel	40,000.00
9. Conferences	25,000.00
10. Printing & Duplicating	12,000.00
11. Other (Miscellaneous)	14,000.00
Total Expenses	$ 1,045,750.00

treatment of budget items. For example, the expense category of *employee-related expenses* (ERE) would be operationally defined as those nonsalary and wage costs associated with each staff position, such as: Social Security payments, federal and state withholding taxes, health and dental insurance costs, and retirement costs.

Identifying all Revenues and Expenses

A social service agency's line-item budgeting format should include a complete presentation of all *anticipated revenues* and all *proposed expenses*. As Table 11.1 illustrates, the line-item budget for Safe Haven is balanced, total anticipated revenues are $1,045,750 and proposed expenses are $1,045,750.

Balancing the Budget

The use of a line-item budgeting system with a standardized budget format that includes all anticipated revenues and proposed expenses clearly indicates whether the budget is balanced or unbalanced. During the budgetary process, the standardized line-item budget format facilitates the identification and discussion of where proposed expenses might be reduced or where additional revenues might be sought in order to bring the finalized budget into balance.

Because balancing the budget can sometimes be a painful experience, a temptation exists to force a budget into balance. A forced balanced budget is created when the management of a social service agency consciously overstates revenues or understates expenses. There is an old story about the director of a religiously affiliated social service agency who forced his agency budget into balance each fiscal year by routinely including a revenue category called "unanticipated income." When asked about this unorthodox approach, the director replied that he preferred to trust in divine intervention rather than go through the pain of balancing the budget. Unless one has connections in high places, forcing the budget of a social service agency into balance is risky business.

Balancing the budget at the beginning of the fiscal year can be a difficult task, but it is preferable to trying to balance an unbalanced budget during the fiscal year. An unbalanced budget must eventually be balanced. Each month that a budget remains unbalanced makes the task more difficult. The actual impact of a budget reduction on the operations of a social service agency is equal to the amount of the necessary reduction multiplied by the number of months elapsed in the fiscal year. For example, a $2,000 budget reduction made in the sixth month of a fiscal year actually has an organizational impact equal to $12,000 on an annualized basis.

To summarize:

- Line-item budgeting systems require the design of a standardized budget format that identifies all anticipated revenues and proposed expenses.
- All budget categories in a line-item budget should be operationally defined.
- Line-item budgets should be balanced: anticipated revenues should be equal to or greater than proposed expenses.
- It is better to balance a line-item budget at the beginning of the fiscal year rather than later.

The Link Between Line-Item Budgeting and Functional and Program Budgeting

The development of either a functional budgeting system or a program budgeting system for a social service agency actually begins with the agency's line-item budget.

The central idea behind both functional and program budgeting systems is to take a social service agency's line-item budget and *assign or allocate all expenses to the agency's various programs in order to determine the total cost of each program.* At this point, functional and program budgeting systems diverge.

Functional budgeting systems are concerned with the outputs, efficiency, and productivity of a social service agency's various programs. Functional budgeting systems address the following questions: How much service do the agency's various programs provide as measured in terms of products and services (intermediate outputs), quality products and services (quality outputs), and service completions (final outputs)? What is the anticipated cost per intermediate output (unit of service), per quality output, and per service completion?

Program budgeting systems are concerned with the outcomes or effectiveness of a social service agency's various programs. Program budgeting systems address such questions as: What outcomes (results, accomplishments, or impacts) do the agency's various programs intend to achieve? And what is the anticipated cost per outcome?

Because both functional and program budgeting systems are concerned with determining the total cost of the various programs operated by a social service agency, they have certain common implementation steps including the following:

1. Developing the line-item budget identifying all anticipated revenues and proposed expenses

2. Determining the agency's program structure

3. Creating the cost allocation plan format

4. Identifying direct and indirect costs

5. Assigning direct costs to programs and indirect costs to the indirect cost pool

6. Allocating indirect costs and determining the total cost of programs

Developing the Line-Item Budget

The first step in implementing either a functional or a program budgeting system in a social service agency is the development of a line-item budget that identifies all anticipated revenues and proposed expenses. This step has already been accomplished (see Table 11.1).

Determining the Agency's Program Structure

Determining the social service agency's program structure is the second step. *Program structure* refers to the number of distinct programs operated by a social service agency. This issue was addressed in earlier chapters.

In our Safe Haven case example, the agency has determined that it has five programs, (1) a shelter program, (2) a case management program, (3) an individual and group counseling program, (4) a financial management training program, and (5) an employment training and placement program. In order to decrease the degree of complexity in discussing budgeting issues, we are going to deal with only three programs: *case management*, *counseling*, and *employment training and placement*.

Creating the Cost Allocation Plan Format

The cost allocation plan format is the primary document or tool used to derive a functional or program budget from a line-item budget (see Table 11.2). In the rows of the cost allocation plan format, the same line-items

Table 11.2   Safe Haven Cost Allocation Plan Format

Budget Line-Item	Case Management Program	Counseling Program	Employment Training & Placement Program	Indirect Cost Pool
1. Salaries & Wages				
Executive Director				
Business Manager				
Accountant				
Case Managers				
Counselors				
Job Training Specialists				
Support Services Supervisor				
Support Services Staff				
Total Salaries & Wages				
2. ERE @ 25%				
3. Rent				
4. Utilities				
5. Equipment				
6. Supplies				
7. Telephone				
8. Travel				
9. Conferences				
10. Printing & Duplicating				
11. Other (Miscellaneous)				

appear that are used in the agency's line-item budget (see Table 11.1). Each of the three programs (case management, counseling, and employment training and placement) appears in a column heading. One column is labeled the *indirect cost pool*. With the aid of this cost allocation plan format, the total cost of each of the three programs can be determined.

Identifying Direct and Indirect Costs

Every item of proposed expense (as identified in a social service agency's line-item budget) can be classified as either a *direct cost* or an *indirect cost*.

Direct costs are those items of expense incurred by a social service agency for the benefit of only *one program*. Examples of direct costs include:

- The salaries and wages of staff who work for only one program
- Materials and supplies used for the benefit of only one program
- Travel costs associated with only one program
- Equipment used exclusively in one program
- Any other costs that benefit only one program

Indirect costs are those items of expense that benefit *two or more programs*. Indirect costs are sometimes referred to as "overhead costs" or "organizational and maintenance (OM) costs." Indirect costs typically involve the salaries, wages, and employee related expenses (ERE) of the executive director and other agency staff who work on all agency programs. Additionally, all operating expenses that benefit two or more agency programs are considered as indirect costs. Other operating costs that are generally treated as indirect costs include:

- Building rent
- Utilities
- Janitorial services
- Telephones
- Auditing

Assigning Direct Costs to Programs and Indirect Costs to the Indirect Cost Pool

For a social service agency to determine the total cost of its various programs, each program's direct costs must be determined, as well as each program's relative share of indirect costs. *The total cost of a social service program is the sum of its direct and indirect costs.* Identifying a program's direct costs is a fairly straightforward activity. If a cost item benefits one program and one program only, the cost is a direct cost to that program. In our Safe Haven case study, we will assume that: (1) the two case managers work exclusively for the case management program, (2) the three counselors work exclusively for the counseling program, and (3) the two job training specialists work exclusively for the employment training and placement program. Consequently, all of these costs are direct costs and are assigned to their respective programs (see Table 11.3).

For the remaining salary and wage items in Table 11.3, the question is asked: Is this item a direct cost or an indirect cost? For example, the work of the executive director benefits all agency programs, so her salary ($75,000) is an indirect cost. As an indirect cost, the executive director's salary cannot be placed in any of the three programs, but must be assigned to the "indirect cost pool." The indirect cost pool is a temporary holding category. The same procedure is followed for all the remaining salary and wage items.

The work of the business manager and the accountant benefits all programs, so these costs are also indirect costs. The support services supervisor and the four support services staff work for all programs. Since different programs have peaks and valleys in their workloads, a decision was made by Safe Haven to have all support services staff work for all programs and to allow the support services supervisor to manage the workload. Therefore, the salaries and wages of the support services supervisor and the four support services staff are indirect costs and are assigned to the indirect cost pool.

Adding across the column "total salaries and wages" in Table 11.3, we arrive at a figure of $655,000 ($84,000 + $141,000 + $94,000 + 336,000). This figure ($655,000) is the same as the figure for total salaries and wages identified in Table 11.1. Thus, we know that the math is correct and that we didn't gain or lose money (something you can't do) when assigning salary and wage costs. It should be noted, however, that rounding errors from multiplying and dividing can affect the computations. Nevertheless, the total of all costs included in a cost allocation plan must equal the total costs of the line-item budget.

Employee related expenses (ERE) follow the salaries and wages they relate to. Thus, the ERE rate 25% is applied to the total salary and wages for each of the three programs as well as the indirect cost pool (see Table 11.4). We have now completed assigning all salary and wage costs and can turn our attention to other operating costs.

Table 11.3   Safe Haven Assigning Salary and Wage Costs

Budget Line-Item	Case Management Program	Counseling Program	Employment Training & Placement Program	Indirect Cost Pool
1. Salaries & Wages				
Executive Director				75,000.00
Business Manager				65,000.00
Accountant				42,000.00
Case Managers	$84,000.00			
Counselors		$141,000.00		
Job Training Specialists			$94,000.00	
Support Services Supervisor				42,000.00
Support Services Staff				112,000.00
Total Salaries & Wages	84,000.00	141,000.00	94,000.00	336,000.00
2. ERE @ 25%				
3. Rent				
4. Utilities				
5. Equipment				
6. Supplies				
7. Telephone				
8. Travel				
9. Conferences				
10. Printing & Duplicating				
11. Other (Miscellaneous)				

Table 11.4   Safe Haven Assigning ERE Costs

Budget Line-Item	Case Management Program	Counseling Program	Employment Training & Placement Program	Indirect Cost Pool
1. Salaries & Wages				
Executive Director				75,000.00
Business Manager				65,000.00
Accountant				42,000.00
Case Managers	$84,000.00			
Counselors		$141,000.00		
Job Training Specialists			$94,000.00	
Support Services Supervisor				42,000.00
Support Services Staff				112,000.00
Total Salaries & Wages	84,000.00	141,000.00	94,000.00	336,000.00
2. ERE @ 25%	21,000.00	35,250.00	23,500.00	84,000.00
3. Rent				
4. Utilities				
5. Equipment				
6. Supplies				
7. Telephone				
8. Travel				
9. Conferences				
10. Printing & Duplicating				
11. Other (Miscellaneous)				

Other operating costs is the term applied to those items of cost in a line-item budget that are not salary and wage related. Other operating costs generally tend to be indirect costs because they benefit all programs. For example, all social service programs benefit to some extent from rent, utilities, supplies, telephone, equipment, printing, and duplicating, and so on. Additionally, all programs generally have at least some travel and conference costs. Thus, all the other operating costs in the Safe Haven budget are indirect costs and are assigned to the indirect cost pool (see Table 11.5).

Each program's total direct costs, as well as the total indirect costs in the cost allocation pool, can now be determined by totaling the columns. The total direct costs of the case management program is $105,000, the counseling program is $176,250, the employment training and placement program is $117,500, and the total of the indirect cost pool is $647,000.00. When the four column amounts are totaled ($105,000 + $176,250 + $117,500 + $647,000) the resulting amount ($1,045,750) is the same as the total Safe Haven line-item budget shown in Table 11.1.

Allocating Indirect Costs to Programs and Determining Total Program Costs

The next step is to allocate the indirect cost pool to individual programs. A method must be determined to apportion the costs in the indirect cost pool to the three programs. The process by which indirect costs are allocated to programs is called *cost allocation*. The actual practice of cost allocation is a technical matter best left to accountants. However; the logic behind cost allocation is not difficult and is essential to a complete understanding of how functional and program budgets are derived from line-item budgets.[1]

Cost allocation involves the selection of a methodology, or base, to be used to allocate the indirect costs to programs. The cost allocation methodologies, or bases, most frequently used by social service agencies are (a) total direct costs, (b) direct labor costs, (c) direct labor hours, and (d) direct costing (Hay & Wilson, 1995; Horngren, Foster, and Datar, 1997; Martin, 2001; Mayers, 2004).

Table 11.5   Safe Haven Determining the Total Direct Costs of Programs and the Total of the Indirect Cost Pool

Budget Line-Item	Case Management Program	Counseling Program	Employment Training & Placement Program	Indirect Cost Pool
1. Salaries & Wages				
Executive Director				75,000.00
Business Manager				65,000.00
Accountant				42,000.00
Case Managers	$84,000.00			
Counselors		$141,000.00		
Job Training Specialists			$94,000.00	
Support Services Supervisor				42,000.00
Support Services Staff				112,000.00
Total Salaries & Wages	84,000.00	141,000.00	94,000.00	336,000.00
2. ERE @ 25%	21,000.00	35,250.00	23,500.00	84,000.00
3. Rent				40,000.00
4. Utilities				17,000.00
5. Equipment				42,000.00
6. Supplies				25,000.00
7. Telephone				12,000.00
8. Travel				40,000.00
9. Conferences				25,000.00
10. Printing & Duplicating				12,000.00
11. Other (Miscellaneous)				14,000.00
TOTALS	$105,000.00	$176,250.00	$117,500.00	$647,000.00

Total Direct Cost Methodology

Cost allocation using the total direct costs methodology involves four steps:

1. Determining each program's share of direct costs
2. Totaling all direct costs
3. Determining each program's relative percentage share of indirect costs
4. Allocating the indirect cost pool to each program, using the derived indirect cost rate

Cost allocation using *total direct costs* as the base involves apportioning, or allocating, the indirect cost pool ($647,000) to the three programs according to each program's relative percentage share of total direct costs (see Table 11.6). The total direct costs of the three programs is $398,750 ($105,000 + $176,250 + $117,500).

To apportion, or allocate, the indirect cost pool ($647,000) to the three programs, an *indirect cost rate* must be computed. An indirect cost rate is a ratio that expresses the relationship between a program's direct costs and indirect costs. Determining the indirect cost rate using the total direct costs methodology or base involves dividing the indirect cost pool ($647,000) by the total direct costs ($398,750) of all three programs. The resulting percentage (162.26%) is the indirect cost rate.

$$\frac{\text{Indirect Cost Pool } (\$647,000)}{\text{Total Direct Costs } (\$105,000 + \$176,250 + \$117,500)} = \frac{647,000}{398,750} = 1.6226 = 162.26\%$$

The indirect cost rate is then applied to the total direct costs of each program. For example, the total direct costs of the case management program ($105,000) is multiplied by the indirect cost rate (1.6226). The result ($170,373) is the case management program's allocated share of indirect costs.

Total Direct Cost of Case Management Program		Indirect Cost Rate		
$105,000	×	1.6226	=	$170,373

Table 11.6   Safe Haven Allocating Indirect Costs to Programs Using the "Total Direct Costs" Methodology and Determining the Total Cost of a Program

Budget Line-Item	Case Management Program	Counseling Program	Employment Training & Placement Program	Indirect Cost Pool
1. Salaries & Wages				
Executive Director				75,000.00
Business Manager				65,000.00
Accountant				42,000.00
Case Managers	$84,000.00			
Counselors		$141,000.00		
Job Training Specialists			$94,000.00	
Support Services Supervisor				42,000.00
Support Services Staff				112,000.00
Total Salaries & Wages	84,000.00	141,000.00	94,000.00	336,000.00
2. ERE @ 25%	21,000.00	35,250.00	23,500.00	84,000.00
3. Rent				40,000.00
4. Utilities				17,000.00
5. Equipment				42,000.00
6. Supplies				25,000.00
7. Telephone				12,000.00
8. Travel				40,000.00
9. Conferences				25,000.00
10. Printing & Duplicating				12,000.00
11. Other (Miscellaneous)				14,000.00
Total Direct Costs	$105,000.00	$176,250.00	$117,500.00	$647,000.00
Allocated Indirect Costs	170,373.00	285,983.00	190,656.00	
Total Direct & Indirect Costs	$275,373.00	$462,233.00	308,156.00	

Each program's *assigned* direct costs and *allocated* indirect costs are then totaled (see Table 11.6). The resulting amounts constitute the full or total costs of each program. For example, the cost of the case management program is $105,000 in direct costs plus $170,373 in indirect costs for a full or total cost of $275,373.

The total costs of the other two programs operated by Safe Haven (counseling and employment, training and placement) are computed following the same process.

Direct Labor Costs Methodology

The second approach to cost allocation is called the *direct labor costs* methodology. The process is essentially the same as the total direct costs methodology, except that instead of finding each program's relative percentage share of total direct costs, each program's relative percentage share of *direct labor costs* is computed and then used as the base. Direct labor costs are those staffing costs, including ERE, that are considered direct costs.

In the total direct costs example shown above, all the direct costs are direct labor costs. Consequently, for purposes of our Safe Haven case example, there is no difference between the results one gets using either the total direct costs methodology or the direct labor costs methodology.

Direct Labor Hours Methodology

The third approach to cost allocation is the *direct labor hours* methodology. Again, the process is essentially the same as for the total direct costs and the total direct labor costs methodologies, except that with this methodology each program's relative percentage share of total *direct labor hours* is determined and then used as the base. *Direct labor hours* means the total annual hours worked by all agency staff that are considered direct costs.

The average work year, taking into consideration weekends and holidays, is generally computed at 2,080 hours. In the Safe Haven case example, the two staff that work full time for the case management program are the program's only direct costs. Thus, the case management program has 4,160 direct labor hours (2 @ 2,080). The counseling program has three staff that work full time and are the program's only direct costs. Consequently, the counseling program has 6,240 direct labor hours (3 @ 2,080). In the same vein, the employment training and placement program has only two full-time staff that are considered direct labor costs. The number of direct labor hours for the training and placement program is 4,160 (2 @ 2,080). Finally, the total direct labor hours (14,560) is computed by adding together the direct labor hours for each of the three programs (4,160 + 6,240 + 4,160).

The indirect cost rate is determined by dividing the indirect cost pool ($647,000) by the total direct labor hours (14,560). The result is an indirect cost rate that represents a dollar value rather than a percentage.

$$\frac{\text{Indirect Cost Pool } (\$647{,}000)}{\text{Total Direct Labor Hours } (4{,}160 + 6{,}240 + 4{,}160)} = \frac{647{,}000}{14{,}560} = \$44.44$$

In the case of our Safe Haven example, the indirect cost pool ($647,000) is divided by 14,560 direct labor hours, which results in a rate of $44.44 per direct labor hour. The amount of indirect costs that is allocated to the case management program is $184,870 ($44.44 × 4,160). The same procedure is utilized to allocate indirect costs to the other two programs (see Table 11.7).

It should be noted that regardless of the cost allocation methodology utilized, the amount of direct costs in each program and the amount in the indirect cost pool always remains constant. The only variable in the computations is the base that is used to allocate indirect costs.

Direct Costing Methodology

The fourth and final approach to cost allocation is *direct costing*. This methodology involves converting indirect costs to direct costs. The direct costing method requires that a unique measure or base be found and used to allocate each item of indirect cost. With this methodology, each item of indirect cost has its own base for allocation purposes. The indirect cost item "telephone" from Table 11.7 can be used to illustrate how an item of indirect cost can be converted to a direct cost. The cost item telephone (defined as basic monthly service charges) is generally treated as an indirect cost because the telephone system of a social service agency benefits all programs. One way of converting this item of indirect cost to a direct cost is to determine the total number of telephones utilized in Safe Haven and the number of telephones used by each of the three programs. Each program's relative percentage share of total telephones then becomes the base for allocating telephone charges to the agency's programs.

Any item of indirect cost can be converted into a direct cost by finding a measure (e.g., hours, square feet, etc.) to serve as the allocation base. The allocation bases shown in Table 11.8 are generally acknowledged as acceptable for purposes of the direct costing methodology.

Table 11.7   Safe Haven Allocating Indirect Costs to Programs Using the "Direct Labor Hours" Methodology and Determining the Total Cost of a Program

Budget Line-Item	Case Management Program	Counseling Program	Employment Training & Placement Program	Indirect Cost Pool
1. Salaries & Wages				
Executive Director				75,000.00
Business Manager				65,000.00
Accountant				42,000.00
Case Managers	$84,000.00			
Counselors		$141,000.00		
Job Training Specialists			$94,000.00	
Support Services Supervisor				42,000.00
Support Services Staff				112,000.00
Total Salaries & Wages	84,000.00	141,000.00	94,000.00	336,000.00
2. ERE @ 25%	21,000.00	35,250.00	23,500.00	84,000.00
3. Rent				40,000.00
4. Utilities				17,000.00
5. Equipment				42,000.00
6. Supplies				25,000.00
7. Telephone				12,000.00
8. Travel				40,000.00
9. Conferences				25,000.00
10. Printing & Duplicating				12,000.00
11. Other (Miscellaneous)				14,000.00
Total Direct Costs	$105,000.00	$176,250.00	$117,500.00	$647,000.00
Allocated Indirect Costs	184,870.00	277,306.00	184,870.00	
Total Direct & Indirect Costs	$289,870.00	$453,556.00	$302,370.00	

Table 11.8   Suggested Bases for the Direct Charging of Indirect Costs

Indirect Cost Item	Allocation Base
Accounting	Number of transactions processed for each program
Auditing	Hours worked on each program
Budgeting	Hours worked on each program
Information Technology	Number of computer workstations
Employees	Hours worked on each program
Insurance	Square feet of office space occupied by each program
Janitorial	Square feet of office space occupied by each program
Legal	Hours worked for each program
Telephone	Number of telephones
Mail	Number of pieces of mail processed
Printing & Duplicating	Number of jobs/number of pages
Utilities	Square feet of office space occupied by each program

Which Cost Allocation Methodology Is Best?

There is no one best cost allocation methodology for a social service agency to use in allocating indirect costs. One methodology may be more appropriate in some situations and less appropriate in others. Some methodologies are more difficult to implement than others. Also, depending upon the nature of the program, different methodologies may result in only marginal if any changes in the actual allocation of indirect costs.

• The *total direct costs* methodology is the simplest approach to implement. The assumption underlining this approach is that there is a strong relationship between the total direct costs of a program and the amount of operations and maintenance or overhead expenses (indirect costs) associated with the oversight of the program.

• The *direct labor costs* methodology is said to be a superior approach when the majority of an agency's programs are labor intensive. Most social service agency programs are labor intensive, with 70% or more of an organization's budget being comprised of salaries, wages, and employee related expenses. This methodology is only slightly more difficult to implement than the total direct costs methodology.

• The *direct labor hours* methodology is said to be even more appropriate for labor intensive agencies then the direct labor costs methodology. Staff in social service programs are frequently paid at differing rates. Consequently, two staff performing the same type of work can have significantly different budget implications. The direct labor hours methodology is slightly more difficult to implement than the direct labor hours methodology.

• The *direct costing* methodology is said to be the most accurate form of cost allocation, because a different and more relevant base is used for each item of indirect costs. Some times a funding source (either government or private) may mandate the use of this methodology. The direct costing methodology is the most difficult to implement.

For some social service agencies, a combination of direct costing for salaries, wages, and ERE combined with another methodology for the remaining costs may be more appropriate. With this "combination of methods," personnel costs can be easily converted to direct costs based on hours worked for each program.

The choice of the most appropriate cost allocation methodology for a social service agency to use is best left to the agency's accountants and auditors after consultation with major funding sources. Nevertheless, the guiding principle in selecting a cost allocation methodology should be to ensure that each program is allocated its fair share of agency indirect costs and that the total program cost figure represents as accurately as possible the real costs of providing agency programs.

It should be noted that once a social serviced agency decides upon a cost allocation methodology, it is required by federal and state regulations as well as generally accepted accounting principles (GAAP) to utilize the same methodology for each program.

Is Cost Allocation Worth the Effort?

Considering the additional work involved with cost allocation, the question is invariably raised: Is cost allocation really worth the effort? The answer is yes! Without resorting to cost allocation, a social service agency does not know the full costs of providing its various programs. In turn, an agency cannot develop accurate costs per unit of service (intermediate output), per quality output, or per service completion (final output). If a social service agency does not know the true unit costs of its various programs, it has no way of determining the service delivery implications of revenue increases or decreases. The knowledge of a program's true unit costs is also necessary for the setting of fees.

Government and foundation funding sources today frequently link contracts and grant payments to the provision of a specified number of units of service (intermediate outputs). If a social service program does not include indirect costs in the computation of its unit costs, then the program is actually underpricing its services. A social service program that consistently underprices its services may find itself committed to a contract or grant that actually causes it to lose money.

In summary:

- Functional and program budgeting systems both begin with a social service agency's line-item budget, but with a focus on expenses.
- Direct and indirect costs are then assigned and allocated respectively to programs.
- Direct costs are those items of cost that benefit only one program.
- Indirect costs are those items of cost that benefit two or more programs.
- Four cost allocation methodologies or bases are generally used by social service agencies: total direct costs, direct labor costs, direct labor hours, and direct costing (converting indirect costs to direct costs).
- Cost allocation is essential to the successful financial management of social service agencies and programs today.

Functional Budgeting Systems

Determining a program's total costs, including both direct and indirect costs, completes the first seven steps required to move from a line-item budgeting system to a functional and program budgeting system. Six additional steps are required to create a functional budgeting system: (1) selecting the program's intermediate output (unit of service) measure, (2) determining the program's intermediate output objective, (3) computing the program's cost per intermediate output, (4) selecting the program's final output (service completion) measure, (5) determining the program's final output (service completion) objective, and (6) computing the program's cost per final output (service completion). For purposes of this section, the focus will be on Safe Haven's case management program.

Selecting the Program's Intermediate
Output (Unit of Service) Measure

The intermediate output (unit-of-service) measure for the case management program is one hour of direct client contact time.

Determining the Program's Intermediate
Output (Unit of Service) Objective

The management of Safe Haven has established an objective for the case management program of 3,500 intermediate outputs (units of service) for the first year.

Computing the Program's Cost Per
Intermediate Output (Unit of Service)

The total cost of the case management program is $275,373. The intermediate output (unit of service) objective is 3,500. The cost per intermediate output (unit of service) is $78.68 per hour of direct client contact time.

$$\frac{\text{Total Case Management Program Cost}}{\text{Intermediate Output (Unit of Service) Objective}} = \frac{\$275,373}{3,500} = \$78.68$$

Selecting the Program's Final
Output (Service Completion) Measure

The final output (service completion) for the case management program is one client receiving a full complement of services.

Determining the Program's Final
Output (Service Completion) Objective

The management of Safe Haven has established an objective for the case management program of 20 service completions for the first year.

Computing the Program's Cost Per Final Output (Service Completion)

The total cost of the case management program is $275,373. The final output (service completion) objective is 20 clients. The cost per final output (service completion) is: $13,768.65.

$$\frac{\text{Total Case Management Program Costs}}{\text{Final Output (Service Completion) Objective}} = \frac{\$275,373}{20} = \$13,768.65$$

The Safe Haven functional budgeting system for the case management program is shown in Table 11.9. The same type of format would also be utilized in constructing a functional budgeting system for Safe Haven's other two programs.

To summarize:

- Functional budgeting systems require the designation of intermediate and final output measures, the establishment of intermediate and final output objectives, and the computation of output costs (both intermediate and final outputs).
- Unit costs are determined by dividing total program cost by total intermediate outputs (units of service) and by total final outputs (service completions).
- The intermediate and final output objectives and output costs determine the types of information that will be available to the management of a social service agency for purposes of monitoring and assessing program operations.

Table 11.9   Case Management Functional Budgeting System

Case Management Program	
Total program cost:	$275,373
Objectives	
− *Intermediate output:*	3,500 units of case management services @ a cost of $78.68 per unit
− *Final output:*	20 service completions @ a cost of $13,768.65 per service completion.

Program Budgeting Systems

Once total program costs have been calculated, the creation of a program budget involves essentially the same steps as the creation of a functional budgeting system. The only difference is that functional budget systems focus on outputs while program budgeting systems focus on outcomes.

Selecting the Program's Intermediate Outcome Measure

The intermediate outcome measure for the case management program is one client completing her "individual rehabilitation plan (IRP)."

Selecting the Program's Intermediate Outcome Objective

The management of Safe Haven has established an objective for the case management program of achieving 18 intermediate outcomes for the first year.

Computing the Program's Cost Per Intermediate Outcome

The total cost of the case management program is $275,373. The intermediate outcome objective is 18. The cost per intermediate outcome is $15,298.50.

$$\frac{\text{Total Case Management Program Cost}}{\text{Intermediate Outcome Objective}} = \frac{\$275,373}{18} = \$15,298.50$$

Selecting the Program's Final Outcome Measure

The final output for the case management program is one client free of violence for one year.

Determining the Program's Final Outcome Objective

The management of Safe Haven has established an objective for the case management program of achieving 15 final outcomes for the first year.

Computing the Program's Cost Per Final Outcome

The total cost of the case management program is $275,373. The final outcome objective is 15. The cost per final output (service completion) is $18,358.20

$$\frac{\text{Total Case Management Program Costs}}{\text{Final Outcome Objective}} = \frac{\$275,373}{15} = \$18,358.20$$

The Safe Haven program budgeting system for the case management program is shown in Table 11.10. The same type of format would be utilized in constructing a program budgeting system budget for Safe Haven's other two programs.

The type of programmatic and financial data and information provided by program budgeting systems is extremely useful for planning purposes. By relating costs to planned outcome (results, accomplishment, or impacts), a social service agency can determine how effective its various

Table 11.10   Case Management Program Budgeting System

Case Management Program	
Total program cost:	$275,373
Objectives	
— *Intermediate outcome:*	18 clients completing their individual rehabilitation plans @ a cost of $15,298.50 per client
— *Final outcome:*	15 clients remaining free of abuse for one year @ a cost of $18,358.20 per client

programs are. Hard data and information on program outcomes will also help to increase the credibility of a social service agency with its funding sources, advocacy groups, and clients.

In summary:

- Program budgeting systems require the determination of program outcome objectives and the computation of cost per outcome.
- When programs share an outcome objective, cost per outcome is computed by dividing the total program cost of all programs that contribute to the outcome by the number of planned outcomes.
- When programs have their own individual outcome objectives, cost per outcome is computed by dividing each program's total cost by the number of outcomes to be achieved.
- Program budgeting systems provide powerful data and information on the effectiveness of programs.

A Comprehensive Budgeting System

As discussed in Chapter 10, the combination of all three budgeting systems (see Figure 11.4) provides a comprehensive view of the operation of a social service agency and its various programs that none can provide by itself. Once a line-item budget system has been created, it takes only a little additional effort to construct a functional budgeting system and a program budgeting system.

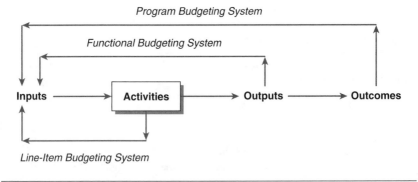

Figure 11.4   Comprehensive Budgeting System

Note

1. For a more detailed discussion of cost allocation, see Office of Management & Budget (OMB) Circular A-122 – "Cost Principles for Non-Profit Organizations" at www.omb.gov.

References

Hay, L., & Wilson, E. (1995). *Accounting for government and nonprofit entities*. Chicago: Irwin.

Horngren, C., Foster, G., & Datar, S. (1997). *Cost accounting: A managerial emphasis*. Englewood Cliffs, NJ: Prentice Hall.

Martin, L. (2001). *Financial management for human service administrators*. Boston: Allyn & Bacon.

Mayers, R. (2004). *Financial management for nonprofit human service organizations*. Springfield, IL: Charles C. Thomas.

Chapter 12

Performance Measurement, Monitoring, and Program Evaluation

Data Requirements

CHAPTER OVERVIEW

The purpose of this chapter is to explain:

- Performance measurement, monitoring, and program evaluation
- The different types of data required to perform these functions
- The ways in which data are used

The following topics are covered in this chapter:

- The link between performance measurement, monitoring, and evaluation and management information systems
- Feedback and self-evaluating systems
- Performance measurement
- Monitoring
- Program evaluation
- Program data requirements
    Coverage data
    Equity data
    Process data
    Effort (output) data
    Cost-efficiency data
    Results (outcome) data
    Cost-effectiveness data
    Impact data
- Performance measurement, monitoring, program evaluation, and program data
- The utility of performance measurement, monitoring, and program evaluation

The Link Between Performance Measurement, Monitoring, and Evaluation and Management Information Systems

Although the topics of performance measurement, monitoring, and program evaluation appear toward the end of this book, they are an integral part of the entire process of effectiveness-based program planning. The material presented in the preceding chapters (including the discussion of needs assessment, planning, program design, and the establishment of goals and objectives) can all be seen as laying the groundwork for a discussion of performance measurement, monitoring, and program evaluation. Through the use of these assessment tools, social service agencies can (1) address the performance accountability requirements demanded by social service funding agencies today, as well as (2) determine if social service programs are working as intended or are in need of refinement.

A strong link needs to exist between a social service agency's performance measurement, monitoring, and program evaluation systems and its management information system (MIS). The nexus here involves specification of the types of performance data a social service agency and its various programs are going to use and the inclusion of that data in the agency's MIS. In the case of monitoring in particular, it is necessary for a social service agency to have current, even real-time, performance data in order to adequately perform this function. Historically, many social service agencies waited until a program was in existence for some time before thinking about performance measurement, monitoring, and program evaluation. This approach virtually ensured that the data necessary to assess the implementation, performance, and impact of programs would not be available. Attempting to reconstruct agency performance measurement, monitoring, and program evaluation data *after the fact* has never been an optimum strategy. To offer an alternative approach, we explicitly introduced evaluation at the beginning of Chapter 9 dealing with management information.

Feedback and Self-Evaluating Systems

Throughout this book, we have used the systems framework as a model for thinking about effectiveness-based program planning. We return to it once more to assist us in thinking about performance measurement, monitoring, and program evaluation. Self-learning systems, sometimes referred to as *heuristic systems*, learn by doing. Self-learning systems take data and information (*feedback*) about their operations, analyze it, and then use it to make adjustments in the way the program operates. For example, a thermostat is a self-learning system. A thermostat monitors the temperature of a room and adjusts the air conditioning as needed to maintain a comfortable environment. If we think of a program as a self-learning system (see Figure 12.1), performance measurement, monitoring, and program evaluation provide feedback about the operations and functioning of the program. This feedback becomes new *input* into the program and can lead to changes, refinements, and improvements in how the program is designed and implemented.

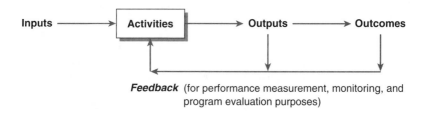

Feedback (for performance measurement, monitoring, and program evaluation purposes)

Figure 12.1   The Systems Framework, Feedback, and Self-Learning Systems

As Figure 12.1 illustrates, feedback is provided on the outputs, quality, and outcomes of a program. It is this feedback that is used for performance measurement purposes, monitoring purposes, and program evaluation purposes.

Performance Measurement

Performance measurement can be defined as the assessment of the outputs (efficiency), quality, and outcomes (effectiveness) of programs (Hatry, 1980; Martin and Kettner, 1996; McDavid and Hawthorn, 2006).

As Table 12.1 indicates, the primary purpose of performance measurement is external reporting. In terms of perspective, performance measurement has both a financial and a managerial orientation, with an equal emphasis on both owing to its roots in accounting and performance auditing. The central idea behind performance measurement is to have government agencies and programs, including social service agencies and programs, collect and report to stakeholders (i.e., funding sources, clients, elected officials, advocacy groups, citizens, and others) data and information on their performance.

Performance measurement seeks to make government-funded programs more *transparent* to stakeholders. Through transparency, stakeholders become

Table 12.1   A Comparison of Performance Measurement, Monitoring, and Program Evaluation

	Performance Measurement	*Monitoring*	*Program Evaluation*
Unit of analysis	Program	Program	Program
Primary purpose(s)	External reporting	Program management	Program and policy improvement
Perspective(s)	Financial/ managerial	Managerial	Policy/planning
Use of data	Feedback on program performance to external stakeholders	Feedback on program operations to agency administrators	Feedback on program results (outcomes) and impacts to policy makers and planners

more knowledgeable about how government-funded programs operate and how they help to improve the lives of citizens. This type of information is helpful in maintaining and increasing stakeholder support for social service programs.

Performance measurement is concerned with providing answers to such frequent stakeholder questions as: How much product or service (outputs or units of service) does the program provide? What is the quality (quality outputs) of the service provided by the program? How many clients completed treatment (service completions)? What outcomes (intermediate and final) does the program achieve? And how cost-efficient and cost-effective is the program?

Performance measurement has become institutionalized at the federal government level through the provisions of the Government Performance and Results Act (GPRA) of 1993 (Pub. L. No. 103–62). GPRA requires all federal agencies to collect and report performance measurement data and information about their various programs. The Governmental Accounting Standards Board (GASB), the organization that establishes what are called "generally accepted accounting principles" for state and local governments, encourages these same governments to also report performance measurement data. GASB believes that state and local governments should report to stakeholders the same types of performance data that businesses report to stockholders. In order for governments to collect and report performance measurement information, they necessarily have to involve their grantees and contractors. Thus, most nonprofit social service organizations today are also involved with performance measurement (Martin, 2005; Martin and Miller, 2006).

It should be noted that performance measurement is concerned only with the collection and reporting of *performance* data and information. Performance measurement does *not* concern itself with such questions as Was the program implemented as planned? Did the program achieve its intended results? And what was the program's impact? For feedback that addresses these types of questions, social service agencies must turn to monitoring and program evaluation.

Monitoring

Monitoring can be defined as an assessment of the extent to which a program is implemented as designed and serves its intended target group (Rossi, Lipsey, and Freeman, 2004). Some program evaluation texts refer to monitoring as "formative evaluation" because it takes place during program implementation (McDavid and Hawthorn, 2006).

The word *monitoring* comes from the Latin word *monere,* meaning "to warn." Monitoring can be compared to the navigation system on an airplane. When a commercial airliner starts to stray off course, an alarm sounds in the cockpit, alerting the pilot, who then takes corrective action to return the plane to its proper course heading. In the same vein, monitoring provides feedback to warn a social service administrator when the implementation of a program starts to deviate from its original design. The administrator can then take corrective action to bring the program back into line with its program design.

The primary purpose (see Table 12.1) of monitoring is program management; consequently, monitoring has a managerial perspective. Monitoring provides social service administrators with feedback on the current status of a program in terms of such questions as: Is the program being implemented as designed? What proportion of the community need is the program meeting? Are only eligible target-group clients being served? Are subgeographical areas and subgroups (e.g., ethnic minorities, women, persons with disabilities, and others) being served in appropriate numbers? What products and services are being provided and in what amounts? And what results are being achieved in terms of outputs and outcomes? In the assessment of program outputs, quality, and outcomes, monitoring and performance measurement overlap somewhat. Performance measurement and monitoring are both concerned with outputs, quality, and outcomes as well as issues of cost-efficiency and cost-effectiveness. The difference between the two is that performance measurement is concerned with the reporting of feedback data and information to external stakeholders, whereas monitoring is concerned with using the feedback data and information to internally track the implementation of programs and to make changes and refinements as needed.

Monitoring also lays the groundwork for program evaluation by helping to ensure that a program is implemented as intended. No useful purpose is served in conducting a program evaluation if a program is not implemented as intended.

Program Evaluation

Program evaluation can be defined as social science techniques applied to determining the workings and effectiveness of social programs (Rossi,

Lipsey, and Freeman, 2004, p. 2). Program evaluation is frequently concerned with determining the impact of a program. Impact assessment necessitates establishing cause-and-effect relationships: The program (the cause), and no other external factors, accounts for the achievement of the program outcomes (the effect). Because cause-and-effect relationships are difficult to establish, the assessment of program impact usually involves the use of social science research techniques and the application of statistics (Rossi, Lipsey, and Freeman, 2004).

The primary purpose of program evaluation (see Table 12.1) is to provide feedback on results (outcomes) and program impacts to inform policy makers and planners about the effectiveness of programs and the appropriateness of the social intervention hypotheses that underline them. Program evaluation addresses such questions as: Did the program work as intended? What results (outcomes) did the program accomplish? What measurable impacts did the program achieve? Is the program cost-effective? Program evaluation can also lead to the discovery of positive as well as negative "unintended consequences," thereby suggesting needed changes and refinements in social policy or program design.

In terms of the assessment of results (outcomes), program evaluation overlaps somewhat with both performance measurement and monitoring. The difference is that program evaluation is not concerned with the reporting of results data and information to external stakeholders (performance measurement) or with tracking a program's success in accomplishing results and impacts during implementation (monitoring) but, rather, is concerned with using program results (outcomes) and impact feedback data and information to improve policy and planning. Program evaluation also overlaps with monitoring in that both are concerned with ensuring that a program is implemented as intended. The difference is that monitoring assesses a program *during implementation,* whereas program evaluation can take place *either during implementation* (formative evaluation) *or after the fact* (summative evaluation).

Program Data Requirements

At this point, the reader has probably already concluded that performance measurement, monitoring, and program evaluation are all important and necessary component parts of what might be called *program assessment.* Through the use of management information systems (MIS) and dashboards, social service agencies only need ensure that they are collecting the necessary assessment data and they should be able to report performance measurement data and information to external stakeholders, perform ongoing program monitoring, and conduct program evaluations.

The types of program data that social service agencies need to collect to satisfy the requirements of performance measurement, monitoring, and program evaluation include: (1) coverage, (2) equity, (3) process, (4) effort, (5) cost-efficiency, (6) results, (7) cost-effectiveness, and (8) impact. These eight types do not constitute the entire universe of program data, but they are the ones that performance measurement, monitoring, and program evaluation are generally most concerned with. Each of these eight data types is discussed below, including the types of assessment questions the data are used to address (see Table 12.2).

Coverage Data

Coverage data provide feedback on the extent to which a program is (a) meeting the community need and (b) reaching its target population. Monitored during program implementation, coverage data can be used not only to determine the extent to which the target group is being reached but also to ensure that individuals ineligible for the program are not served. Conducted at the end of a program, or at some defined end point (e.g., the end of the fiscal year), coverage data can be used in a program evaluation mode to document that only eligible clients were served and to assess the adequacy, or inadequacy, of current program funding and service levels to meet the community need.

Equity Data

Equity data provide feedback on the extent to which specific subgeographical areas of a community as well as specific subgroups (such as ethnic minorities, women, persons with disabilities, children, or the elderly) are being served by a program. Unless a program is targeted at a specific subgeographical area or specific subgroup of a community, all other things being equal, geographical subareas and subgroups should be served by a program in roughly the same proportion as their composition in the community. Equity data can be used to ensure adequate coverage of subgeographical areas and subgroups during implementation (monitoring) or at the end of a program (program evaluation) to document that a program is or is not reaching some geographical subarea or subgroup. Utilized in a performance measurement approach, coverage

Table 12.2   Types of Program Data and Related Assessment Questions

Type of Program Data	Related Assessment Questions
Coverage	To what extent is the program meeting the community need?
Equity	To what extent is the program adequately serving subgeographical areas and subgroups (ethnic minorities, women, persons with disabilities, etc.)?
Process	To what extent is the program being implemented as intended in terms of: service definitions? service tasks? standards? other service delivery requirements?
Effort (outputs)	To what extent is the program producing: products and services (intermediate outputs)? quality products and services (quality outputs)? service completions (final outputs)?
Cost-Efficiency	What is the: cost per intermediate outputs? cost per quality outputs? cost per service completion?
Results (outcomes)	To what is extent is the program achieving: intermediate outcomes? final outcomes?
Cost-Effectiveness	What is the: cost per intermediate outcome? cost per final outcome?
Impact	To what extent is the program achieving a measurable impact?

data provides stakeholders with information about the distribution of outputs, quality outputs, and outcomes across subgeographical areas and subgroups.

Process Data

Process data provide feedback on the extent to which a program is implemented as designed. During implementation (monitoring), process data can be used to compare actual service delivery to planned service design to ensure conformance with such items as service definitions, service tasks, service standards, work statements, service specifications, and other service requirements. At the end of a program, process data can be used to determine and document (program evaluation) that a program was implemented as intended.

Effort (Output) Data

Effort (output) data provide feedback on the amount of products and services (intermediate outputs) provided, the amount of quality products and services (quality outputs) provided, and the number of service completions (final outputs) achieved. Effort (output) data can be monitored during implementation to compare actual effort to planned effort and to take corrective action when actual effort fails to coincide with planned effort. Effort (output) data can be used at the end of a program year to document service delivery levels (program evaluation) and for purposes of performance measurement reporting. Effort (output) data are also used in determining a program's cost-efficiency. Effort (output) data is one of the three major types of performance measurement information that would routinely be reported to stakeholders.

Cost-Efficiency Data

Cost-efficiency data provide feedback on the costs of providing program products and services, including intermediate outputs, quality outputs, and final outputs (service completions). Cost-efficiency data are developed by computing costs per output: intermediate, quality, and final. During implementation, actual cost data can be compared with planned costs (monitoring). At the end of a program year, cost-efficiency data can be used to assess a program's productivity and are also required for purposes of performance measurement reporting.

Results (Outcome) Data

Results (outcome) data provide feedback on the extent to which a program achieves its intended results (outcomes), both intermediate and final. Results (outcome) data can be monitored during implementation to compare actual results achieved with planned results. Used at the end of a program year, results (outcome) data document for policy and planning purposes the results achieved by a program. Results (outcome) data are also required for purposes of performance measurement reporting. Finally, results (outcome) data are used in determining a program's cost-effectiveness.

Cost-Effectiveness Data

Cost-effectiveness data provide feedback on the costs of achieving program results (outcomes), both intermediate and final. Cost-effectiveness data are developed by computing cost per intermediate outcome and cost per final outcome. Cost-effectiveness data are usually available only at the end of the program year (program evaluation) and are used to document the costs of achieving results (outcomes) for policy and planning purposes and for purposes of performance measurement reporting.

Impact Data

Impact data provide feedback on the most difficult assessment question of all: What happened to clients as a result of participation in a program that would not have happened in the program's absence? To address this question, impact data are usually generated using social science research techniques, including the creation of a control group for comparison purposes and the use of statistics to measure the magnitude of the impact. The development of impact data is a difficult undertaking. Nevertheless, limitations on program and agency resources make it imperative that available resources be put to the best use possible. Impact data can provide social service administrators with hard social science-based information that demonstrates the extent to which a program achieves measurable impacts with its clients.

Performance Measurement, Monitoring, Program Evaluation, and Program Data

As illustrated in Table 12.3, performance measurement, monitoring, and program evaluation overlap in terms of their use of program data. In particular, considerable program data overlap exists between monitoring and program evaluation, and performance measurement overlaps somewhat with both monitoring and program evaluation.

Table 12.3   Performance Measurement, Monitoring, Program Evaluation, and Type of Program Data

Type of Assessment Data	Performance Measurement	Monitoring	Program Evaluation
Coverage		X	X
Equity		X	X
Process		X	X
Effort	X	X	
Cost-Efficiency	X	X	
Results	X	X	X
Cost-Effectiveness	X	X	X
Impact	X		X

The overlap in terms of types of program data leads to an important observation: To a great extent, the differences between performance measurement, monitoring, and program evaluation are not so much differences in the *types* of program data used as differences in *when and how* program data are used. Performance measurement uses program data for *external reporting purposes.* Monitoring uses program data during implementation for *management purposes.* Program evaluation uses program data after implementation for *policy and planning purposes.*

The Utility of Performance Measurement, Monitoring, and Program Evaluation

The test of any feedback system is the usefulness of the resulting data and information. As we have repeatedly stressed in earlier chapters, the critical questions to effectiveness-based program planning are these:

- What types of clients?
- With what types of problems?
- Receive what types of services?

- With what results?
- At what cost?

The program feedback data and information produced by the answers to the above questions are useful for a number of purposes.

First, and most importantly, program feedback data provide information needed by social service administrators and front-line managers. These are the individuals most immediately responsible for implementing programs, and it is critical that they have current data and information on which to base decisions.

Second, program feedback data satisfy the reporting requirements of social service-funding agencies.

Third, program feedback data meet the needs of external stakeholders. The political environment of the social services today is often turbulent, irrational, demanding, and frustrating. Every social service administrator has experienced the helpless feeling of not being able to respond to questions about why his or her agency is, or is not, doing something that a particular politician, reporter, or interest group favors or opposes. Program assessment data and information represent tools that can be used by social service administrators to respond to inquiries about their programs. Data and information, of course, do not guarantee that all community and political interests will be satisfied, but at least they provide a sound, data-based response. Data and information can also be used to sell a program and to enlarge its support base in a community.

To summarize:

- Performance measurement, monitoring, and program evaluation are three major approaches to assessing the implementation, performance, results, and impacts of programs.
- The data and information generated by performance measurement, monitoring, and program evaluation constitute feedback that can be used to improve programs.
- Performance measurement is principally concerned with using feedback on program efficiency, quality, and effectiveness for external reporting purposes.
- Monitoring is principally concerned with using feedback during program implementation for managerial purposes, including (a) ensuring that programs are delivered as intended and (b) assessing program efficiency, quality, effectiveness, cost-efficiency, and cost-effectiveness.
- Program evaluation is principally concerned with using feedback for policy and planning purposes, including the assessment of program results (outcomes) and the determination and measurement of program impact.

References

Hatry, H. (1980). *Performance measurement: A guide for local elected officials.* Washington, DC: Urban Institute Press.

Martin, L. (2005). Performance based contracting for human services: Does it work? *Administration in Social Work, 29,* 63–77.

Martin, L., & Kettner, P. (1996). *Measuring the performance of human service programs.* Thousand Oaks, CA: Sage.

Martin, L., & Miller, J. (2006). *Contracting for public sector services.* Herndon, VA: National Institute of Governmental Purchasing.

McDavid, J., & Hawthorn, L. (2006). *Program evaluation and performance measurement: An introduction to practice.* Thousand Oaks, CA: Sage.

Rossi, P., Lipsey, M., & Freeman, H. (2004). *Evaluation: A systematic approach* (7th ed.). Thousand Oaks, CA: Sage.

Chapter 13

Program Impact Evaluation and Hypothesis Testing

CHAPTER OVERVIEW

The purpose of this chapter is to explain:

- Program evaluation in more detail
- The key differences between program evaluation and performance measurement
- Theory success, theory failure, and program failure
- The major types of impact program evaluations
- The logic model relationship between theory (cause), intervention (program), and result (effect)
- The two major reasons why programs fail
- Pre-experimental, quasi-experimental, and experimental impact program evaluation designs

The following topics are covered in this chapter:

- Differentiating program evaluation from performance measurement
- Impact program evaluation
- Impact program evaluation and hypothesis testing

> - Research designs for impact program evaluation
>   Pre-experimental impact program evaluation designs
>   Quasi-experimental impact program evaluation designs
>   Experimental impact program evaluation designs

Differentiating Program Evaluation From Performance Measurement

Before beginning a detailed discussion of program evaluation, it is useful to further distinguish it from performance measurement. Because program evaluation and performance measurement can, and frequently do, utilize the same types of data and information, some confusion exists over how these two approaches differ.

McDavid and Hawthorn (2006, p. 293) identify a few key features that are important in distinguishing program evaluation from performance measurement: (1) frequency, (2) issue(s), and (3) attribution of outcomes.

- *Frequency* - program evaluation tends to be episodic, while performance measurement in an on going activity.

- *Issue(s)* - program evaluation is frequently driven by specific stakeholder questions, while performance measurement deals with more general performance issues that are relatively constant over time.

- *Attribution of outcomes* - program evaluation is concerned with determining if the program actually accounts for the outcome (result) achieved or if the outcome is attributable to some other factor. In performance measurement, attribution is generally assumed. For the purposes of this chapter, we will equate a concern with the attribution of outcomes to "impact program evaluation."

Impact Program Evaluation

An impact program evaluation attempts to demonstrate that the outcome (results) is directly attributable to the program and is not related to some other variable. An impact program evaluation seeks to establish *a cause-and-effect relationship* between a program and its outcome (results).

Table 13.1   Differences Between Program Evaluation and Performance
Measurement

	Program Evaluation	*Performance Measurement*
Frequency	Episodic	Ongoing
Issue(s)	Designed to address *specific* stakeholder questions at a particular point in time	Designed to address more *general* performance issues that are constant over time
Attribution of Outcomes	To be determined	Assumed

SOURCE: Adapted from McDavid, J., & Hawthorn, L. (2006). *Program Evaluation & Performance Measurement*. Thousand Oaks, CA: Sage Publications, Inc. Reprinted with permission.

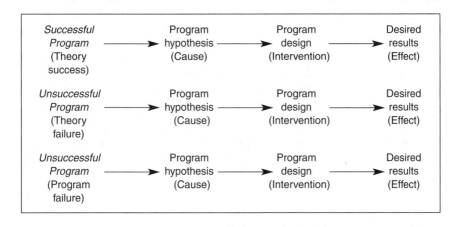

Figure 13.1   The Relationship Between Program Hypothesis and Program Results

An impact program evaluation can demonstrate that (1) a program is successful, (2) a program is unsuccessful due to theory failure, or (3) a program is unsuccessful due to program failure (see Figure 13.1). All three of these results are related to the intervention hypothesis that underpins a program and the way in which a program is implemented.

Using logic model terminology, a successful program is one where there is alignment between the program hypothesis (*theory*) and the program design (*cause*) which produces the desired outcome (*effect*). We can call this result: *theory success.* An unsuccessful program usually occurs for one of two reasons: *theory failure* or *program failure.*

• Theory failure occurs when there is alignment between the program hypothesis (theory) and the program design (intervention), but the program does not produce the desired outcome (effects). When this situation occurs, it can be called theory failure because *if* the hypotheses had been valid, *then* the program design should have produced the desired outcome (results). Because the desired outcome was not produced, the hypothesis is not supported and a different hypothesis must be considered.

• Program failure occurs when there is misalignment between the program hypothesis (cause) and the program design (intervention), and the program fails to produce the desired outcome (effects). This situation should not come as a surprise. When a program is created that is not driven by a valid program hypothesis, program failure is the likely result.

The important point here is that when a program fails to achieve its desired outcome (result) due to theory failure, *the result is nevertheless still a valid test of the program.* We can make inferences about the program because the test itself is valid. Consequently, we can learn from theory failure just as we learn from a successful program. However, when a program fails to achieve the desired result due to program failure, *the program has not been properly tested.* We cannot draw any inferences about the success or failure of a program when it is not implemented as planned.

Impact Program Evaluation and Hypothesis Testing

In Chapter 6, we discussed program planning as a hypothesis-generating activity and program evaluation as a hypothesis-testing activity. A program hypothesis

- Makes explicit the assumptions about program expectations (outcome)
- Establishes a framework to bring internal consistency to a program
- Enables inputs, activities, outputs, and outcomes to be examined for internal consistency

We offered a fairly detailed hypothesis in Chapter 6 related to the issue of domestic abuse. We argued that women who are the victims of domestic violence face a number of barriers to self-sufficiency (e.g., low self-esteem, social isolation, lack of financial resources, lack of basic education, and marketable skills). The suggestion was made that *if* we could identify the major barriers (hypothesis) and *if* we could successfully eliminate those barriers, *then* we would see positive changes leading to an increase in self-sufficiency. Now let's look again at the three tracks presented in Figure 13.1.

The first track, labeled "successful program," depicts an ideal situation. Let's assume that the hypothesis here is that *if* basic education and job training services are provided, *then* women who are victims of domestic abuse will be able to get jobs and become more self-sufficient. The program is implemented as designed (basic education and job training services are provided), and the desired outcome (result) is achieved: the participants get jobs and become more self-sufficient. Given this finding, we conclude that the hypothesis is supported or validated. But programs can also fail to achieve their desired outcome (result) due to flaws in either the theory or the program.

The second track in Figure 13.1, labeled "theory failure," describes a situation in which a program is implemented as designed, but the anticipated outcome (result) is not achieved. *Theory failure* comes about because of a flaw in the intervention hypothesis underlying the program: namely, that certain causal processes will lead directly to the desired outcome (result). The hypothesis is the same: *if* basic education and job training services are provided, *then* women who are victims of domestic abuse will be able to get jobs and become more self-sufficient. The program is implemented as designed, but few participants get jobs and become more self-sufficient. Given this finding, we conclude that the hypothesis is not supported or validated.

The third track in Figure 13.1, labeled "program failure," describes a situation where a program is not implemented as designed. In such a case, we can say nothing about the achievement of program outcome (result). Program outcome may or may not be achieved, but neither success nor failure can be attributed to the program. For example, the hypothesis is the same: *if* basic education and job training services are provided, *then* women who are victims of domestic abuse will be able to get jobs and become more self-sufficient. But let's say that due to funding reductions only basic education services are provided; no job training services are provided. The program hypothesis may or may not be correct; we will never know because it was not properly tested. Failure in this case is attributable not to flaws in the theory, but due to deficiencies in program implementation.

Research Designs for Impact Program Evaluation

The essence of impact program evaluation is comparison. What is compared with what was or probably would have been in the absence of a particular program. Typically, comparisons are based on observations of (1) different groups at the same time or (2) the same group at different points over time. Impact program evaluations seek to measure and compare these observations with one another in such a way as to be able to attribute any differences in outcome (result) to the program.

A variety of impact evaluation designs are available for use depending on the particular environmental situation and the resources available. These research designs vary in complexity, timeliness, cost, feasibility, and potential usefulness. Impact program evaluation is a complicated, demanding, and difficult undertaking that, to be successful, must be approached with realism, commitment, and considerable knowledge. Table 13.2 presents three basic impact program evaluation designs:

- Pre-experimental designs
- Quasi-experimental designs
- Experimental designs

Table 13.2   Types of Impact Program Evaluations

Type 1 - Pre-Experimental Designs				
One-shot case study			X	0
Single group pretest/posttest		01	X	02
Type 2 - Quasi-Experimental Designs				
Nonequivalent comparison group		01	X	02
		03		04
Type 3 - Experimental Designs				
Pretest/posttest control group	R	01	X	02
	R	03	X	04

Each "X" in Table 13.2 represents a program (an intervention) provided to a defined client group. Each "0" refers to an observation—the actual measurement of a defined client attitude, behavior, or condition that is intended to be changed by a program. Random assignment of clients (the process of selecting individuals in such a way that each client has an equal chance of being included in either the control or the treatment group) is indicated by an "R" preceding the row. A row not preceded by "R" indicates that the groups to be compared are not formed by random assignment. Letters in the same row (horizontally) indicate that the same group is participating in the program and being observed. Vertical alignment of letters with the same design indicate events occurring at the same time. Temporal order is left to right.

With the exception of the one-shot case study, each design is based on either (a) a comparison of observations before participation in the program and again after completion of the program or the receipt of a full complement of services or (b) a comparison of observations of a group that participated in the program and a similar group that did not. These basic comparisons are elaborated or combined in the more complex designs to allow for a comparison of the outcomes (results) of different programs.

Pre-Experimental Impact Program Evaluation Designs

The first program impact evaluation design to be discussed is the *one-shot case study*. Unfortunately, this design is quite common in the social services. The problem is that the one-shot case study is not a true impact program evaluation design. After clients have completed a program or received a full complement of services, data are collected on outcome (result) achieved. For example, adolescent mothers are provided parent training. After completion of the program, their parenting knowledge is tested. Any increase in test scores are *attributed* to knowledge gained from the program. However, because the young women were not tested before they started the program (to create a baseline for comparison purposes), it is impossible to determine if parenting knowledge was truly increased or not. In this instance attributing any increase in parenting knowledge to the program is not based on any supportable evidence. The one-shot case study design is more reflective of performance measurement than impact program evaluation.

The second impact program evaluation design, the *single-group pretest/ posttest design*, creates a baseline for comparison purposes. Each young mother is tested on her parenting knowledge before she enters the program and again after she completes the program or receives a full complement of services. Diagrammatically, we can depict the results as follows:

$$Change = O2 - O1$$

The measure of program impact is determined by subtracting the pretest score from the posttest score; the difference is attributable to the program. For example, if a young mother scores 50 on the pretest and 75 on the posttest, we can conclude that there was an improvement of 25 points in her case. For confidentiality purposes, we would of course talk not about individual clients but about aggregate client data. In this instance, we might compare the means (the arithmetic average designated by the symbol $\bar{X}$) of the pretest and posttest scores for all the young mothers in the parent training class:

$$Change = \bar{X}O2 - \bar{X}O1$$

Although this design resolves the problem (lack of a baseline) raised in the one-shot case study, it fails to deal with another important problem. Granted, we did observe improvement in the parenting skills of the young mothers as measured by changes after participation in the program, but we still cannot conclude that these changes were produced by the program. This problem, known as the *competing hypothesis dilemma*, asserts that although changes were observed, factors other than the program could have produced them. These "other factors" might range from the young women's being exposed to television shows or school programs dealing with parenting knowledge to the young women "learning" how to take the test (i.e., being taught, by the first test, how to respond to the second test).

Quasi-Experimental Impact Program Evaluation Designs

The third impact program evaluation design falls into the category of a quasi-experimental design and is called: the *nonequivalent comparison group design*. This design begins to deal with the competing hypothesis dilemma. In this design, a comparison group is created of individuals who are "statistically similar" to the clients in the program. *Statistically similar* means that the comparison group is the same on all characteristics hypothesized to be relevant to achieving the program outcome (result).

For example, subjects for the comparison group could be (a) people who are eligible for the program and apply, but who are denied access because demand exceeds supply; (b) people who are eligible for the program but are unaware of its existence; or (c) people who are technically eligible for the program and would like to participate, but who are not residents of the community or target area.

The comparison (or nontreated) group usually receives some other type of program rather than no program at all. This practice avoids the ethical problem of withholding services from some clients for the purposes of experimentation. With the nonequivalent comparison group design, the potential problem of competing hypotheses is minimized in that factors outside the program are likely to affect both groups in the same ways; also the effect of testing (the pretest effect) is minimized in that both groups are exposed to the same tests. The measurement of impact analysis consists of (a) subtracting the mean pretest score from the posttest score for the control group, (b) doing the same for the experimental group, and (c) comparing the results.

$$Change\ (treatment)\quad =\ \bar{X}O2 - \bar{X}O1$$

$$Change\ (comparison)\ =\ \bar{X}O4 - \bar{X}O3$$

If any difference exists between the control group and the program participants, that difference is said to constitute the program's impact, provided the difference is statistically significant (i.e., there is little probability that the difference is due to chance).

Experimental Impact Program Evaluation Designs

The final impact program evaluation design to be discussed is called the *experimental design*. This design is the strongest in that randomization is used to assign participants, or subjects, either to the control group or to participation in the program. *Random assignment* means that each participant, or subject, has an equal chance of being assigned to the control group or to participation in the program. Random assignment ensures that the two groups are likely to be similar on all characteristics and that any differences between the two groups are likely to be due to the program and not to external factors.[1]

Once random assignment has occurred, the process and analysis are the same as for the quasi-experimental design. Although this design holds the promise for producing data that clearly and unequivocally demonstrate the impact of a program, if randomization were the sine qua non for evaluating the impact of social programs (as some authors argue) few impact program evaluations would ever be conducted. Beyond the ethical issues involved in withholding participation in a program from clients, it is legally difficult to withhold services from any individual who meets the eligibility criteria for public programs and for private programs supported by public funds. For these reasons, social service administrators tend to rely more on quasi-experimental and other less rigorous designs when conducting impact program evaluation.

A Concluding Comment

The underlying thrust of this book has been to outline a process that encourages mutual respect between direct service practitioners and social service administrators and managers, a process that assumes a partnership relationship between or among administrators, managers, practitioners, and clients through the development of a supportive and open problem-solving environment.

Effectiveness-based program planning may appear to be linear—that is, problem analysis precedes the development of the program hypothesis, which in turn precedes the development of goals and objectives, and so forth—it is, in reality, more of an iterative process. Our belief is that all problem solving should be viewed as a process of social learning through social transactions and not just as adherence to a set of cookbook-type rules. We recognize the reality of the ever-changing and nonstable environments in which social services administration is conducted, and it is this reality that has guided our development of this effectiveness-based program planning model.

Note

1. True experimental designs include random assignment of clients to ensure that no selection bias (e.g., screening for those clients most likely to benefit) influences the measurement of the program's impact. Readers who would like more complete listings and critiques of experimental and quasi-experimental designs are referred to Gabor, Unrau, and Grinnel (1998) and Rossi, Lipsey, and Freeman (2004).

References

Gabor, P., Unrau, Y., & Grinnel, R. (1998). *Evaluation for social worker*s. Needham Heights, MA: Allyn & Bacon.

McDavid, J., & Hawthorn, L. (2006). *Program evaluation & performance measurement.* Thousand Oaks, CA: Sage.

Rossi, P., Lipsey, M., & Freeman, H. (2004). *Evaluation: A systematic approach* (7th ed.). Thousand Oaks, CA: Sage.

Author Index

Anderson, J., 49
Andringa, R., 121
Appleby, G., 49
Austin, M., 6, 118

Babbie, B., 82
Banfield, E., 32
Bazron, B. J., 49
Bell, J. B., 6
Bell, W., 88 (table), 89 (table)
Bennett, L, 192
Berry, B., 88
Bradshaw, J., 15, 59
Brody, R., 121, 122, 124, 126, 150

Campbell, J., 30
Carrilio, T., 178
Carter, R., 49
Chen, S., 192
Clindblom, C., 32
Cloward, R., 49
Coley, S., 123, 124
Colon, E., 49
Corcoran, K., 165, 188
Crosby, P., 161
Cross, T. L., 49

Daley, J., 121
Datar, S., 234
Delbecq, A., 82
Deming, W., 161
Dennis, K. W., 49
Department of Economic Security
    (Arizona), 148

Department of Human Services, 62, 74
Dill, L., 30
Dooley, S., 89

Eckerson, W., 179
Engstrom, T., 121
Ezell, M., 120

Faludi, A., 29
Federal Register, 44
Ferraro, K., 30, 119
Fischer, J., 165, 188
Fishback, R., 30
Flett, H., 192
Foster, G., 234
Freeman, H., 255, 257, 274 (n1)

Gabor, P., 274 (n1)
Gamble, D. N., 49
Gold, E., 89
Goldsmith, H., 89
Gonzales, H. F., 49
Greenway, M., 143, 147
Grinnel, R., 274 (n1)
Gundersdorf, J., 218 (n1)
Gustafson, D., 85

Harris, A., 73 (table)
Hatry, H., 143, 147, 167, 254
Hawthorn, L., 254, 256, 266, 267 (table)
Hay, L., 234
Herbert, B., 30
Hobbs, N., 71
Horngren, C., 234

Subject Index

About the Authors

Peter M. Kettner is Professor Emeritus at the Arizona State University School of Social Work. He is the author of six books, four of which have been translated into multiple languages. He has also authored over 50 articles, monographs, and book chapters on the topics of purchase-of-service contracting, privatization, macro practice in social work, human services planning, and social work administration. Over his 30-year career in academia he served as consultant to five different state human service agencies and dozens of local nonprofit agencies on their purchase of service contracting practices and in the design and implementation of effectiveness-based planning systems. In retirement he has continued his writing and consultation with local government and nonprofit agencies.

Robert M. Moroney is Professor of Social Policy and Planning at the School of Social Work at Arizona State University. He is the author of 10 books and over 60 articles and book chapters on various aspects of policy, planning, and program evaluation. He has been associated with a number of policy centers, including the Bush Institute at the University of North Carolina and the Vanderbilt Institute of Public Policy Institutes. He also spent a year at the invitation of the Joseph Rountree Memorial Trust and the Department of Health and Human Services, England, examining that country's social policies affecting the family. He recently was a Senior Fulbright Scholar with the Department of Social Policy and Social Work, University College Dublin, and more recently a Senior Fulbright Scholar at Vilnius Pedagogical University. He currently serves as a board member of the Rosalyn Carter Institute for Human Development. He does extensive consultation with numerous national, state, and local human service organizations.

Lawrence L. Martin is Professor of Public Affairs, Social Work and Public Administration at the University of Central Florida in Orlando. He was previously on the faculty of the Columbia University School of Social Work in New York City where he directed the program in social work administration. He is the author or coauthor of 17 books and major monographs and over 100 articles and book chapters on human services administration, procurement and contracting, performance measurement, and budgeting and financial management. His works have been translated and reprinted in Chinese, French, Korean, Portuguese, Russian, and Mongolian. He has provided consultation and training to numerous state and local governments and nonprofit organizations throughout the United States. He has also worked internationally with governmental and nongovernmental organizations (NGOs) in Canada, France, Germany, Sweden, and Mongolia. He currently serves on the board of directors of the National Network for Social Work Managers and the editorial board of *Administration in Social Work.*